The Avant-(
Feature F

The Avant-Garde Feature Film

A Critical History

WILLIAM E. B. VERRONE

McFarland & Company, Inc., Publishers
Jefferson, North Carolina, and London

LIBRARY OF CONGRESS CATALOGUING-IN-PUBLICATION DATA

Verrone, William.
    The avant-garde feature film : a critical history / William
E. B. Verrone.
        p.   cm.
    Includes bibliographical references and index.

    ISBN 978-0-7864-5910-0
    softcover : 50# alkaline paper ∞

    1. Experimental films—History and criticism.   I. Title.
PN1995.9.E96V48   2012
791.43'611—dc23   2011034633

BRITISH LIBRARY CATALOGUING DATA ARE AVAILABLE

Front cover image: Jack Nance in *Eraserhead*, 1977 (Photofest);
cover design by David K. Landis (Shake It Loose Graphics)

Manufactured in the United States of America

McFarland & Company, Inc., Publishers
  Box 611, Jefferson, North Carolina 28640
  www.mcfarlandpub.com

Table of Contents

Acknowledgments

I would like to thank my peers and the administration at my university for their support during the writing of this book. I would like to thank my wife and my daughter who, in particular, made every day of work worthwhile and fun. Every ker-plop was needed and welcomed with a smile.

Preface

The Avant-Garde Feature Film:
An Overview and Explanation

There are many feature films one might call avant-garde. They can range from cut-out animation to video experiments, surrealism to expressionism, foreign-language to silent. With so many films produced around the world, it is difficult assessing all films that are in some way avant-garde. This book does not attempt to detail them — that would be an impossibly complex and tricky endeavor. So, in order to consider the contemporary avant-garde feature film, a type of film that not only naturally fits into the larger genre of avant-garde and experimental cinema, but also crosses boundaries— to become aligned with art-house cinema, feminist film, or cult film, for example — one must be rather open-minded. To understand how broad the net may be cast to include many films in the category of contemporary avant-garde feature film, it is necessary and even quite essential to be willing to embrace the *very idea* of avant-gardism foremost before accepting and allowing for the many films that can be considered as such.

If one were to trace the trajectory of avant-garde and experimental filmmaking over cinema history, it would be *relatively* unproblematic to discover that certain films "stand out" among others, that they have become well-known and therefore have become influential. Hence, much of what follows is a discussion primarily of the avant-garde films that might already be generally accepted as prime examples of alternative approaches to cinematic form, style, and content. The filmmakers who have made such films take the art and aesthetics of filmmaking to be an undertaking that shuns cultural and economic influence, which simply means they are concerned with creating an audio-visual film that is purely different — sometimes at odds with or reactionary to the kinds of films that generate public pleasure. So in the basic, fundamental sense, avant-garde films are just that: *different*.

It is, therefore, somewhat undemanding to identify films that are experimental and avant-garde; any seasoned filmgoer can recognize and possibly even categorize films that are dissimilar to the ones that serve the innocuous contentment mainstream film offers. However, just knowing there is an alternative is not enough; I believe it is essential to view the avant-garde as the most creative, imaginary, visionary, and aesthetically challenging form of film practice, and therefore it should be viewed not only as "the alternative" but as the *best* avenue for exploring the cinema.

But where to begin? There are many different types of avant-garde films, something I explore later, but perhaps it can be argued that within the experimental realm of filmmaking there are far more variations on typical, accepted genres (in addition to the outright defying of genres) that avant-garde films participate in. For this reason we should keep in mind the enormity of *types* that (perhaps) constitute the major genre of avant-garde film and especially *feature films*. Among others, there is surrealist, essayistic, women's experimental, collage, animation, video installation, city symphony, abstract, structural, or diary films that exist in avant-garde. So when discussing avant-garde feature films, one may include something from the silent era, like Benjamin Christensen's expressionistic and fragmentary docu-essay *Häxan: Witchcraft Through the Ages* (1922), or, more recently, Apichatpong Weerasethakul's surreal, experimental documentary *Mysterious Object at Noon* (2000). Similarly, one may claim seminal, canonical films like *The Cabinet of Dr. Caligari* (1919) is both an expressionistic and avant-garde film, or that Dziga Vertov's *Man with a Movie Camera* (1929) is the first great city symphony picture. Or, one might include "traditional" experimental and avant-garde filmmakers and films, such as Jonas Mekas's *As I Was Moving Ahead Occasionally I Saw Brief Glimpses of Beauty* (2000) or Ken Jacobs's *Star Spangled to Death* (1957–1961, 2003–2004). And then there is Stan Brakhage, the most acknowledged and acclaimed avant-gardist of the past half century, who, in addition to making several cycle films that when viewed together, create longer features, also made the seminal *Dog Star Man* (1961–1964). All of these can be considered avant-garde feature films (with *Caligari* arguably being the least, perhaps), which is partly why locating and describing feature films as avant-garde is sometimes a subjective endeavor. The films I discuss are ones that I believe can be considered avant-garde, mainly because of their entirely unorthodox uses of stylistic and formal devices or techniques, and also because of the subject matter and how it is represented. I should note, too, that my focus is predominately on European and North American cinema. This is not a bias, but more because readers will have greater access to these films. And detailing avant-garde films from every continent, multiple countries, or specific regions requires much more space than I have here.

Avant-garde and experimental cinema has received much critical analysis and appraisal, especially since the 1970s. I cite some of these analyses—but certainly not all of them — here to aid readers with the fundamental issues, definitions, and historical treatment of the genre. From the early assessments of Gene Youngblood (*Expanded Cinema*, 1970) to P. Adams Sitney (*Visionary Film*,

1974), or Parker Tyler (*Underground Film*, 1969) to Jonas Mekas (*Movie Journal: The Rise of a New American Cinema, 1959–1971*, 1972) or David Curtis (*Experimental Cinema*, 1971); to more recent studies, such as Paul Arthur (*A Line of Sight*, 2005) or A.L Rees (*A History of Experimental Film and Video*, 1999), to Jean Petrolle and Virginia Wright Wexman (*Women and Experimental Filmmaking*, 2005) or Michael O'Pray (*Avant-Garde Film*, 2003), there are many texts that offer invaluable insight into the history and culture of the avant-garde film. Many of these texts do discuss longer films, but most of the films I address in the last part of this book — the contemporary avant-garde feature film — are *not* discussed, primarily because they are not seen as canonical avant-garde films. And indeed they are not; they are of a different *type* than the historical avant-gardes, something I hope to make clear over the course of the book.

The focus of this volume is on feature-length avant-garde films. I am interested in contemporary avant-garde feature films in particular, and also the historical and cultural parameters that help establish and maintain the very idea of an avant-garde cinema. To this end, the book is also about defining the various types of avant-garde and experimental films. I feel this is an important area of interest because it is largely a neglected one; most accounts of the avant-garde focus on short films. I clarify this in both the introduction and in Parts I and II of the book. My approach to contemporary avant-garde films acknowledges the fact that the way I define them is similar to the way one may consider other genres, like independent cinema or art-house cinema. My general interest in the contemporary avant-garde feature stems in part from much research and teaching in cinema and directors "outside" the mainstream; avant-garde film is a particular area of interest because of its variety, its historical and cultural significance, and because of its capacity to engage us on cognitive levels that are more intellectual and emotional.

This book is not theoretical in nature. I simply want to provide an overview of feature-length avant-garde films. There will be many films missing from my discussion; as mentioned, there are many types one could address as avant-garde. I have only chosen a handful to analyze specifically. There are other texts that address specific directors and films, and I would suggest readers seek them out if interested. Most of my research and attention is to the films themselves, and also some of the books that have become standard examinations of avant-garde and experimental cinema — incidentally, two categories that I admit to sometimes using interchangeably. I have included a bibliography, and I urge readers to consult it. The main difference between this book and others is that (a) I focus on feature-length films, whereas traditional discussions of avant-garde cinema, and especially textbooks on avant-garde films, focus on short, canonical films (and their filmmakers); and (b) I address many types of films one could consider avant-garde, which in part takes me away from the canonical avant-gardes.

Introduction

Since the beginning of cinema there have always been attempts by film-makers to seek alternative methods of approaching cinematic form, style, and thematic content. Both amateurs and professionals alike have been driven to produce films that embrace unconventional methods and styles in order to render a particular and unique vision. The alternative is the avant-garde. The avant-garde has existed in a peripheral position to more formally accepted genres of cinema. A history of the avant-garde encompasses many movements, schools of thought, nationalities, attitudes, and theoretical speculation. The dialogic criticism circling the avant-garde is rather tenuous because there are no "exact" definitions of it, and also there are certain connotations that arise whenever the term is mentioned: offbeat, weird, strange, offensive, experimental, to name but a few epithets. Given this, the history of the avant-garde film is wrought with complications: There are literally thousands of short films that are characterized as "avant-garde," and these multitudes of films are either embraced by the artistic community as being overtly typical of certain avant-garde "movements" (such as abstract, surrealist, or structuralist) or they are hardly ever seen and therefore exist more for their creators, other filmmakers, scholars, or collectors. Most studies of the history of avant-garde cinema tend to focus on the massive amount of short films that have been produced for over a century.[1] While these studies are extremely important in aiding the understanding of the characteristics of the avant-garde film, they are not inclusive. Defining the avant-garde film is a rather complex and tricky area, made more decisive — and divisive — by the fact that there are also many types of avant-garde films, and also because the discourses surrounding them almost always focus predominately on short films. Many well-known practitioners of alternative cinema, particularly avant-garde short films, also write about their works (e.g., Stan Brakhage, Maya Deren, or James Broughton), which both complicates and instructs us how to think about them. By "short film" I mean ones that have a running time of less than an hour. What then of longer films that have the characteristics of avant-garde cinema?

This study is an overview of the avant-garde feature film, with a particular interest in and focus on contemporary filmmakers and films. Feature films that contain avant-garde characteristics are plentiful, whereas ones that are entirely avant-garde are rare. There are large numbers of films that are certainly "alternative to the mainstream" and are therefore labeled as an avant-garde, underground, or cult film. Modernism, or modernist aesthetics, has also been described as being dialectically antithetical to avant-garde, but there are critics who discuss avant-garde films as being reasonable examples of high modernism, mainly because the advent of the avant-garde in the 1920s coincided with the widely used term "modernism" employed to discuss the historical moment and certain artistic practices. Because there are so many terms and ideas associated with the avant-garde, perfecting a definition is difficult. My goal is to analyze and critically discuss feature-length avant-garde films, a largely neglected area of film studies and therefore worthy of fresh insight and evaluation. There are numerous filmmakers who are typically called avant-gardists, including Guy Maddin, Peter Greenaway, and Jan Svankmajer, all of whom I will discuss; but there are also many types of feature films that should be considered avant-garde, from surrealist exercises to found-footage films to essay films, all constructed by a variety of directors who can be thought of as making avant-garde features. Because I am interested in the avant-garde feature film as it exists in contemporary cinema, I will only briefly address feature-length experimental films from the "canonical" avant-gardes, e.g., filmmakers from the 1930s to the 1960s, whose work is traditionally held as the best examples of avant-garde filmmaking and therefore have been written about extensively. Using these figures as touchstones is helpful, but they are directors primarily known for their shorter works, even when "compiling" a longer film. (The features made by these avant-garde filmmakers are also well-known, mainly because the directors—like Cocteau, Buñuel, Frampton, or Mekas—*did* make feature films.) Other figures, like Deren, Anger, and Brakhage, focused almost exclusively on shorter films (though both Brakhage and Anger did make longer ones). Still, their output is enormously influential and cannot be overlooked. Contemporary or modern feature-length avant-garde films share many of the characteristics of the popular and well-known short films of the avant-garde, but they are also decidedly more multifaceted, more intricate, and unconditionally more difficult to categorize. For example, many contemporary filmmakers have utilized "avant-garde" aesthetics in their films. There are moments, that is, of strange, dream-like, or surreal instances that occur in feature films.[2] Using avant-garde techniques, like superimposition, rapid montage, continuity errors, or nonlinear storytelling, occasionally signify a mainstream film as "different." Additionally, many films use historically significant cinematic stylistic choices, like expressionism or surrealism. An avant-garde feature film may have a recognizable narrative structure, but it is often occluded by such stylistic or formal characteristics of the historical avant-gardes, or they are deliberately different in approach or execution. A feature-length avant-garde film's style, form, and technique are unequivocally different.

The avant-garde feature film is one whose entire structure is based upon certain principles of the various avant-gardes, and not just moments in the narrative that seem "unusual." Even when a feature-length avant-garde picture appears rather "common," which they very often do, it is important to understand why the filmmaker has chosen to incorporate varying styles, methods, or strategies within the film. It is not necessarily done in the hopes of reaching a larger audience, but rather to visualize the objective and subjective realities that distinguish the films themselves. Many traces of avant-garde techniques also can be found in numerous international cinemas, from the French New Wave to Czechoslovakian animation. These pictures are extremely important in aiding an overall understanding of feature-length avant-garde films, so I want to discuss them as significant historical instances of the avant-garde. Avant-garde filmmakers tend to work in a particular and highly personal way, making films that are consciously anti-mainstream, deliberately aesthetically challenging, and purposefully intellectually and emotionally demanding. Inasmuch as they are making a film, they are also provoking the spectator. But it is a very good thing to be provoked by the cinema. Rarely is the spectator challenged to think and, more importantly, *to see* differently than when engaged by an avant-garde film. Avant-garde features are theoretically oppositional to mainstream films. The filmmaker's attitude toward the capabilities of cinema directly influences the spectator's attitude, which could be aggravating just as much as it is invigorating. Even more importantly, "avant-garde" is an attitude — one that stirs, instigates, irritates, and incites.

Avant-garde cinema has existed since the advent of moving images, even if the label has been retroactively applied. Many short works produced by Thomas Edison or Edwin S. Porter or Georges Méliès have been described as avant-garde, mainly because, at that time (between 1895 and 1903), these and other filmmakers were simply figuring out the equipment and what exactly to film, which resulted in fragmentary shorts that appeared "unusual." Gaumont films from the 1910s also occasionally had unusual narratives and film styles. Again, these films, though, were not deliberately made as "avant-garde." After World War I, more typical and characteristic examples emerged in the 1920s, when "avant-garde" was used to describe certain artistic practices. The 1920s gave rise to Surrealism, Expressionism, and Abstraction, all important attributes of the avant-garde film that I will detail in Chapter 2. The 1940s and 1950s demonstrated a wide variety of personal films, while the 1960s and 1970s gave rise to underground and cult cinema, two important areas of cinema history that, while not completely assuming the moniker of "avant-garde," nevertheless consist of films that share many general qualities of avant-garde cinema as a whole. While it is helpful to draw a trajectory of the historical avant-gardes, and also to recognize certain films and movements that help shape the contemporary avant-garde feature film, it still is imperative to acknowledge that because of the conflicting views on the cultural and social significance of the various avant-gardes, a concise history proves elusive. What I will aim to do in this study is provide a more thorough understanding of the feature-length avant-garde film by outlining the various film techniques, styles, forms, and strategies that shape the contemporary avant-garde feature film.

Avant-garde films often give rise to debates concerning formalism and realism. Certainly the formal aspects of filmmaking are apparent — and often deliberately so — in avant-garde pictures, but I also think that a great many avant-garde films are realistic in the sense that they not only present us with a unique subjective representation of reality (a phenomenological perspective), but, theoretically and ontologically speaking, they deal with the material reality of the filmstrip itself. Essentially, avant-garde filmmakers appreciate the capabilities of film (and video), which makes their often bare-bones aesthetic approach *real*. At the same time, however, it is very clear when watching an avant-garde film, and sometimes with a feature-length film, that spectators are keenly aware of the artifice of the film. This scenario presents us with a unique dialectic; avant-garde filmmakers very deliberately are aware of the medium (anyone from Cocteau to Godard to Greenaway argues this), but their works also embrace a realist attitude — their own *vision of reality*. For example, even surrealist films are, in a roundabout way, "interpretations" of reality; Godard's *A Woman Is a Woman* (1961) deconstructs and rebuilds the generic tropes of the musical, melodrama, and romance to reflect reality. While I am not equating the two (i.e., avant-garde/realism), it does seem that avant-garde films can be identified as types of films that approach reality from an alternative perspective. This alternative perspective crops up in the many varieties of feature-length avant-garde films, from outright surrealist films to psychodramas, diary films, and even structuralist films.[3] Simply put (for now), many feature-length avant-garde films offer an array of styles, techniques, and themes that present us with a highly important, yet appropriated, view of everyday events or dream worlds that are ostensibly "real."

Avant-garde films take an anti-establishment stance, a position that enables the filmmakers to address any subject matter on their own terms. For this reason I want to use the term "avant-garde" as an artistic category, an aesthetic approach, and an attitude. First, films that are avant-garde are in their own genre; and like in other more mainstream genres (i.e., Romantic Comedy, Science Fiction, etc.), there are subgenres and hybrid genres, but I will refer to them as "types" of avant-garde film. Certain types, that is, become common practice for certain filmmakers. These might include the Essay Film or Collage Film or Surrealist Film. The unique aspect about the artistic category of the avant-grade is that it encompasses not just films, but paintings, music, sculpture, architecture, and even literature. This broadening of the term might help us understand a bit more about the unique aspects it has in regards to cinematic practice. To categorize avant-garde films into subgenres helps demarcate them, even if the boundaries are somewhat arbitrary. As mentioned previously, ascribing a work of art as "avant-garde" immediately gives rise to questions over intent, meaning, and craft. But it also suggests a far more profound work of art as well, which is beneficial to an overall understanding of the significance of an avant-garde work, like a film. Second, "avant-garde" denotes a particular aesthetic approach to the craft. In filmmaking, it signifies a conscious shift from conventional tropes to more experimental ones. Embracing unusual methods in order to render a vision elucidates both historical and cultural attitudes about avant-garde works. A surrealist film from the 1920s, for example, like the highly influential *Un Chien Andalou* (1929), makes us recognize and appreciate the audacity of the style and the absurdities of the narrative. Finally, a filmmaker (or other artist) can have an avant-garde attitude. Having this mind-set suggests an outsider positioning, but it also connotes an iconoclastic and visionary creator, someone who works external to the limits of tradition.

In order to understand the aspects of a feature-length film that is avant-garde, it may be helpful to interrogate the term itself. Before the term "avant-garde" was co-opted and used to describe artistic practices, it generally referred to a military advancement. "Avant-Garde" is a French term, which, when translated, means "advance guard." The term was originally used to describe troops who were ahead of the rest of the army and "led the way" to the battlefield, or at least surveyed the battleground before the rest of the army advanced with them. The job of the advance guard, or vanguard, as it was also known, was to plan a particular course for the army to follow. Since they were scouting the area, they had to be highly skilled. They also had to search for and identify danger, and therefore protect the ones they were leading. "Vanguard" also means forerunner or forefront. If we take the term literally, then, and change "army" to "filmmaker," it implies that filmmakers who are part of the avant-garde "lead the way" for all other filmmakers to follow, and also that they were in danger or at least participated in dangerous maneuvering. This is not how the avant-garde is traditionally considered. The avant-garde is usually discussed as being on the margins or fringes, and not *leading the way* as forerunners of form and style, as I think they do. A quick syllogism:

> The avant-garde is in advance of other filmmakers.
> Other filmmakers follow the avant-garde as it leads.
> Therefore, the other filmmakers are "behind" the avant-garde.

This is not a perfect syllogism, but the point is that the rest of the filmmaking world — the mainstream — is being led by the avant-garde. It is the filmmakers working within the aesthetic milieu of the various avant-gardes who are foremost and principally "ahead" of more traditional filmmakers, and so the rest of the filmmaking world is following their lead, even trying to catch up. They lead by example. Essentially, the avant-garde is *better than* the traditions of the mainstream; the films within the avant-garde are therefore more artistic and more skillfully made, are "dangerous," and, as a result, are more aesthetically demanding. These possibly overused metaphors notwithstanding, the avant-garde feature film is also one that is unavoidable; any time an avant-garde filmmaker creates a new work, he or she is signaled out as being in opposition to the center, which, in terms of success and recognition, puts the avant-garde filmmaker at a disadvantage — but only if he or she courts the mainstream, which is extremely rare. Instead, existing on the periphery has its advantages. A benefit to being on the outside looking in is that the outsider — the avant-garde filmmaker — is free from constraint. There is a higher amount of freedom, a greater degree of independence, a wider divide between art and the "culture industry." Mass culture in particular tends to swallow up more mainstream filmmaking with endless tie-ins, star-driven vehicles, and the bombardment of advertising. Avant-garde cinema is, therefore, a highly important area of artistic achievement that needs (re)consideration, especially when it comes to the feature film. Feature-length avant-garde films are rarely discussed outside of very small cinephilic circles, if even then, and thus warrant an analysis that situates them as important and significance instances of cinema history and culture.[4] An avant-garde feature film can be defined as one that has (a) an idiosyncratic personal vision; (b) stylistic or formal innovation; and (c) a sustained or decipherable narrative. These traits are simple enough but need further investigation.

Almost any film could be labeled as personal, but in the world of the avant-garde it means something different. Personal ambition and artistry are different motivations; the avant-garde feature filmmaker is far more interested in artistry than monetary or mainstream success. These filmmakers create films that adhere to personal visions of what cinema can accomplish that is far removed and beyond the technically-infused cinema of the mainstream. This is not to say the avant-garde feature does not welcome technology. Indeed, many avant-garde feature films embrace technology in order to craft unique stories. Still, the avant-garde feature film very rarely has ties to studio financing, so the technology is either "primitive," such as scratching the surface of the film itself (like Stan Brakhage) or tinting it (like Guy Maddin), or is created completely by the filmmaker (like Jan Svankmajer's puppets and animation techniques). A personal vision of cinema also suggests the necessity to be creative. Again, this is a rather simplistic notion, but the avant-garde filmmaker radically re-examines the creative process, asking questions of the medium itself. What can film do? What can film accomplish? How can film articulate the unique and peculiar visions of the uncanny, the unconscious, the imaginative? Interestingly, avant-garde films are not typically embraced by the mainstream like other avant-garde arts. Painting, for instance, is routinely applauded whenever a consciously new voice is heard.[5] Similarly, music has also forged a niche for avant-garde composers.[6] Even choreographers are studied intently for their highly individualistic interpretations of the body and movement.[7] The avant-garde feature filmmaker is only studied by serious cinèastes or academics; their films are not "on display" like works of art in a museum. Traditionally speaking, directors whose works are considered avant-garde are accepted at certain film festivals (particularly Toronto, Berlin, Cannes, and Venice, but minor ones as well), but rarely are they welcomed on larger stages. Their world is uniquely their own; hence they are creating personal films for personal gratification, with little regard to ever achieving success, be it nominal or not. In addition, most of these filmmakers embrace their outsider status and recognize the ardent followers their work has gathered. Some of the films and filmmakers I will discuss are actually well-known, as they have either received a larger critical assessment or because they straddle the margins and the mainstream.

A personal cinema can also be exemplified by ideological or political positions. Peter Wollen has detailed Jean-Luc Godard's "counter-cinema" in this regard. The original avant-gardes of the1920s (Impressionism, Dadaism, Surrealism) were in large part an ideological assault on the mainstream. These types of films aimed to deconstruct the "typical." They were anti-aesthetic and anti-bourgeois, and often had nonlinear plots or didactic tones. (Godard's "Vertov" films of the late 1960s and early 1970s are often discussed in a similar fashion. I will discuss Godard further, addressing his films that are indeed avant-garde, ones that I call "theoretical-dialectic films.") Luis Buñuel's *L'Age d'Or* (1930), for example, an early paradigm of the avant-garde feature film, is one of his characteristic condemnations of the bourgeoisie. It embraces its blasphemy while also instigating provocation based on the ideological stance it takes. Spectators see the problems instigated by the middle class based on the ideological nature of the film. Buñuel's personal, subjective view is the driving force behind the film, and it is a vision he would return to again and again.

Being personal also connotes the almost compulsive certainty of presenting a visual inner landscape. In essence, the avant-garde filmmaker has a very distinctive idea about the film he or she creates. Personal (short) films of the avant-garde have been described as poetic, which implies a higher degree of imagination, idealism, and subjectivity, and certain rudiments of Romanticism, elements that do not usually creep into the mainstream. Certain film directors who have a personal poetic vision but are not regarded as avant-garde undoubtedly work in their own meticulous ways, utilizing methods that are applicable to their own visions. Ingmar Bergman is one such director. His works are not really avant-garde, but they are extremely personal. (The one exception may be *Persona* [1966], a film that is sometimes labeled as avant-garde.) Avant-garde filmmakers whose films are entirely unconventional possess a poetic sense of filmmaking; almost all of their cinematic output is avant-garde, rather than having one or two films that are nontraditional. This is the case with the feature film as well. Very rarely will the avant-garde feature filmmaker venture into the mainstream (though, as mentioned, it does occur). The explosion of American avant-garde film in the 1940s through 1960s, which was primarily focused on filmmakers like Kenneth Anger, Maya Deren, and Stan Brakhage, was a "personal cinema in which expression, improvisation and spontaneity were to be paramount, a poetry of private passions ... [it was] an attempt to deal with the self by using mythical themes and images, and the filmmaker as narrative protagonist."[8] By contrast, contemporary avant-garde feature films do not star the director, nor do they actively seek to uncover the unconscious, though they delve into unconscious states of being/existence through uncanny effects. (Guy Maddin, who I will discuss in an analysis of his film *Archangel*, does make auto-biographical films where he also addresses his memories—but he has other people appear as "Guy Maddin," and his films are somewhat surrealist, like many of the shorter, personal American avant-garde films were.) The essential and fundamental quality of feature-length avant-garde films is the easily recognizable style of the director. The directors I will be discussing, therefore, could be considered auteurs.

A familiar style of filmmaking implies that a collection of avant-garde feature films by the same director are easy to identify. This is undoubtedly true. Whatever stylistic choices someone makes, inevitably those choices impact their creativity. In other words, when considering the avant-garde feature film, it is necessary to consider how the film's language produces a particular topography. The directors I will be focusing on have a deliberate and peculiar style; the mise-en-scène, cinematography, and narrative structure of their films indicate both a radical departure from the norm and also a fundamental and far-reaching aesthetic that signifies their work. Very often the style of the avant-garde filmmaker is used to subvert the classical norms of typical mainstream cinema. Many of the films I will address routinely ask us to re-think fundamentally our preconceptions about cinema. The auteur director of the avant-garde typically eschews genre conventions, relying solely on his or her vision (or re-vision) of generic topoi. The style of the avant-garde filmmaker is habitually described as modernist, which implies a need to break away from tradition while seeking alternative forms and forging a pervasive self-consciousness. For instance, the historical avant-gardes of the 1920s and 1930s designate a distinction "between a high-modernist avant-garde preoccupied with autotelic form, and a 'low' carnivalized, anti-institutional, and anti-grammatical avant-garde which attacked the art system."[9] While this also distinguishes a more political slant characteristic of the earlier avant-gardes, many contemporary feature-length films also demonstrate an "autotelic" or "anti-" attitude. An auteuristic filmmaker who makes avant-garde feature films is particularly well-suited to abstain from rules that govern more traditional kinds of filmmaking, whether studio-era films or more recent Hollywood blockbusters. Finally, auteurism denotes a particular style, a recognizable method of filmmaking by a single director. It is easy to get hemmed in by the "auteur theory," but when considering feature-length avant-garde films, it can be useful simply because auteurism also implies an individualistic approach, the director-as-producer-of-meaning, and a clear indication of film-as-art, which I will discuss further in Chapter 2.

One final characteristic of the feature-length avant-garde film is the narrative structure. Many short avant-garde films have nonlinear plots, which means they are more associative than direct. Montage, collage, and even "regular" linear editing practices also help structure the narrative of the avant-garde feature film. Most feature films usually have a discernable plot, although it may be suggestive, convoluted, or presented more visually than narratively. It may be argued, perhaps more fittingly, that the narrative of the avant-garde feature "has been displaced, deformed, and reformed, rather than simply expunged altogether."[10] Recognizing the narrative in the feature is easier than in shorter avant-garde films. Simply put, they do have stories to tell. There may be a good deal of interpretation on the part of the spectator, but here again lies the notion of provoking the spectator. Instead of simply being the passive receiver of the film's narrative, the spectator of the avant-garde feature often has to work more aggressively to uncover the narrative idioms at play. Feature-length avant-garde films may have unusual narrative structures, but they still inherently focus on the story itself, even when rendered in an "offbeat" fashion. Jan Svankmajer's *Conspirators of Pleasure* (1996), for example, has no dialogue, but the episodic construction of the narrative, combined with the striking visuals, make the film entirely unique and imminently enjoyable — far more than a film loaded with dialogue that tackles the same perverse subject matter. An alternative film narrative also presents reality in an unusual way. The ostensible nature of realism is often questioned in an avant-garde film narrative, though the events are very much a part of the "real" world of the filmmaker's vision. Even though there is direct observation of the world, avant-garde filmmakers challenge the idea of an objective reality and therefore focus more on subjectivity. This is not to say that many avant-garde features do not utilize objectivity. As mentioned previously, I would say that most avant-garde features do in fact present us with an objective truth, but it is highly tempered through the artist's own subjective perspective. Experimental avant-garde narratives can be associative, structural, participatory, critical, confrontational, or expressive.[11] Hans-Jürgen Syberberg's *Hitler, a Film from Germany* (1977), which I will discuss further, for example, utilizes Brechtian distanciation in an attempt to deliberately force the spectator into serious contemplation of the film's ideas and form.

The avant-garde feature film is unique to cinema history. It is an innovative and original work that inspires and aggravates. These types of films are often relegated to the margins because they are so different from what audiences expect when they go to the movies. In fact, it is very rare that an avant-garde feature film will ever actually play in any market. They are screened at festivals, museums, universities, or art-house theaters in large cities. The only way many of these films gain notice is simply from the analyses they receive from critics or scholars. Many avant-garde features become cult or underground "classics," which also means they accumulate a rabid following over a period of time. Still others are screened maybe once or twice, are seen by relatively few people, and become the stuff of legends. The exhibition, distribution, and promotion of avant-garde features is a thorny undertaking; directors of the avant-garde are used to being heralded at festivals, but beyond that they realize their films will not be embraced by middle America. But that is okay. If they ever gain a degree of popularity, it potentially compromises their vision. Remaining independent is just as important as maintaining the integrity of their work.

I have detailed several important areas of the avant-garde feature film, which I will elaborate on in chapters 1 and 2. They are not exhaustive characteristics, but they do help us form a general outline of certain qualities that denote their unique nature. In discussing a variety of films and particular filmmakers, I hope to show the historical, aesthetic, and social significance of the avant-garde feature film. Avant-garde films are pedagogical interventions that allow us to see cinema from an entirely different perspective. They operate in a world where the cultural value systems of the mainstream are almost nonexistent. Avant-garde feature films are fraught with ambiguities, paradoxes, and multivalent messages. They are also far more imaginative than the majority of films that constitute the popular. For this reason alone we should value their inventiveness, their unapologetic styles, and their combination of playful and serious attitudes that outweigh the conventional. Indeed, the directors of the avant-garde feature film are leading the way.

The book is divided into several parts with individual chapters addressing particular areas of the avant-garde feature film; and each section is presented chronologically, so as to offer an historical trajectory of the avant-garde feature film. Part I is divided into three chapters. Chapter 1 offers a more thorough definition of avant-garde film in order to clarify how the contemporary feature films I will discuss (as case studies in Part III) adhere to certain tropes or characteristics of the better-known historical avant-gardes. In Chapter 2, I provide an overview of several key stylistic and formal filmmaking practices that help identify the avant-garde feature film. These practices, which include Expressionism, Surrealism, Abstraction, and Montage, are all important areas of film history and culture, and they signify a certain link between formal practices of the 1920s with later avant-garde films. Chapter 3 offers analyses of four important early avant-garde feature films: Luis Buñuel and Salvador Dalí's *L'Age d'Or* (1930), Jean Cocteau's *The Blood of a Poet* (1930), Hans Richter's *Dreams That Money Can Buy* (1947) and Jean Isidore Isou's *Venom and Eternity* (1951). Each of these films provides early examples of alternative approaches to narrative, form, and theme.

Part II is divided into two chapters. Chapter 4 addresses the *real* avant-garde, by which I mean those films and filmmakers traditionally accepted and studied as the most significant and influential avant-gardists of the twentieth century. These include Stan Brakhage, Kenneth Anger, Maya Deren, Ken Jacobs, James Broughton, Michael Snow, and others. These filmmakers are considered *pure* avant-garde and experimental filmmakers, best known for their *shorter* films. I will discuss them briefly (as they have been chronicled in full elsewhere) in order to show their lasting influence on feature-length avant-garde films and filmmakers. To exemplify this, Chapter 5 offers case studies of longer avant-garde films made by these well-known artists. I will discuss Harry Smith's *Heaven and Earth Magic* (1957–1962), Andy Warhol's *Sleep* (1963), Jonas Mekas's *Walden (Diaries, Notes, Sketches)* (1969), and Hollis Frampton's *Zorns Lemma* (1970) as examples of the best kind of avant-garde feature filmmaking that are all influential yet vastly different from the contemporary avant-garde feature film.

With Part III the focus is shifted to the contemporary avant-garde feature film, detailing more recent (1960s to the present) moments and movements of avant-garde feature filmmaking. In the introductory section I detail particular historical/cultural occurrences in film that helped shape and define avant-garde films. Chapter 6 is an overview of Underground Film and how it relates to contemporary avant-garde feature films. Chapter 7 delineates different types or subgenres of the avant-garde feature film, including the Essay Film (or the Theoretical-Dialectic Film), Women's Experimental Cinema (itself a genre), and the City Symphony Film. My reason for focusing only on these three is because their methods and approach overlap: All are essentially avant-garde docufictions. There are certainly other "types" of avant-garde films, which hopefully will have been made clear in the first two parts of the book, and also in the section on recent films.

Chapter 8 brings the book full circle by examining several key filmmakers and a handful of representative avant-garde feature films. This chapter offers analyses of contemporary modern avant-garde feature films. Each case study is unique and offers ways of defining and describing certain films as avant-garde or experimental and antithetical to the mainstream, and each have some ties to traditional forms of avant-garde filmmaking.

I should make clear, too, that I am not putting forth a theory of avant-garde film; rather, I am *engaging* with current and historical ideas and issues in avant-garde criticism. In many ways this book is meant as an introduction to avant-garde film, experimental filmmaking, and what I am arguing for — the feature-length avant-garde film. The astute student of avant-garde film history and culture might therefore find this material relevant and hopefully insightful.

PART I

AVANT-GARDE FILM: HISTORY, THEORY AND CRITICISM

Part of the appeal of avant-garde film stems from its sheer unconventionality, its boldness, its difference. There is a long tradition of aesthetic practice that stands in opposition to tradition, whether to prevailing modes of discourse, methodological approach, dominant ideology, or rules of construction. Avant-garde filmmaking practices are part of this tradition. Constructing a work of art (here, a film), is a process of decision-making, and for the avant-garde filmmaker or those that wish to experiment with the medium and its materiality, there is a conscious decision to avoid tradition. The reasons for this vary, of course, but ultimately certain filmmakers may embrace artistic movements (surrealism or Dadaism, for instance), or they may create a unique path themselves, combining forms, techniques, motifs, and highly personal concerns. This leads to a sensibility based on advanced (i.e., *avant-garde*) vision — the vision to expand the capabilities of film. There are many rich examples of artists who shun mainstream practice — whether in film, music, literature, or painting — and because of this one may indeed be able to trace a certain historical or cultural arc of specific types of alternative approaches to aesthetic creation, again whether it be film, music, literature, painting, etc. In the end, what one may discover is a fascinating trajectory of non-mainstream art. The avant-garde and experimental film tradition follows such a path. In order to recognize the ways contemporary filmmakers create experimental films, it is beneficial to trace aesthetic practices that helped shape avant-garde film over cinematic history. It is also beneficial to consider these types of films *as films themselves*— that is, what exactly do they show and depict, how do they communicate, how are they different, how do they present conceptual and perceptual ideas, and so forth. Understanding these lines of inquiry might also lead to a greater appreciation of avant-garde film in general. Thus, it is critically important to explore and consider the various ways that avant-garde films have both evolved *and* remained consistent in their decisive means of investigating the cinematic medium and the world around us.

𝔖 Chapter 1 𝔢

What Is an
Avant-Garde Film?

Avant-garde films necessitate a different kind of viewing experience, one that requires discipline, patience, and enthusiasm for alternative forms of representation and presentation. Avant-garde films involve the senses in ways that are atypical of mainstream films; nothing is ever clearly denoted for you, so you have to work. This is not to say that all avant-garde films are completely strange and have no form of narrative continuity or plot construction. Many do, especially feature films. But the processes involved in discovering all the nuances of form/style/theme in avant-garde feature films is unique to cinema culture. Avant-garde films do not necessarily fit easily into particular genres, nor do they often constitute a tight or secure genre on their own (an issue I address later). Still, when one visualizes or thinks of an avant-garde film, it typically manifests as something *different*—a work that is antithetical to the mainstream, is produced outside economic and cultural channels of discourse, is (sometimes) deliberately political in nature, and is uniformly diverse in its multiple variations and forms. Avant-garde films are "understood as interventionist, existing to confront and transform the dominant culture by putting aesthetic practice at the service of social and political change."[1] Still, "avant-garde" is hard to define precisely; but it is perhaps easy to recognize an avant-garde film, simply because it is so dissimilar to what is generally expected from going to the movies or even watching films at home.

Avant-garde films differ from more mainstream genre films because they do not have easily proscribed generic traits or characteristics in them that identify them according to a straightforward genre, though they do engage genre(s). A classic Western, for example, has readily identifiable iconography: broad outdoor vistas; clearly delineated good guys and bad guys; horses; six-shooters; saloons; etc. But an avant-garde film does not have these kinds of markers. Instead, most — but not all — can be identified according to the following:

1. an experimental style or form
2. a non-linear, achronological, or non-narrative story

3. an unusual manner of representation (of reality or otherwise)
4. a particular voice/vision of the director
5. poetic or lyrical flourishes
6. the mixing of styles/genres
7. ambiguity, in terms of characterization or narrative or thematic closure
8. a decidedly different kind of demand for contrary spectatorial expectations
9. when available/known, alternative production/distribution/exhibition practices
10. an appearance that signifies an "other"

It goes without saying that not all of these indicators are stable, that not every avant-garde film has all or even as few as two of these characteristics. And certainly other attributes may be added to this list. But on average, many avant-garde films adhere to at least one of these (mainstream films might also, but not always deliberately). What, then, makes an avant-garde film essentially different? It really comes down to viewing and thinking — perception and contemplation. Those viewers wanting to be challenged by an aesthetic that is artful, demanding, idiosyncratic, and peculiarly odd, and who desire an active viewing experience, seek the avant-garde film. However, the best-known avant-garde films are short in length and are "canonical," something I will address in Part II. So what then of the feature-length avant-garde film? What makes them unique, special, and dissimilar to other films? In some regard, the distinctiveness of the avant-garde feature film lies in its capacity to attract filmmakers who want to experiment. That is, anyone who really wants to attempt an alternative film project *can*— mainstream filmmaker or not — but only if he or she is willing to risk everything for the sake of personal vision and creativity. (It goes without saying, perhaps, that most feature-length avant-garde films are made by filmmakers who are already practicing avant-gardists; most, if not all, of their films are avant-garde.) The contemporary directors and films I will discuss in Part III all are filmmakers who actively seek alternative modes of engagement. A feature-length avant-garde film is one that is ambitious in scope, execution, and presentation. Its style and form is unquestionably different, its thematic content distinct and personal, and its level of engagement is extremely dynamic, even when there is a discernable narrative or one that is nonlinear or achronological or defies spatial/temporal and causal logic.

Some Considerations of Style/Form

Avant-garde feature films use film language in different ways. The essential elements of any film —cinematography, mise-en-scène, editing, sound — are often deployed and employed in ways that make them stand out. Most avant-garde features intentionally try to destabilize the characteristics that define classical Hollywood style, like causal logic, narrative linearity, and unobtrusive craftsmanship. The production conventions that define mainstream film are antithetical to the individualistic, experimental, or visionary principles that help define avant-garde features. These types of films can take various forms; there may be structural films (Frampton's *Zorns Lemma*); surrealist excursions (Cocteau's *Blood of a Poet* or Svankmajer's *Conspirators of Pleasure*); anachronistic blendings of styles (Maddin's *Archangel*); or essayistic efforts (Friedrich's *The Ties That Bind* or Jarman's *Blue*). In all such cases, what one recognizes is a sensorial experience unlike the bland passivity of mainstream cinema. These films (and others) force us to contemplate the theoretical and practical applications of film language because they apply and exploit them in ways so dialectically opposed to typical film; watching them not only engages us emotionally but also intellectually. Avant-garde features exist in the margins, often unaffected by the culture industry that drives the commercial realm of film production. (Some films or filmmakers might "slip" into the center, like David Lynch, but only because of their/his growing cult status and not because they/he embrace[s] the mainstream.) Avant-garde feature films focus on a wide array of cinematic tropes and formal styles. They may address issues concerning simultaneity and temporal/spatial logic or disorientation; subjectivity; the unconscious potential of the film itself (as opposed to the psychoanalysis of a character); abstractness; or questions concerning film-as-art. They may draw attention to their signifying practices or question the stability of accepted signs and referents; they may address the potential for alternative point of views; and they may distort the traits of narrative cinema, such as setting, character, or plot. They may engage in modernist, postmodernist, or anti-modernist aesthetics. They may be hostile toward other films ("virtually all verbal proclamations of avant-garde filmmakers show a lesser or greater amount of hostility toward commercial filmmaking"[2]). By not participating in the commercial film industry that defines the cultural capital of mainstream filmmaking, the avant-garde feature film is aligned with forms of artistic expression aimed at countering, reacting against, or destabilizing the accepted norms and values of art and filmmaking.

Film styles vary through genre, but the most important aspects of determining a particular film's style is through its language: mise-en-scène, cinematography, editing, and sound. Considerations of the multiple techniques involved in constructing a film are essential in understanding its style or stylistic devices. So when considering an avant-garde feature film, one should be mindful of how the filmmaker is using the traits of film language to create a particular style. Style, according to David Bordwell, is

> A film's systematic and significant use of techniques of the medium. Those techniques fall into broad domains: mise en scène (staging, lighting, performance, and setting); framing, focus, control of color values, and other aspects of cinematography; editing;

and sound. Style is, minimally, the texture of the film's images and sounds, the result of choices made by the filmmaker(s) in particular historical circumstances.[3]

This categorization of style is essentially a delineation of the language of film, and it bears repeating only because it allows for a way of interpreting and distinguishing modes of cinematic practice, like avant-garde films that are distinct because they engage forms differently and separately from traditional narrative histories of cinema. In other words, when considering style it is helpful to be able to analyze an avant-garde film based upon the styles it participates with, challenges, and/or modifies. Film form is often questioned in avant-garde films. In contrast with more mainstream films, avant-garde films emphasize form first: "Ideological implications may follow, but the most distinctive aspect of [avant-garde] film is its stress on form. The form of the work, which continuity editing in fiction and stress on an eternal referent in documentary deemphasize, takes on primary importance."[4] An examination of the history of the avant-garde almost always establishes a line of opposition to mainstream film practices, which are, in most regards, "easier" to trace through film history. An avant-garde film flies in the face of tradition; it has ties to modernist art (also an oppositional aesthetic force), and, when introduced into the mainstream (like Duchamp's urinal or Buñuel's *Un Chien Andalou* or Warhol's Brillo boxes), it initiates a divide while simultaneously and ironically bridging the gap between mainstream and oppositional art, a paradox that leaves many avant-garde films (and other forms of art) unknown. As Robert Ray suggests, when "the art world began to assume that because the introduction of a new style and its acceptance by the public [happens], a gap would inevitably exist."[5] The oppositional stance of avant-garde films already indicate another line of inquiry, not just from a stylistic front, but also formalist, thematic, aesthetic, ideological, or critical/theoretical ones as well.

Avant-garde films can also be defined — or at least recognized — by their industrial practices. The way they are produced, distributed, and exhibited (if they are at all distributed and shown) differs vastly from commercialized mass-market cinema. This inevitably affects spectatorship because the importance of where and when someone sees a film (let alone avant-garde) can influence their understanding of it. Still, the majority of avant-garde films are produced outside standard industrial practices. (It should be noted that some do receive financing and are often funded through state-supported film cooperatives, which gives them certain recognition at film festivals, museums, or college campuses.) According to Jeffrey Skoller, avant-garde filmmakers are largely the ones responsible for the distribution and exhibition of their films, either through private funding/screenings, or through "artist-run, not-for-profit production, distribution, or exhibition collectives and organizations." He continues,

> This mode of production reflects another defining principle of modernist avant-gardism, that of its aspiration for autonomy from critical and economic institutionalization. Central to this idea is that individually authored and independently

produced media can be seen as an authentic popular-culture form offering an alternative and antidote to the consumerist media of the for-profit mass-culture industry. This desire for viable forms of cultural production that are autonomous from both the art world and the mass-culture industry continues to be seen as a primary signifier of contemporary avant-garde media practices.[6]

According to Skoller, there is in some regards a dialectic between the desire for autonomy and the viability of the films themselves. While this may be true to a certain extent, most avant-garde filmmakers are content satisfying their own personal ambitions rather than participating in the mainstream, though their films inevitably will be viewed as counterpoint to mainstream films.

Avant-garde films are know for their originality, their precise and dedicated attempts at reinventing what we think we know about how films construct and communicate meaning through the audio-visual experience. Many avant-garde feature films exist in contrary — even reactionary — relationships with dominant cinematic practice, which means they are unique because they address concerns perhaps similar to other films, but do so in completely different ways. Avant-garde films participate in dialogues with all forms of media. In some regards, avant-garde films are an investigation into the ways film can be conceived differently, which essentially is a practice of *innovation*. A fundamental question then might arise: "What exactly is innovative about avant-garde films?" The answer is both historically and culturally grounded. According to Robert Ray,

> Although the avant-garde carries the reputation of irresponsible rebellion, it, in fact, amounts to the humanist's equivalent of science's pure research. Having derived its name from the military (particularly, from the term for the advance troops entrusted with opening holes in the enemy position) and having repeatedly committed itself to scientifically conceived projects (e.g. Zola's "Experimental Novel," Breton's "Surrealist Manifesto"), the avant-garde has always had its practical side. Indeed, in many ways, it amounts to a laboratory of creativity itself. Thus, the question "How do you start an avant-garde?" has implications for any undertaking where innovation is valuable.[7]

The focus on innovation is key in accepting the avant-garde feature film. By understanding the innovativeness of all aspects of the film, from narrative to style, one begins the process of appreciation and comprehension of the avant-garde film, filmmaker, and mode of representation that possibly signifies a genre. Many avant-garde feature films are counterintuitive to what being innovative even connotes, but it suggests an explicit desire for a countercultural "other" that raises consciousness about its relationship to other forms of media practice. As Skoller suggests, avant-garde films are traditionally understood to be "structured by the notion of an aesthetic vanguard leading the way by social critique and aesthetic innovation toward a progressive re-thinking of the relationship of art to the social order."[8] The discourse surrounding avant-garde film as an *innovative force* serves as a tool for critique and knowledge.

Avant-garde films have also been defined by description. For example, Bill Nichols describes almost all non-narrative, experimental, avant-garde films as "poetic." Certain connotations come from a label (lyricism, subjectivity, personal endeavor/labor, and so forth), but nevertheless can prove fruitful in categorizing certain aspects of different avant-garde feature films. According to Nichols, "The poetic mode is a major link between the documentary and avant-garde film. It stresses form or pattern over an explicit argument, even though it may well have an implicit perspective on some aspect of the historical world."[9] In other words, "Avant-garde films, for example, may include elements of logic and aspects of storytelling but they also give great emphasis to the poetic qualities of film language."[10] The poetic sensibilities of the filmmaker — here typically ascribed to an avant-garde filmmaker — are present in the finished "poetic" film and are recognized through an analysis of the film's style. Watching avant-garde films, and especially ones that are longer, means becoming involved in the categories of spectatorship (like emotional involvement or detachment; intellectual engagement; or ideological confrontation) that are both conflicting and contemplative. A "typical" avant-garde film is one that is short and often non-narrative. Feature-length avant-garde films very often have narratives, though they may be presented in an unusual manner. For example, Sergei Paradjanov's *The Color of Pomegranates* (1968) presents the life of a poet, but mainly through vivid tableaux. An avant-garde bio-film like Dusan Makavejev's *W.R.: Mysteries of the Organism* (1971) presents associative vignettes more so than a linear plot, even though it tells a story. And finally, something like Guy Maddin's *Brand Upon the Brain!* (2006) has a very recognizable story, but its manner of presentation — as separate, small-film chapters told like a silent film — differs vastly from mainstream film. This is why the viewing process for avant-garde films is so different and undeniably restless. As Scott MacDonald suggests, "For most people ... avant-garde films are so entirely unlike 'real movies' that they demand a full-scale revaluation of our cinematic preconceptions; they are closer to being 'purely' critical."[11] Avant-garde films serve as guides to viewing processes just as much as they reveal themselves through narrative, image, or audio. Watching films like these, as well as other feature-length avant-garde films, focuses our attention on style and form, and often our knowledge of the world around us. Indeed,

> In poetic film there is often little pretense that what we see resembles the world we already know. The force of the filmmaker's distinctive vision and formal preoccupations give considerable shape to what appears on the screen. Continuity editing is seldom a guiding principle. Poetic films may jump from one place to another, one character to another, and one object to another. They find their coherence in the patterns created from such jumps and in other departures from convention.[12]

The play of cinematic tropes is a means by which the avant-garde filmmaker articulates a particular vision. As Nichols says of the poetic capabilities of many avant-garde film examples, "As poetic works, these films offer the viewer a heightened awareness of the very form and structure of cinema. Like paintings that emphasize brushstrokes in the flatness of the canvas, these works remind the viewer of the material basis for signification in film and related audiovisual media-sounds and images that pass across the screen."[13] What this suggests is that when watching a feature-length avant-garde film, one has to work at discovering or uncovering meaning(s) that emerge from the *texture* of the film: Its form signifies a particular organization that reveals itself through its use of film language — that is, its use or manipulation of sound, editing, mise-en-scène, or cinematography. Most importantly, avant-garde films force us to reconceptualize, reevaluate, and redefine our experience of cinema that we thought we understood based upon the conventions we are already familiar with from viewing mainstream films. As MacDonald says, "The [viewing] experience provides us with the opportunity (an opportunity much of our training has taught us to resist) to come to a clearer, more complete understanding of what the cinematic experience actually can be, and what — for all the pleasure and inspiration it may give us — the conventional movie experience is *not*."[14] In many ways, watching an avant-garde film allows for *uncorrupted* spectatorship, an expression of pleasure generated from the immediacy of the film rather than filtered through the public sphere like mainstream cinema.

Watching and Perceiving

Avant-garde feature films deliberately provoke the spectator. Avant-garde feature films address and interact with ideas and issues surrounding principles of perception; and often the filmmakers choose to do this, bur more frequently the films themselves raise questions concerning them. Dudley Andrew has noted, "Avant-garde filmmakers over the years have disrupted the codes of perception by altering the usual focus, framing, and even the speed and direction of visual recording."[15] This assertion points to the overriding idea that almost all avant-garde feature films are produced and distributed in opposition to the status quo because they "alter the usual"— that is, as Andrew says, they disturb viewer expectations. The avant-garde feature film constantly challenges conventional aesthetic tastes because it is already established as an "other," and it forces us to reexamine the fundamental precepts of perceiving reality as well, which is why I think most avant-garde films are about altering perception. "The viewer's social assumptions and viewing expectations may be thrown into question," states Nichols.[16] In addition, avant-garde feature films allow us to see how cinema can be perceived by showing us a medium ripe for intervention.

Avant-garde feature films may be a genre unto itself, but I suggest that since there are so many different examples of the types of filmmaking associated with experimental and avant-garde filmmaking, perhaps it is best to say that there are relatively few directors whose complete filmic output is entirely avant-garde or even feature-length; Svankmajer, Maddin, and Jarman all made shorts, and Svankmajer and Maddin continue to do so. Feature-length avant-garde films adhere to and subvert traditional narrative continuity and linearity, challenging notions of convention. Sometimes there are mixes of styles and techniques, such as slow motion, superimposition, montage, long takes, or a mix of subjective and objective storytelling. There may be minimalism or extravagance. There may be naturalism or theatrical performance. Some feature-length avant-garde films may be overtly political or ideological in nature, while others simply are pure fantasy. In most cases the narrative structures and formal techniques employed in feature-length avant-garde films are based on the notion of direct self-expression. I will discuss auteurism a bit more in the next chapter, but, generally speaking, the avant-garde filmmaker has a personal vision that he/she brings to the screen in ways atypical of traditional, conventional films. The emphasis on the director as creator of meaning, in addition to the images and sounds (the verbal/visual assault) of the avant-garde feature film, make it untraditional and unorthodox — but, and this is important to remember, *fun.*

Being challenged by cinema is a rewarding experience. Art cinema affords possibilities of constant reflection, and so does avant-garde film. In many ways, an avant-garde film turns us back to the norms and traditions of narrative cinema because we look for correlations, discrepancies, gaps, or omissions in film history and culture as a result of the always-existing tangential experimental realm of art. Most filmgoers are familiar with tropes of classical cinema (on an unconscious level), so when confronted by the avant-garde, they rely upon what they know to help uncover meanings on stylistic and thematic levels. Skoller points out that "as an ideal, avant-garde film is a cosmopolitan movement, at once marginalized and dependent on these more visible fields [of industry, cultural activism, the art world, and academia], but exerting the force of limitless possibility to them."[17] Knowing the avant-garde means knowing the mainstream and being able to speak critically of it. This helps with any viewing position, since formal patterns help one perceive cognitively the film's particular world. According to Scott MacDonald, viewers already inherently know the avant-garde because they know mainstream film. He suggests:

> No one — or certainly almost no one — sees avant-garde films without first having seen mass-market commercial films. In fact, by the time most people see their first avant-garde film, they have already seen hundreds of films in commercial theaters and on television, and their sense of what a movie is has been almost indelibly imprinted in their conscious and unconscious minds by their training as children ... and by the continual reconfirmation of this training during adolescence and adulthood. The result is that whatever particular manipulations of imagery, sound, and time define these first avant-garde film experiences as alternatives to the commercial cinema are recognizable only because of the conventionalized context viewers have already developed.[18]

It is important, then, to consider that spectators are, in some fashion, already attuned to alternative viewing practices simply because of avant-garde film's conflicting presence with the mainstream. In other words, keen cinema spectators are aware of the differences that emerge from a comparison between mainstream Hollywood film and those films existing in the margins, which include avant-garde films. While this might be a slight exaggeration, for the most part it does point to the always-conflicting stands of cinematic practice (the mainstream versus the alternative) that do define many considerations of spectatorship. Avant-garde film plays a defining role in contemporary cultural criticism because it will always be political-by-association and defiantly anti-authoritarian in nature, either through its formal innovation or thematic content, even when spectators are unfamiliar with its conventions, or familiar with them by default (through knowing the conventions of mainstream, commercial cinema). And Robert Ray suggests that avant-garde artists (including filmmakers) must "reduce the gap" between the mainstream and the avant-garde if it (the avant-garde) is ever to be taken seriously, or at least if it is ever to be formally "accepted." He says, "Mass taste must be educated to accept what it does not already know. Of course, most mass art (Hollywood, for example) avoids taking on that project and merely reproduces variations of familiar forms."[19] In other words, avant-garde filmmakers, according to Ray, should strive to become somewhat like the mainstream in order to be recognized. While this is a valid point, I do not think it is the goal for most avant-garde filmmakers. Most, I would suggest, are not at all concerned about "closing the gap" with the mainstream. They are too concerned with their own personal creativity and subjectivity, and the many manipulations of film form that makes them individually unique. As Bill Nichols points out,

> Many poetic or avant-garde films invite criticism that locates them in a formal context. This formal context helps explain the conventions each film adopts, challenges, or subverts, the alternative forms of perception it invites, and the implications these choices have for the development of the art of film. Such criticism often pays close attention to the form and structure of the film, even at the level of examining individual shots and the patterns they form. The metaphorical relationship between a story world and the actual world becomes secondary to the experiential relationship between the viewer and the screen.[20]

This visceral, immediate experience occurs when viewing many types of films, but avant-garde films *interact* with the viewer on more personal levels, ones that require a spectatorial urgency and directness wholly and qualitatively different from — and greater than — commercial narrative cinema. Challenging perception is an important part of the avant-garde filmmaker's goal; what we think we know and what we think we can perceive and comprehend is thwarted, subverted, or destabilized with most avant-garde films, which is, again, a welcoming and new concept for most cinemagoers. For the filmmakers of the 1920s — the first avant-garde — which I will discuss further in the next section, one of the crucial theoretical and practical ideas hinged on the very notion of discomforting the spectator, either through new forms and styles, abstruse (or nonexistent) themes, or militant ideological viewpoints typically reserved for manifestoes or (later) documentaries.

Watching an avant-garde feature film heightens an awareness of the act of seeing and thinking, a combination of the sensorial and the cognitive functions of accepted ideas of perception and cognition. Almost all films require a form of participation, but avant-garde films allow us to *create* as well. In discussing viewership (that is, to understand), "We can define making sense as discerning the overall meaning and the overall schematic structure. Or, to put it in slightly more formal terms, we can say that viewers have made sense of a film when they have established sufficient coherence among the film's elements by matching those elements to template schemata."[21] Avant-garde films allow for a constant interrogation of the film: "Avant-garde filmmakers continue to take up complicated and difficult material by confronting their concerns head on, rather than making their difficulties by surrendering to the silence of the seeming impossibility of representation" (Skoller xxxii). For this reason (and others) the viewer actively participates in the construction of meaning while confronting the film, just as the filmmaker does him or herself. This is why some scholars see a direct line of influence from the earliest film experiments ("attractions") with avant-garde film. The origins of film centered on the direct presentation of the film image and its *foreignness*. Film historian Tom Gunning asserts that the spectacle of films, from the very beginning of film history, were "attractions"— moving pictures that present/show rather than represent/tell. According to Gunning, these attractions can be traced to the kinds of formal displays of the later avant-garde film movements. He says, "It is precisely this harnessing of visibility, this act of showing and exhibition which I feel cinema before 1906 displays most intensely. Its inspiration for the avant-garde of the early decades of [the twentieth] century needs to be re-explored."[23] This lineage is enough for a critic like Paul Arthur to suggest, "To put it bluntly, the avant-garde in its essential outlines still conforms to cinematic modalities put into place by the time of Lumiere and Melies."[24] In essence, then, for some critics, watching avant-garde films is similar to watching the earliest forms of cinematic expression because they were/are new, spectacular, and disarming in their directness and confrontation.

Genre and Genre Expectation

As distinguished in Chapter 1, there is no one particular way of defining any avant-garde film. There are far too many characteristics and peculiarities that signify an alternative approach to filmmaking. Still, there can be traces of certain things filmmakers do that enables us to place them into sub-categories. P. Adams Sitney, for example, has discussed the mythopoetic film, the trance film, and the structural film, all examples of certain "types" of avant-garde cinema.[25] Jan-Christopher Horak has recognized city films, dance films, and parody films as avant-garde.[26] Perhaps the most important thing one must recognize and remember about avant-garde film is that even when the subject matter is similar to mainstream films, they are fundamentally dissimilar. This almost goes without saying—and I have already stressed it several times—but those spectators unaccustomed to viewing avant-garde film, and particularly longer avant-garde films, may find them off-putting since they are used to a particular kind of viewing practice formed through years of watching mainstream cinema, predicated on familiarity and comfort, which oftentimes does not occur in the world of the avant-garde. With avant-garde film, one must foster a different kind of viewing experience both prior to and during the film. Avant-garde films are knowingly eccentric and free-spirited, highlighting their nonconformist nature through many different types of rhetorical strategies, narratives schemes, or stylistic innovations. They are unique because the filmmakers who create them are most certainly and decidedly individualistic in their approaches to what the cinema is capable of doing and also what the cinema *does*. In other words, filmmakers who create avant-garde films pay little attention to any set standards, generic formulas, or common assumptions. If they do, they often deliberately subvert them through uncanny effects or nonlinear narratives.

All of this is to say that watching an avant-garde film opens the mind; there are no real generic expectations involved. Genre implies a set of codes, familiar (and expected) iconography, and a certain narrative coherency. Genre really is a function of the culture machine; the "economics of predictability"— a phrase created to study the spending habits of ordinary American citizens— suggests that people will come back to what is familiar to them. During the studio era, such predictability was the standard way of knowing *what* genre film to create *when*. As Timothy Corrigan and Patricia White tell us, "Film genres follow an economics of predictability—that is, the production, regulation, and distribution of materials—in ways that anticipate the desires for those materials and the efficient delivery of them."[27] There is a certain discourse associated with any particular genre. With avant-garde film, though, the discourse is not as forthcoming. The only possible general expectation for one may be that it will undoubtedly be "different." But that still does not indicate the kind of viewing experience one desires—necessarily. Any cultural product, film or otherwise, participates in genre, even if it is "by default." Avant-garde films do this. According to Jacques Derrida, "Every text participates in one or several genres, there is no genreless text"; however, "participation never amounts to belonging."[28] So while it may be okay or even justified to call something like *Venom and Eternity* (1951) a "Surrealist" film and therefore possibly of the surrealist genre, it nevertheless acts in a participatory manner more so than being a *genre film*.

The avant-garde has been positioned outside of and alongside the mainstream, which generally consists of Hollywood and/or traditional filmmaking. This quite possibly might make it a genre; it creates its generic tropes—if there can be any—through oppositional terms/ideas/customs prevalent in mainstream film. Nichols suggests that there may be two distinct types of avant-garde film, which he believes might help viewers interpret them. He distinguishes the two as "the formal avant-garde that is primarily concerned with the nature of the cinematic signifier, the basic raw material of sound and image ... and the political avant-garde that concerns itself with social reality and seeks to reveal aspects of this reality in formally innovative ways."[29] While these two categories are helpful in determining some aspects of the historical avant-gardes, they do not always help define contemporary feature-length avant-garde films (though some, like Maddin's films or Svankmajer's are exercises in form, and those of Jarman, Friedrich, or Godard could be political). Perhaps these two categories (or genres) of avant-garde film can be isolated based on their relations with mainstream cinema. Steve Neale even suggests about avant-garde or "non-institutionalized" films, "Though different in many ways from the means by which Hollywood genres are made and known, they nevertheless perform a similar institutional function; they help provide a generic framework within which to comprehend films."[30] This may be true to some extent, but I would suggest the process of formulating a set of criteria for placing avant-garde film neatly into one genre is difficult — almost too difficult. Edward Small also suggests, "Direct Theory [sic] contends that experimental film/video is a coordinate category and that its aesthetic is best understood when it is considered as a major genre coordinate to (but separate from) other major genres like fictive features or documentaries."[31] It *can* be helpful, of course, to call a group of films "avant-garde or experimental" because it does inevitably conjure definite thoughts about the films existing within the group. But, as I will outline later, there are subgenres or "types" of avant-garde film that do contain certain common characteristics that possibly generate a preconceived viewing experience.

Avant-garde films actively challenge expectations and therefore remain unorthodox. Genres might challenge us — think hybrid genre — but, generally, formulas are followed and expectations are met. If there is an avant-garde genre, then its conventions are multifaceted and can only be used as labels or criteria when discussing particular types, which is the best method, I believe, to distinguish such types. Surrealist film, for example, may defy ordinary narrative logic in favor of "dream-like" narratives; they may contain obscure metaphoric or symbolic imagery; and they may manipulate time/space. Perhaps instead of — or in addition to — calling the avant-garde a genre, it may be better suited to consider it as a movement, a method, and an ideology. Avant-garde film has typically been addressed in terms of its periodization, its "set" list of acknowledged filmmakers, and its critical reception and opposition to the mainstream. As a whole, then, its history is best observed as relating to time periods — movements and moments — during which certain filmmakers emerged and created a body of work that has traditionally been examined as a teleological process of the evolution of film art. Some of these artists may be lumped together in certain subgenres (the mythopoetic film, for example), which in turn help establish a particular historical trajectory of avant-garde film practice. Alternatively, avant-garde films do not respond well to the boundaries that are somewhat imposed by genre, nor do they work well within the confines of the commercial industry. Avant-garde films, like films in other genres, engage in an intertextual discourse with one another: the surrealist, abstract, or city symphony films constantly interact with later films and moments in experimental and avant-garde film history. Any film genre evolves over time (e.g., comedy — from the 1930s screwball comedies to 1990s gross-out comedies). Avant-garde film, as a genre, also has evolved; but, more interestingly, it also maintains much of its original energy and technological experimentation, its narrative discontinuity, and its formal and stylistic uniqueness that has marked each historical moment, from the 1920s to the 1940s to the 1960s. In other words, just as much as avant-garde film develops, it also (mostly) *remains the same*, which is a way of establishing a way of expectation. According to Steve Neale,

> [There] is a difference between films which are designed to conform, however broadly, to pre-existing categories, expectations and models, and those, like *Un Chien Andalou*, which are not. The latter may encounter expectations and those expectations may be based on previous films or on the tenets of a movement or a group. They may conform to labels or descriptions circulated in advance by critics, distributors, reviewers, perhaps even filmmakers themselves. And they may all establish their own internal norms and hence become more familiar — and more predictable — as they unfold. But many of these norms are unique to the films themselves. Thus the films are less predictable in advance, and at more or less every level.[32]

This statement is mostly true; however, I would suggest that avant-garde films, and especially even with "canonical" ones like *Un Chien andalou*, are never easy to predict even after having seen many and many types. And that is what makes them *special*, unique. Its purpose as a genre, if one can admit to a genre's "purpose," is to constantly challenge expectations and offer complex formal/thematic innovations. Avant-garde films do establish "internal norms," but they still never quite function as predictable genre films. Many genres cannot and do not challenge expectations because of their inherent and established body of tropes. So, to return to where I started, one can never *really* know what to expect when watching an avant-garde film, even when the *type* of avant-garde film is known.

Traditional genres that drive the commercial film industry are based upon a specific guideline for narrative comprehension. According to Barry Keith Grant, "Genre movies are those commercial feature films which, through repetition and variation, tell familiar stories with familiar characters in familiar situations."[33] Avant-garde films do not adhere to this formulation; they are not commercial films made for mass consumption and enjoyment. Their pleasure comes from discovery — of finding, viewing, and contemplating them beyond the strictures of "rules."

My aim in this book is to discuss feature-length avant-garde films, which might present a conundrum in terms of genre specificity. Some of the films I address may actually *be* of a major genre (e.g., is *Conspirators of Pleasure* [1996] a Romance film?), so I will discuss some of the more recognizable tropes when analyzing the films individually. It may not be entirely imperative to consider genre when discussing avant-garde film. My inclusion of it here, though, is simply to suggest that while it, as a whole, may be considered a genre, it does not act like or "behave" as a typical genre should. And while there may be many instances of overlap among certain types of avant-garde films, there still is a broad disconnect among so many films simply because their creators—the film-makers themselves—are so individualistic and forward-thinking that seeing how they are related only generates further discussion of how they are not approximate at all. All of this notwithstanding, there still remains the fact that there really is not an *avant-garde feature film genre*, or there is perhaps a loose one at best. Unlike the historical avant-gardes, feature films that are avant-garde (or experimental) are often one-offs, except in the case of directors who choose to work entirely or nearly completely in the avant-garde sector. Other filmmakers who have made an avant-garde feature film might also have made traditional narrative (or documentary) films as well. But avant-garde as a genre creates a new language of comprehension, a "renewing [of] the language of cinema for a renewed audience."[34] Andrew does equate avant-garde film with other genres just from the very nature that they are *called* avant-garde; rightfully so, but as a genre, avant-garde film constantly works in the processes of upend-ing all expectations that other genres might provide. Because avant-garde film confronts spectator knowledge, or at least *actively adds to it*, the viewing of avant-garde feature films requires discipline as much as it does patience.

What Are Avant-Garde Films About?

The themes addressed in avant-garde feature films vary, but almost always there is something the filmmaker wants to discuss. The best-known short films of the avant-garde are very often up for multiple interpretations (e.g., *Meshes of the Afternoon, Un Chien Andalou, Wavelength*), while others are far more explicit in their themes (e.g., *Fireworks, Window Water Baby Moving*). Feature-length avant-garde films are typically explicit, which means they have a narra-tive and they have situations that can be analyzed in terms of theme. But they also can be explained through various interpretations (e.g., *Eraserhead, The Falls*). Most feature films that are experimental have something to say about the material world around us, whether in a clearly ideological manner (*The Ties That Bind*), an associative or metaphoric manner (e.g., *Blood Tea and Red String, Glass Lips*), or in a fashion deliberately devoid of coherent narrativity (e.g., *Last Year at Marienbad*). But I would also say that what makes feature-length avant-garde films pleasurable is their very destabilization of what can or should be expected. In short, these films engage us because we recognize (and hopefully appreciate) the formal and stylistic innovations, and also because we read them as texts in subjective ways, even when an apparent theme might be recognized. So to say that avant-garde films are "about" something simply means that they generate meaning(s) through their often complicated notions concerning film form, culture, history, ideology, spectatorship, and anything else one might bring to or decipher from the films themselves. And that is what makes them fun.

৩ Chapter 2 ৫

The Historical Avant-Gardes and the Styles of Influence for the Avant-Garde Feature Film

This chapter is meant to elucidate several key historical moments of the first avant-garde of the 1920s, as well as clarify some of the more prescient concerns of feature-length avant-garde films that stem from the second historical avant-gardes of the 1940s through the 1960s. Many of the forms taken by contemporary avant-garde features have looked back to the early practices that surfaced in experimental filmmaking during the 1920s, and later the 1940s and 1960s. At the same time, many contemporary features build upon existing models of theory and practice of experimental and avant-garde cinema, but those initial experiments with narrative and film language and film form — generally considered to be the "first historical avant-garde" — is vital in understanding the modern avant-garde feature film. Hence, this chapter covers a few fundamental and critical ideas surrounding the avant-gardes and their subsequent significance on the historical trajectory of avant-garde filmmaking. The importance of different styles, particularly surrealism, which developed during the 1920s, would come to dominate avant-garde feature film production (as limited as it was for a half century). But other manifestations of style also influenced avant-garde practice, from the 1920s until today. Understanding this trajectory is essential because it helps us recognize the reasons many contemporary avant-garde feature films have direct ties to historical aesthetic practices that stem from the 1920s, when modernist forms of art transformed much artistic practice. As Bill Nichols points out,

> The avant-garde, heavily indebted to modernist principles, stressed the poetic dimension of cinema over storytelling. Since the 1920s, avant-garde filmmakers have identified their efforts with various modernist currents such as surrealism, Dada, constructivism, and German expressionism more than with realism.... The Soviet period [1917–20s] stressed the principle of montage to engage the viewer in a radically

new way, whereas the European postwar period [1950s–60s] stressed the interiority or subjectivity of characters who no longer seemed to belong to a shared social reality.[1]

While I tend to think that avant-garde filmmakers do indeed engage with reality and "reality" as literal and figurative constructs, Nichols does suggest, correctly, that particular modes of filmmaking identified with modernism, from surrealism to montage to interiority, are ways to identify avant-garde films. In still another estimation of the significance of the early (1920s) avant-gardes, Scott MacDonald writes,

> The first film avant-garde fueled at least two different critical responses to the mass commercial cinema. Not surprisingly, these responses parallel two of the more salient tendencies in the fine arts during the first decades of [the twentieth century]: abstraction and surrealism. Both tendencies resulted in films that are memorable enough to continue to inspire and inform critical filmmaking in Western Europe, North America, Japan, and elsewhere.[2]

Abstraction is fundamentally important to many avant-garde filmmakers, and MacDonald is also correct to note that both it and surrealism continue to inspire avant-garde filmmakers. The modernist impulse of the early avant-gardes, which was predicated on the idea of the shock of the new, still resonates today in feature-length avant-garde films. Additionally, "The importance of identifying an essential 'nature' of a medium — that what the artwork expresses uniquely lies in the particularity of the medium used — has been a hallmark of modernist art in general."[3] These ideas are crucial in determining the significance of contemporary avant-garde feature films.

The Historical Avant-Gardes: The 1920s

The historical avant-gardes, which are generally reserved to the 1920s and the 1940s through the 1960s, are important from both theoretical and practical standpoints in understanding the types of avant-garde feature films I will discuss throughout this book. Generally speaking, the 1920s was a time of innovation in filmmaking, and, in particular, was when experimental and avant-garde film flourished in terms of developing particular styles and forms that were different from or even directly reactionary to standard, mainstream film practice. The significance of the development of avant-garde film has been chronicled elsewhere very well, so all I will mention in this brief interlude is some of the ideas surrounding its development and how they are important to avant-garde feature film construction.

The avant-garde cinemas of the 1920s — the first film avant-garde — was instigated by a variety of people in different circumstances and countries. In some instances, the filmmakers were basically responding to the various forms of new artistic creation and applying them to film; in others, they were politically, ideologically, or aesthetically motivated, wishing to challenge the norms of tradition or bourgeois society. The new forms of artistic creation stemmed mainly from the visual arts, but also encompassed sculpture and literature. These ideas/new aesthetics were expressionism, surrealism, Dadaism, and abstraction, all of which I will detail a bit more fully below, and they inspired and motivated amateur filmmakers to attempt like-minded representations of society and culture through cinema. Such filmmaking practices occurred in both the United States and in Europe, but the real hub of activity was in Europe.

During the late 1910s there was a small movement of artists wishing to overthrow the confines of cinema from its already-growing commercial base. The essential motivation was to free the cinema — a liberation that would raise film to art. These movements occurred in France and Germany primarily, but also later in Great Britain and the United States, and eventually in the Soviet Union (but theirs was a different sort of film revolution). According to Duncan Reekie,

> Within this dynamic pioneer movement there was a diversity of debate about film form and a diverse range of agents were involved: commercial narrative feature filmmakers, abstract animators, Dadaists and Surrealists, artists and anti-artists. There were both groups and individuals who were engaged in radical political activity and who articulated genuine understanding of the popular. Moreover, there were films produced that would influence all subsequent experimental cinema.[4]

This miscellaneous group of creators also established the ciné-clubs and film journals that discussed the nature and purpose of (film) art. A common interest and passion in new forms linked these seemingly disparate groups together, and avant-garde film blossomed and flourished from such creativity and inventiveness, where "the gallery or club rather than the movie-house was their site, outside the space and conventions of cinema."[5] Working in the margins gave these filmmakers a space and place to articulate credos that reflected the aesthetic current of the other arts, and it also helped establish the popularity of the "art film" as an opposition to the mainstream in terms of production and exhibition. Further, it promulgated the cause of avant-garde resistance and creativity seen then, and in many ways today, as the underbelly of art. But what these filmmakers did, and why they are so very important, was to establish a new means of audio/visual communication.

The European avant-gardes experimented with cinematography, editing, and narrative. They also played with abstract (non)representation, either through shapes or animation. One thing to remember is that almost all of these pictures were short. Rarely was there any film that lasted more than a few minutes. (Later productions in the 1920s began to grow in length.) Perhaps more importantly, these diverse artists and filmmakers helped theorize the moving image. The debates over film form versus realism may be attributed to the avant-garde filmmakers of the 1920s, though the debate can certainly be traced to the contrasting styles and films of Edison and the Lumière brothers. But because the avant-garde filmmakers of the 1920s were influenced by other arts, there were already manifestoes or other forms of written articulation about the very ontology and epistemology of the cinema that helped establish the (future) significance of these artists as groundbreaking and original. In other words, the progenitors of the 1920s essentially created the discourse of avant-garde film-making, an influence that stamps almost any contemporary feature film. The movement may have been short-lived (sound trumped many efforts at experimentation), but "the unresolved instabilities and contradictions of the first avant-garde were perpetuated into the history of avant-garde film."[6]

The 1920s European avant-gardes firmly established the idea of a contrary mode of representation, something that remains with the feature-length avant-garde films of the present. The collection of ideas and different styles that sprang from such a varied amount of individuals and films remains highly powerful when considering the trajectory of avant-garde filmmaking. As Michael O'Pray notes, "Abstraction, collage/montage, anti-narrative, poetic, text and image, were all first intimated — even explored — in this period."[7] One of the things I will suggest about feature-length avant-garde films is the inherent interest in presenting narratives that defy causal logic, making them both similar to and somewhat different from the experimentations of the 1920s. For instance, there are ostensible narratives in films like *Tetsuo: The Iron Man* (1989) or *Blood Tea and Red String* (2006), but their presentational method and storytelling clarity are fairly hidden through their unique formal innovations, which include cinematography and sound manipulations.

Jan-Christopher Horak, in his *Lovers of Cinema: The First American Film Avant-Garde, 1919–1945* (1995), traces the essential formation of an oppositional cinema in the United States. Horak establishes a framework for examining the origins of an American-based avant-garde cinema, one that was more or less established by European expatriates. One important distinction he makes is that many of the avant-garde filmmakers of the 1920s (and beyond) can be considered "amateurs," a term that might imply a sort of unprofessionalism or even a lack of sophistication or "control" of the medium. But, as he informs us, this moniker proves quite apt when describing these filmmakers as different from the "professionals" working in Hollywood. He suggests,

> Earlier [pre–1940s avant-garde] filmmakers thought of themselves primarily as film amateurs rather than professionals. The professional was an employee of Hollywood, producing for hire a profit benefiting the corporate hierarchy, while the amateur was concerned with the cause of film art. Given this self-image, the agenda of the first American film avant-garde could be much broader: to improve the quality of all films, whether personal or professional, to create structures for distribution and exhibition, and to further reception through publications.[8]

Another important distinction made here is the idea of independence and self-dependence, the fact that as amateurs the initial avant-garde filmmakers of the 1920s relied more on themselves than others in the commercial industry. Perhaps even more importantly, these avant-garde filmmakers were concerned with the "cause of film art." There was a convinced attitude that commercial cinema was industry-based and economically-driven. Mainstream narrative cinema was meant to please, placate, and conform. Art Cinema emerged as an alternative form, one that flies in the face of convention while striving for a more formal and thematically innovative cinema. (The "culmination" of Art Cinema would be, of course, the French New Wave and other new wave cinemas of the 1950s through the 1970s.) The "art" in cinema of the avant-gardes during the 1920s was not necessarily the same as it was in later cinemas, but it was based upon the notion that there was a *need* for art in cinema as an opposition to the "non-art" commercial film. Designating film as art also gave amateur/avant-garde film-makers an opportunity to be as creative and imaginative as possible, and allowed for a bit of cultural credence, like with other forms of art (from visual work to architecture to music to literature), even when they were never really recognized outside of their own small circles of ciné-clubs. As Horak notes, "Professionalism was equated with commercialism, while amateurism connoted artistic integrity. This discourse also identifies personal expression with formal experimentation, a dualism repeated continually in contemporary aesthetic manifestoes and reviews, and echoed in the polemics of the second American avant-garde."[9]

Besides the do-it-yourself approach of amateurism, the avant-gardists of the 1920s exhibited an adventurous spirit, something wholly translatable to feature filmmakers of the more contemporary film era. Taking liberties, keeping mistakes, trumping narrative for poeticism — the avant-gardes of the 1920s generated specific areas of film form still utilized by many avant-garde filmmakers today. From the seminal works of Man Ray and Hans Richter in Europe to the city poetics of Strand and Sheeler in the United States, the filmmakers who celebrated the alternative were ones who indulged in audacious styles and themes. Surrealism, of course, embraced the playfulness of the unconscious, depicting wondrous excursions of unorthodox images and actions. Still, it should be noted, many of the avant-gardists of the 1920s were simply "playing" with the form itself, which caused many to see them as disingenuous or uncreative, or certainly lacking any ostensible "skills." In discussing the American avant-garde films of the 1920s, Horak points out,

> The very fact that they were born out of the *reception* of European avant-garde films *in America* inscribed their position: while often borrowing or quoting the formal techniques of the European avant-garde, they demonstrated a certain wild eclecticism, innovativeness, and at times naiveté that was only possible for American filmmakers working far from Paris and Berlin, the centers of Western high culture.[10]

Indeed, the formal explorations generated from cubism, surrealism, expressionism, abstraction, and Dadaism influenced the avant-garde filmmakers of the 1920s in the United States—and continues to do so. For example, David Lynch's *Eraserhead* (1977), which I will discuss in Part III, has the expressionism and abstract poeticism garnered from the films of the 1920s. Many films, too, display the uncanny effect of balancing traditions and styles. There may be, for example, a co-mingling of high and low art, realism and surrealism, or narrative and non-narrative. As O'Pray notes of the fertile 1920s avant-garde scene,

> The 1920s are also characterized by the cross-fertilization of forms—ballet, painting, poetry, music, sculpture, fashion, literature. These high-art sources are matched by an avant-garde fascination with and love of the "low-arts" of circus, vaudeville, Hollywood silent comedies and puppetry. Thus, in many ways, the avant-gardes saw their role as being both in opposition to high art and attempting to displace it, to become a new "high art" so to speak.[11]

If this indeed was the case with the filmmakers of the 1920s, then the same can be said about the later avant-gardes of the 1940s and 1960s, where there was a deliberate attempt (and success) to undermine the pervasive and unattractive world of mainstream cinema. In other words, there was—and is—an effort by the avant-garde to thwart the ideology and aesthetic prominence of the mainstream center, to dislodge it and to criticize it for being bland, ineffective, or simply unoriginal. Avant-garde feature films create a discourse that supplies armor for attack; in other words, to be able to stand alone and alongside typical Hollywood or other commercial production, the avant-garde must be reactionary, mainly because it always has been and has always been perceived that way since its provocating heyday of the 1920s. One thing I will suggest throughout the book is that avant-garde feature films are more artistic than other, mainstream productions. They need to be if we should consider them as a *successful* alternative. As Reekie rightly points out,

> The avant-garde movement [of the 1920s] advocated its own centrality and necessity to the future of cinema. The justification for this stems from two interdependent assumptions. First it was proposed that cinema, when perfected, could and must become art, but this could only be achieved through the pioneering work of dedicated artists and intellectuals. Second the creation of cinema art was conceived as not simply a birth but also a redemption; cinema had to be rescued from its vulgar origins.[12]

I would suggest that the contemporary avant-garde feature film participates in the redemption of the vulgar cinema of the present. When CGI-driven films and blockbuster formulas proliferate at the multiplexes, there needs to be an option or substitute that redeems film. While this may cause some apprehension in people—that cinema even *needs* redemption—it seems clear that seeking out "anti-" forms can quite possibly allow us to see the "art" in avant-garde cinema as opposed to the bland commercialism of its other self. The historical avant-gardes of the 1940s and 1960s also made efforts to see that an alternative kind of filmmaking practice would be welcomed and understood as both a return to the formalism of its roots and its essence as personal expression.

The Historical Avant-Gardes: The 1940s and 1960s

The most comprehensive study of the second American avant-garde is P. Adams Sitney's influential *Visionary Film: The American Avant-Garde, 1943–2000*. This work chronicles the filmmakers best known in the avant-garde world — people like Stan Brakhage, Maya Deren, James Broughton, Sidney Person, and Kenneth Anger, to name some — and particular avant-garde film types, like the mythopoeia film and the structural film. This second era of avant-garde filmmaking is often confined to the United States because these filmmakers (and others) were creating a new form of personal expression that seemed best suited to the tropes of avant-garde filmmaking. While this does not rule out any advancements in avant-garde filmmaking emerging in Europe and elsewhere, the influence of these American filmmakers is too vast, their vision too uncompromised, and their dedication to new styles and forms too unprecedented to not see their lasting authority over the medium. Indeed, "[The] postwar period in America heralded the emergence of a clutch of young men and women dedicated to avant-garde film but removed from the Europeans by geography, culture and their relative youth."[13]

Like their forbearers, the artists of this second wave of avant-garde filmmaking worked entirely outside the studios, with little economic or distribution status. This independence is shared to some extent with contemporary filmmakers who make feature-length avant-garde films. (Many working today have far better resources, including financing, equipment, and assistance.) Largely working alone or in collaboration, these artists strove for a new film enterprise, one where personal ambitions and freedoms, the unconscious desire, and dreams, wishes, and states of unbridled imagination roamed freely and often dictated the content of the films. While there was a wide variety of experimentation (everything from abstract to lyrical to surreal), the vast majority of the films produced in the United States during the 1940s (and into the 1950s) was based upon the self-as-dreamer, or the inner self as locus of convergence. As Sitney suggests, "The central tradition of the American avant-garde film begins with a dream unfolded within shifting perspectives. Much of the subsequent history of that tradition will move toward a metaphysics of cinematic perspective itself."[14] This central notion is present in the films of Svankmajer, Maddin, Jarman, Rainer, Friedrich, and others; and the highly personal nature of the filmmaker's "dream" becomes metaphoric and literal in the avant-garde feature film. Citing Anger, O'Pray states, "[Anger] proclaimed a 'personal cinema' in which expression, improvisation and spontaneity were to be paramount, a poetry of private passions."[15] The films of this era — and we need to remember they were short films — were all mainly forms of interior expression, or were certainly experimental narratives hinging upon the psychic states of their creators, where myth, dream, and reality conflated. Of course there were exceptions, but the idea of a personalized cinema

heavily influenced both the theory of auteurism and the contemporary avant-
garde feature film in terms of the individualized and unique *vision* of the filmmaker. According to Rees,

> Along with the revival of synaesthetic abstraction, U.S. filmmakers reinvented the
> narrative film-poem. The "psycho-drama" (or "trance-film") was modeled on dream,
> lyric verse and contemporary dance. Typically, it enacts the personal conflicts of a
> central subject or protagonist. A scenario of desire and loss, seen from the point of
> view of a single guiding consciousness, ends in either redemption or death. Against
> the grain of realism, montage-editing evokes swift transitions in space and time.
> The subjective, fluid camera is more often a participant in the action than its neutral
> recording agent.[16]

These attributes could very easily describe many avant-garde artists working
today, and certainly can be applicable to many of the feature filmmakers I will
describe later in the book. Similar to Rees's and Sitney's descriptions of the
American avant-garde in the post-war time frame, Reekie, in an echo of Rees,
also states that

> The revitalized experimental film culture that developed in the first decades of post-
> war America was relatively disengaged from the tension of the European avant-garde
> project — it was loose and dispersed; there was no centralized programme, movement
> or manifesto. The work produced was diverse, ranging from modernist mystical
> synaesthetic abstraction to poetic narrative, but a defining feature was an intense
> and personal exploration of myth, ritual, dream and the psyche.[17]

Again, here is the idea of a personalized cinema, where subjectivity, experimentation, and dream-like narrative structure (or ambiguity) proliferates in the
contemporary avant-garde feature film, as it did with early examples like
Cocteau's *The Blood of a Poet*. The boom in experimental filmmaking by
women during the 1970s especially has connection with this form of cinema.
The "trance film" in particular, which Sitney says "deals with visionary
experience," aptly correlates to the visionary films of the avant-garde feature
film.[18] Perhaps most importantly, what the films and filmmakers give us
is the sincere belief in the triumph of the imagination. And while that
may seem commonplace for any type of film production, the avant-garde
feature film readily taps into the imagination — perhaps even in the
Coleridgeian sense — to give us something beyond the literal and beyond
the realm of the sensorial even, though it does evoke and heighten sensory
awareness and participation. For the means by which these filmmakers afford
us these opportunities, I will now briefly outline and describe four categories
of experimentation in film that influence the contemporary avant-garde feature
film: Expression, Surrealism, Abstraction, and Montage. These four styles have
dominated avant-garde filmmaking and have characterized many aspects of
the contemporary avant-garde feature film.

Expression, Surrealism, Abstraction, and Montage

EXPRESSIONISM

Expressionism in cinema stems mainly from Germany, especially the visual arts and the theater. German Expressionism is identified through its carefully constructed and highly stylized mise-en-scène, particularly the sets, shadowy lighting techniques, and performative acting style that was characterized less by realism and more by an affected, jerky, dance-like movement. The most famous Expressionistic film is *The Cabinet of Dr. Caligari* (1920), a phantasmagoric feature that emphasizes a graphic, abstract composition and a stylistic distortion of space. As David Bordwell and Kristin Thompson recognize, "German Expressionist films emphasize the composition of individual shots to an exceptional degree."[19] The effect is uncanny: *Caligari* is known for its jarring, jagged sets, the manipulation of narrative continuity (using a flashback structure), the strong interplay of light and shadow, and the exaggerated acting style. That the story is also strange — a somnambulist who kills on command — doesn't hurt its status as strange yet entirely fascinating. It is also structured in a dream-like fashion, something very important to many longer avant-garde films. Part of the goal of expressionism in the arts (prior to cinema's adoption of it) was to convey heightened emotion, "Making the true essence of things and people emerge into a visible form."[20] In part, the set designs of films like *Caligari* were meant to reflect inner psychic states. To some extent, other expressionistic films, like *Nosferatu* (1921) or *The Last Laugh* (1924), did so as well but focused more on other aspects of expressionism. *The Last Laugh* in particular utilized a freer camera, one that moved around; it also featured montage editing, something *Caligari* did not. This is not always the case, but expressionistic set designs very often mirror narrative patterns developed from character actions. Also, expressionistic sets emphasize shapes, patterns, and designs. Other characteristics include chiaroscuro lighting, slanted/canted camera angles, incongruous settings, odd framings, mechanical acting, and gothic sensibilities. Many of these traits are seen in feature-length avant-garde films. (I should note that *Caligari*, *Nosferatu*, and *The Last Laugh* are *not* generally "accepted" as avant-garde films.) Guy Maddin's cinema uses many, if not all, of the traits of expressionism. *Eraserhead* is both stylistically and thematically similar to expressionist films.

Expressionism was a short-lived phenomenon in cinema, and it has been regularly debated as to exactly when it began and when it died out. Typically, the first half of the 1920s saw a handful of German films that were expressionistic, which heavily influenced the avant-gardes abroad, particularly in the United States. Watson and Webber's *The Fall of the House of Usher* (1928) and Charles Klein's *The Tell-Tale Heart* (1928) both used many of the traits of expressionism. Klein's film version of Poe in particular echoes *Caligari*'s narrative and set design. Expressionism distorts reality, often presenting a non-reality-like atmosphere to create a particular dark mood. Often described as films with "morbid psychological states and troubled dreams," expressionism is, in some regards, a precursor to the psychological terrain that is often mined in surrealism.[21] (Edvard Munch's *The Scream* is the text of expressionist painting.) Subjectivity becomes an objective reality in expressionist films. In sum, "German Expressionism attempted to express interior realities through the means of exterior realities, or to treat subjective states in what was widely regarded at the time as a purely objective medium of representation."[22] The key thing I would like to stress is that the techniques associated with expressionism find their way into more modern films, often creating disturbing realities akin to their 1920s predecessors. Not all avant-garde films utilize expressionism, and likewise, many mainstream films do use expressionistic techniques (albeit in "dream sequences" or, more appropriately, in film noirs). I would even say that expressionism actually remains very vital as a formal and stylistic choice for avant-garde filmmakers interested in creating a very specific mise-en-scène or narrative that certainly distinguishes the film (and filmmaker) from a host of other films.

SURREALISM

If expressionism epitomizes inner turmoil through graphic abstract representation and stylistic exaggeration, then surrealism offers a counterpoint by depicting dreams and the unconscious wishes and desires of the protagonists that fill the non-narratives of the films. Surrealism, like expressionism, rejects realism in favor of dream logic, which implies that with surrealist film almost anything goes, much like a dream. But beyond dreams, surrealist films constantly thwart viewer expectation through illogic, the absurd, the uncanny, and the irrational. In Sitney's words, "The Surrealist cinema depends upon the power of film to evoke a mad voyeurism and to imitate the very discontinuity, the horror, and the irrationality of the unconsciousness."[23] Surrealist film is characterized by a blending of the real and the bizarre, conscious and unconscious states, militarism and a degree of calm, and disorientation, nonlinearity, and unexplained phenomena, including character motivation and action and coherence in terms of narrative, editing, cinematography, and mise-en-scène. In its essence, surrealist cinema (of the 1920s, when it was started and at its height) reveled in — and revealed — the power of the cinema to poeticize the disorder of dream-logic in visual terms.

The surrealists of the 1920s were born of a political movement, much like the expressionists. The other arts informed their agenda, and they were not in complete anathema to mainstream Hollywood production. According to Scott MacDonald, "Using elements of plot, character, and location moviegoers could be expected to recognize, [the surrealists] relentlessly undercut the expectations their inclusion of these elements inevitably created, in the hope of depicting and affecting layers of the conscious and unconscious mind too problematic for the commercial cinema."[24] The Surrealists, in fact, led by Andre Breton, famously would stroll from one movie house to another in the middle of films, connecting disparate narratives and images together to recognize the play of the unconscious in typical films. This idea of seeking the hidden in the everyday is something crucial to surrealist films, and informs the feature films I will discuss, especially those of Jan Svankmajer, who uncovers or discovers the hidden life of objects in his film by animating them and often letting them interact or overtake their human counterparts. As Rees tells us, "While surrealist cinema is often understood as a search for the excessive and spectacular image (as in dream sequences modeled on surrealism, as in some films by Hitchcock), the group were in fact drawn to find the marvelous in the banal, which explains their fascination with Hollywood as well as their refusal to imitate it."[25] Finding "truth" buried in the everyday/normal was a *fun* activity for the surrealists, whose strange and odd imagery visualized this endeavor. The surrealists were champions of what has been called anti-art, a moniker that is both political and reactionary. Anti-art flies in the face of convention and seeks to show the inherent banality of mainstream art (like Hollywood film) by dismantling it. Joseph Cornell's *Rose Hobart* (1936) is a famous example of collage filmmaking that practices the surrealist notion of deconstruction and critique. The film, a re-editing of a Hollywood production, which employs only shots of the heroine and other characters from the film, exemplifies the surrealistic idea of debasing narrative causality by showing reaction shots instead of two people conversing, bizarre images that are out of context, and fragmentation of coherent scenes.

If Surrealism is to be understood as a radical political movement, it is because the filmmakers wanted to expose the hypocrisy of bourgeois codes that dominated mainstream film, and because they actively sought to undermine the ideology of the conventional forms of representation. Surrealism disdained orthodox art. But the surrealists wanted to create films that had a narrative; it was just that the story was illogical and based upon the reveries, hallucinations, and trances associated with dreaming. Many surrealists' tendencies find their way into feature-length avant-garde films. There are many examples, for instance, of films that depict the liberating force of unconscious desires, or ones that highlight the irrationality of reality by focusing on the libidinal forces that become manifest through visual imagery or character behavior. Additionally, "Surrealist visual hallmarks are a scathing documentary eye, 'trick-effects' in the simple and direct manner of their admired 'primitive' cinema (often made in the camera) and an avoidance of overt montage rhythm (seen as too seductive)."[26] Surrealist films are also known to be interpreted by unpacking their symbols, which sometimes is true but very often not. That is, certain films may be read as containing an elaborate symbolic terrain, but many times the filmmaker may claim not to have any interest at all in symbols. It is often "easy" to discover symbols in surrealist film, mainly because of the things that interested the Surrealist group. As Graeme Harper and Rob Stone surmise, regarding the essential interests of the Surrealists,

> The surrealists favored an orientation that was defined by dream-logic, chance, superstition, coincidence, absurdity and challenge. They aimed to recreate links with primal thoughts and emotions in order to recast human needs away from materialism, mass culture and social order towards immersion in the revolutionary hagiography of mankind's dark side.[27]

Films that may contain any semblance of these characteristics might very well supply the spectator with ample ammunition to interpret them in terms of symbol, metaphor, and allegory.

Surrealist imagery is often meant to shock (think of *Un Chien Andalou*'s razor-sliced eyeball) as well as enthrall and perplex. Making sense of the imagery is not often easy, but it certainly provokes, which is another key idea with surrealism in general. Surrealism aims to provoke on many practical and cognitive levels. As Skoller points out,

> The surrealists trafficked in the shock of the discontinuities of daily life in which conscious and unconscious worlds blur, disrupt, and confuse. The colliding montages of such fragmented worlds are seen in the modern city, the non-rational juxtapositions of the images and ideas of mass culture and the resurrection of discarded objects made new as they become connected to the construction of new works of art.[28]

Provocation means having an active viewing experience, a fundamental trait of avant-garde films, and one of the more important ideas of the avant-garde feature film. Spectators *have* to be cognizant of actively participating in the film as they view it, where the blurring of the conscious and unconscious, or the co-mingling of the real and the illogical are normal. In terms of surrealism being an anti-art, perhaps I should mention briefly surrealism's close-but-distant cousin, Dadaism, which in most regards was far more anti- in its agenda. Dadaism suggested that (bourgeois) art must be destroyed before its utopian potential could be attained and practiced. In film, this meant the destruction of the mainstream, or at least the complete annihilation of any kind of traditional filmmaking practice. Dadaist films are small in number, but the theoretical implications of it as a movement (again, from the 1920s) is important in terms of feature-length avant-garde films because of the inherent nature of its anti-authoritarian stance. Moreover, as Reekie surmises, "In its brief and glorious rage the Dada movement developed a repertoire of brilliant subversive techniques, but also initiated a historic dialectic which far from eliminating art effectively vaccinated it against subversion, modernized its technology and expanded and liberated the functionless gaze."[29] This is both a critique and summation of the Dadaist movement; but in its critique, it points to how mainstream cinema has co-opted the subversion that is so fundamentally important to avant-garde films and especially avant-garde feature films that seek to subvert the tropes and expectations of mainstream commercial feature films.

ABSTRACTION

Abstract films are mainly concerned with film form — that is, how the medium itself may be manipulated or present abstract images through shapes, colors, tinting, or scratching the surface of the filmstrip. Often referred to as Abstract Expressionism (later used in the pictorial arts), these types of films showcased a sort of primitivism based solely on the notion of the artist-as-creator, where spontaneity (of creation and of the images themselves) were at play. Abstract films employ cut-outs, animation, and displayed objects, and also hand-painted film frames, or even holes punched in the filmstrip. Sometimes there are no images but simply black and white frames run through the projector. Filmmakers also shot objects as abstract designs, enhancing our perception of everyday phenomena. In O'Pray's summation,

> Two views of abstraction can be seen to operate at [the interstices of early abstraction and the iconoclasm of Dada]. First, there is the fairly purist Platonic notion in which the essence of reality was taken to be abstract geometric forms like circles, cubes, cylinders, spheres, etc. In this type of film the result is the representation of a representation — the basic state of animation. This vied with the rather different idea of revealing the abstract or forms existent in reality — a form of abstractionism. In this way constructivist aesthetics mingled with a Dadaist upturning of normal perceptions and prejudices.[30]

In its essential form, then, the abstract film focuses purely on shapes and objects and designs, and therefore makes us reconsider their function and interaction within everyday reality. Abstract forms rarely focus on anything other than the mingling of forms in their purest states, whereas other narrative films typically are expressive because they focus on the actions and interactions of characters. Contemporary avant-garde feature films are rarely completely abstract; they have characters and narratives. Still, many pay close attention to the arrangement of the mise-en-scène in terms of spatial formations. *The Color of Pomegranates* (1968), for example, which I will detail in Part III, has many tableaux scenes where formal composition is heightened. We recognize how shapes respond to or inform situations and scenes. Similarly, a non-narrative film like *Last Year at Marienbad* (1961) contains many repetitions in geometric shapes and figure placements, including hallways, gardens, and people. Abstraction in film compels us to focus on the meanings derived from forms: shapes, diagonals, colors, rhythms, movements, depths, sizes — all draw our attention in ways not typical of mainstream cinema. The major practitioners of abstract film rarely make longer films, so discovering instances of abstraction in feature-length films is rare, though the ideas associated with Abstract Expressionism in general — personal freedom and formalism in particular — do help shed light on particular filmmaking practices in contemporary cinema.

Abstract films resonate because the characteristics at play in them are readily available in animation, especially computer animation today, and through optical printing processes. These kinds of films tend to be nonrepresentational, hence the focus on shapes and forms and patterns, but representations of *something* can be guessed at, if one is willing. Using varieties of colors and shapes to signify does occur in everyday interaction and observation, so conceptualizing some meaning is not completely absent from some longer abstract films, though the overriding tendency of them is simply to allow creative imagination to run freely, enabling the spectator to engage with rhythms — often analogous to music — in order to focus on abstractions visible *and* imagined.

MONTAGE

One of the most important and theoretical concepts in cinema is montage. Much has been written about montage as theory and practice, so I will limit myself to clarifying a few things in relation to avant-garde film and especially the avant-garde feature film. Montage comes from the Soviet experiments of the 1920s, when filmmakers like Eisenstein and Vertov essentially created a new form of editing called montage. Montage is the rapid juxtaposition of images that when viewed is meant to be jarring, shocking and overwhelming to the spectator. Montage is both an intellectual and emotional practice, a form of editing that stresses the collision of images and de-stresses continuity, though narrative is important (especially in Eisenstein's works). Montage is also an associative practice that calls for an equally associative response: Metaphoric, symbolic, and ideological interpretations stem from the succession of images in montage editing. In many instances, disparate images are joined or juxtaposed through montage. Montage emphasizes the shot — the very basic nature of film itself — as the fundamental essence of cinematic art. Montage also emphasizes the recognition of the editing of the film. Where commercial narrative very often creates classical seamless editing, montage calls attention to the process as a stimulating intellectual/emotional activity.

There can be no overestimation or exaggeration concerning the importance and value of montage to cinematic history. For the avant-garde, the idea of presenting images through juxtaposition was very appealing. It signified another break from typical styles of editing practice, and it also allowed for the thematic and formal explorations found in abstract or surrealist films. Montage is all about movement and the priority of movement in audio-visual terms to engage and push the spectator into a critical consciousness with the elements of the film. Eisenstein is the progenitor of montage. In sum,

> His conception was that cinematic meaning is produced by the combination of discrete elements. In opposition to other contemporary montagists, Eisenstein held that meaning is not assembled by linking frame to frame, shot to shot, rather it is produced by the dialectical conflict between the different elements. Montage is creation by juxtaposition; the meaning produced by the collision of elements cannot be reduced to the sum of the parts, it is a new qualitatively different creation. Moreover, montage is not only located in the juxtaposition between shots and frames, it also takes place within the elements of a single frame's composition.[31]

This complex form of editing and piecing together films is important to many avant-garde filmmakers, in that the way the film is put together or the way the shots *interact* creates specific viewing responses, a fundamental and crucial aspect of avant-garde spectatorship. Feature-length avant-garde films often employ sequences of montage that disorient, engage, and provoke the spectator. *Tetsuo: The Iron Man* and *Glass Lips* (2007) both employ montage, and both immediately force the spectator into compromising viewing positions. Montage, of course, has been co-opted by mainstream cinema and really runs rampant in Hollywood production — which is fine. Avant-garde films simply use montage in ways different from a blockbuster or spectacular picture.

Montage consists of extrapolating shots taken from the totality of a given take. A long take, for example, does not produce a collision, but when shots are examined individually, the natural rhythms of shot-conflict can be utilized more fully. A rectangular frame may contain an elaborate mise-en-scène wherein the use of diagonals, parallels, and asymmetrical patterns form a montage-within, something similar to abstract composition. Eisenstein mastered this idea and also developed the concept of four separate types of montage: metric, rhythmic, tonal, and overtonal. All deal specifically with *movement* and the movement produced by shots. The Soviet "montage-theorists" observed "the filmic shot as being without intrinsic meaning prior to its placement within a montage structure. The shot gained meaning, in other words, only relationally, as part of a larger system."[32] Counterpoints of conflict are essential to discovering the way montage produces ideological, emotional, and intellectual responses from spectators. The dialectic involved in shot juxtaposition enabled Eisenstein (and Vertov and Pudovkin) to craft film sequences that are alive with tension, motion, discontinuity, and ideational creativity. This idea is so very important to how certain avant-garde filmmakers create films that are deliberate means of provocation. Inasmuch as emotions are evoked, the real issue becomes Eisenstein's fifth mode of montage: intellectual. Montage ultimately seeks to control/manipulate spectators' thought processes through images.

Auteurism and Auteur Theory

One final consideration for the avant-garde feature film is auteurism, or the notion that films are "authored" by an individual, the filmmaker. This idea has been widely written about, so I will limit myself to a few of its concepts and their significance to avant-garde film, an area ripe for discussion of the power of the individual artist/author as sole creator.

Auteurism focuses primarily on style, examining a director's films for similarities that can enable the concept of authorship based firstly on the way a filmmaker's approach or method of production creates stylistic tendencies throughout all his/her films. This theory also suggests one can find thematic recurrences throughout an individual's film oeuvre. Auteur theory — first formulated by the French New Wave directors and later made popular in the United States—was "animated by a desire to show that film could transcend its artisanal, industrial form of production and incorporate a singular, signed vision."[33] Auteurism allows for a close examination of certain stylistic traits (mise-en-scène, cinematography, editing) and thematic concerns that any director might have or use in his/her films. One reason why this idea of authorship may be useful to the world of the avant-garde is because the avant-garde filmmaker is essentially the sole creator, the visionary filmmaker who not only creates the scenario but often shoots it and edits it as well. This "mythic" power has been discussed — and debated —for some time, but many of the best-known avant-garde artists (Stan Brakhage, Maya Deren, Harry Smith, Michael Snow, Kenneth Anger, et. al.) might readily be analyzed based on their authorship. Perhaps in no other type of film (or genre) is there a better case made for the auteur than in avant-garde film. Auteurism gives credence to the cinematic artist, and avant-garde film is an area that suggests both a collectivity of artists and the romanticized ideal of the lone artist. Many disagree with the concept of auteurism, but I think it may be well-served when discussing particular avant-garde directors (and especially individual contemporary avant-garde feature films by certain directors) because we can trace specific and individualized stylistic and thematic concerns that sometimes may prove difficult in the mainstream arena (though it should be noted many auteur critics have done exactly that: elevate the studio-system director to the status of auteur).

As auteurism as a concept and theory became scrutinized and attacked by the theorists of the 1970s, its meaning and significance shifted and/or diminished. A new emphasis on "texts" and textual analysis of films both aided and challenged the idea of authorship. Psychoanalysis, feminist theory, structuralism — all became weapons of attack against the auteur theory. But the auteur theory has not gone away, hence its significance to avant-garde film. It is hard to argue that someone like Stan Brakhage is not an auteur, or that a contemporary avant-garde filmmaker like surrealist Jan Svankmajer or a radical like Dusan Makavejev are not as well. Auteur theory suggests that a filmmaker's personal vision stamps any/all of his/her films, which is the initial idea of the auteur developed by Truffaut. Film auteurs are the exception rather than the rule. Given this, maybe it is appropriate to call avant-garde filmmakers true auteurs: They are the ones who most often "author" their film texts, create a specific and individualized mise-en-scène, and address personal concerns. As we shall see in Part III when I look at several directors and films more closely, the idea of the recognizable style — the major idea of auteurism — is crucial in understanding the nuances of the avant-garde feature film.

*   *   *

The ideas put forth here are already well-known in film studies and art history. I emphasize them mainly because they shed light on the types of films

I will later analyze. Additionally, knowing a bit about the historical period of the 1920s lets us consider and evaluate a few examples from that particular era of filmmaking and through the 1940s and 1950s. What I will examine later in Part II is the second avant-garde more fully, often considered as the *definitive* avant-garde: the filmmakers of the 1940s and 1960s who radically altered film history (much more so, perhaps, than the artists of the 1920s). But the developments made during the 1920s), and especially the "schools" of thought — expressionism, surrealism, abstraction, and montage — heavily influenced all film production to such a deep-seated and far-reaching extent that it is necessary to see how the ideas were used in four separate avant-garde feature films, which is where I turn my attention in chapter three. These case studies will hopefully illustrate the summative ideas put forth in these first two chapters.

Case Studies

There have only been a few outright avant-garde feature films that have been produced between the turn of the twentieth century and the mid-twentieth century. There are, of course, examples of films that have *moments* of avant-gardism in them; these include well-known films like *The Cabinet of Dr. Caligari*, *The Last Laugh*, *Sherlock Jr.*, *Häxan: Witchcraft Through the Ages*, and *Napoleon*. While each of these pictures are very important to the evolution of film history at large, they could also be examined in terms of their individual styles that potentially make them avant-garde. That is, they can be determined or classified by what types of avant-garde filmmaking make them exist outside mainstream cinema. However, instead of detailing every small instance of avant-gardism that does in fact occur in such films (I have, to a certain extent, already elaborated on the motifs found in expressionism or surrealism that occur in these types of films), I will instead look at four feature-length avant-garde films that typify certain tendencies found in shorter films of the era. Their styles, forms, and themes can be considered avant-garde because they have specific scenes that are experimental and also because their overall narrative patterns establish levels of discontinuity and disjunction. A more detailed list of avant-garde features that were produced during the silent era and through to the 1950s is found in the appendix.

L'Age d'Or

Luis Buñuel's scandalous (for its time) and surrealist film *L'Age d'Or* (1930) caused such a sensation at its premiere that people rioted, threw ink at the screen, tossed rotten eggs into the crowd of spectators, and physically attacked others. Such a reaction can only come from something that provokes as much as it instigates; and like with another avant-garde masterpiece, Stravinsky's *The Rite of Spring*, when confronted with such a radical aesthetic, people do not know how to react because their ideals have been challenged, and their notions of filmmaking (or musical composition) have been disrupted or eradicated completely. If a film is simply bad, viewers may walk out. But when a riot ensues, something else is going on — something avant-garde in and of itself. As a result of its premiere and its subject matter, and outrage and hostility from political and religious groups, the film was pulled from the screen by the police and banned, only being re-released nearly fifty years later.

L'Age d'Or is a film that blatantly and also subversely attacks the core values of bourgeois society. In it, "Narrative, poetic, and documentary conventions are mixed together into a unique and sacrilegious stew."[1] Its plot is somewhat simple: Two lovers are constantly thwarted in their attempts at intimacy and desire, so they essentially confront the bourgeois society that continuously keeps them from uniting, wanting to overturn the value system that keeps people like them apart in the first place. The film is full of images that can offend, from skeletal bishops to an orgy led by Jesus Christ. The film is a meditation on *L'Amour Fou*, and its style leans heavily toward surrealism, a potent form of critical interpretation of reality, conditioned in part by the avant-gardes of the 1920s. Buñuel's film has "taken up residence in the pantheon of modernist aesthetic scandals," mainly because it is wildly inventive in style and form, its thematic core is both blasphemous and revelatory, and its provocative images still resonate because they provoke contemplation, anger, beauty, and even laughter.[2] Its well-known premiere aside, the film shocks because — like its predecessor, *Un Chien Andalou* — it forces us to consider its unique avant-garde aesthetic in terms of both theme and style.

Buñuel and Salvador Dalí's *Un Chien Andalou* (1929) is one of the most famous avant-garde films ever made. It has no discernable plot, surrealist imagery, illogical spatial/temporal schemes, and a heavy reliance on dream logic. *L'Age d'Or*, which also was created by both Buñuel and Dalí, though Dalí left the project early on and is really only credited with some of the story ideas, follows the same pattern, even if its narrative is a bit more straightforward (but strange and strangely patterned). Buñuel wanted to make a feature film that expanded some of the ideas in *Un Chien Andalou* — namely, an extended treatise on "mad love" and society's repression of sexuality; physical violence; surrealism and surrealistic imagery that becomes part of everyday reality; and finally, a shock to the system of middle-class art and mores (religion and politics). The film has been described as "a sadistic, anti-clerical travesty whose nightmarish imagery was grounded in Rabelaisian wit."[3] Indeed, in its uncomplicated story of a man and woman told through a series of vignettes, there emerges the wit of surrealist surprise and desire, manifested in outrageous images and the play of unconscious ideas made real. Surrealist film attempts "to enhance the impression of film as visual exploration of the unconscious."[4] What a film like *L'Age d'Or* does, then, is engage us on levels that do not simply "exist" as passive acceptance of the images onscreen. Rather, the discordant and juxtaposed images that comprise the narrative force us into reflection because they are so uncanny and provocative. And, as Sophy Williams suggests, "*L'Age d'Or* is a destructive and anarchic response to the strategies of containment and repression of what the surrealist movement of the late 1920s considered the corrupt technological age."[5]

The film opens with a documentary-like prelude about scorpions. Buñuel notes in his autobiography that he had read somewhere that scorpions commit suicide when surrounded by fire, and this thematic tie reverberates throughout the film. The scorpion may represent the lovers' fate as having no chance for survival among the bourgeois ideology. Perhaps as well, this opening signifies a more surrealist tendency of juxtaposing different images for emotional wallop. As Allen Weiss suggests,

> [The] archetypal Surrealist film, *L'Age d'Or* ... opens with a quasi-documentary about scorpions, where we learn of their venomousness, aggressiveness, unsociability and hatred of the sun.... [The] function of this prologue must not be understood simply in terms of a startling diegetic rupture within the film, but rather as a symbolic protasis in which is prefigured a surrealist "theory" of culture where the established values of sublimation are consistently challenged by the disruptive effects of perversion.[6]

The opening may be read allegorically, as the plan of the upper classes, as a condemnation of desire as perpetuated by the upper classes, or as a surrealist theory about perversion, subversion, and the fate of real lovers. After this prologue of sorts, the film abruptly cuts to a beach, where we see four bishops worship alongside a mountain peak before rotting to skeletons on the rocks below. A bandit appears on the beach (played by surrealist conspirator Max Ernst) and revolts against a group of Majorcans and dies — before he even makes any physical contact with the enemy group. Amidst all of this chaos, the two lovers writhe in a pile of mud, attempting to make love. They are torn away from each other by a group of men, and then spend the rest of the film trying desperately to reunite and make love. Also on the beach, a group of dignitaries arrive and proclaim they have come to "found the Roman Empire." Accompanying shots of a modern-day Rome appear. This bizarre opening sequence is wrought with surrealist iconography and sacrilegious imagery, but it is also laced with a kind of subversive humor found often in the avant-garde. *L'Age d'Or* is the kind of film where you might laugh at the absurdity and audacity of the images. In one famous shot, the couple — known simply as the Man and the Woman — is at a party and are trying desperately to consummate their love. As they inch closer, the Man is whisked off to greet people as they arrive at the party. The woman, full of passion and desire, sucks the toes of a nearby statue. It is at once arresting and titillating, as erotic as any mainstream film's claim to love and yearning. This erotic displacement underscores the theme of thwarted passion, a passion that is often stifled by the middle or upper class in their constant need to disrupt union for the sake of rational stability. The Woman's fellatio of the statue's toe shows just how blasphemous Buñuel was — or was accused of being. The irony of the scene, and the source of its biting criticism of the bourgeoisie, stems from the fact that the lowly Woman has done this to a "high" work of art; her corruption of it signifies how the upper classes remain emotionless (the statue's face never changes, of course) while pleasure is served.

L'Age d'Or is a complex work about religion, power, and desire. It filters these themes through a surrealist lens that makes the seriousness of the issues both prescient and satiric. It is full of surrealist juxtapositions: a poor beggar is seen in the street asking for alms and is savagely beaten by the Man; a proud dowager is slapped around for fun; and a father shoots his son. When the film premiered, it caused a sensation, so much so that the surrealists who conspired with Buñuel (Dalí, Ernst, Man Ray, Breton) all agreed upon a declaration of surrealism — a manifesto, really — that accompanied the written descriptions of the film. The fact that a film would be released with an accompanying diatribe is an avant-garde tactic, and serves an avant-garde film in many ways. In part, it read:

> In this age of so-called prosperity, the social function of *L'Age d'Or* must be to urge the oppressed to satisfy their hunger for destruction and perhaps even to cater for the masochism of the oppressor. In spite of all the threats to suppress this film, we believe that it will win out in the end and open new horizons in a sky which can never match in beauty that sky it showed us in a mirror.[7]

Clearly Buñuel and the other avant-gardists who were supporters of the film upon its initial release wanted to incite people into taking a stance against the societal constraints that limit them from participating in particular self-serving acts — just like the couple in the film. This sort of harangue — really a criticism — is hard to imagine today, let alone ever in the mainstream. (The Dogme 95 movement possibly being an exception, but that movement was certainly outsider art as well.) But certain avant-garde films that have a platform or agenda, and many surrealist escapades of the 1920s and 1930s did, have the potency and determinacy to spark moral and political and aesthetic outrage, to cause spectators to become self-aware and socially aware.

L'Age d'Or is a film about displaced desire, "yet it is precisely the perverse manifestations of desire that disrupt the established exigencies of sublimation."[8] As a surrealist exercise in desire, the film can be interpreted as a nightmarish Freudian psychoanalytic excursion of dream-like disassociations. But it is mainly about how desire conflicts and interacts with the powers that try to rend it asunder. The couple in the film are continually thwarted in all attempts to fulfill their desires, but nevertheless, they reflect the desires of many who seek something beyond the stale, bland reality where most people reside. Surrealist film often contains imagery that "corresponds to a discourse of transgression, and an attempt at expressing something which, whether consciously or unconsciously, remains unattainable."[9] This transgression is very important in terms of understanding both the creation of something like *L'Age d'Or* and also the ensuing reaction to it. Chris Jenks, in his book *Transgression*, makes the connection between surrealist forms of art and the philosophical (and practical) application or idea of transgression explicit, which I think is applicable to *L'Age d'Or*. He says:

> The Surrealists demand that we should [let our imaginations run away with us].
> Thus imagination (untrustworthy), the unconscious (inarticulate), and desire
> (unspoken) should now become trustworthy, articulate and find voice, they should
> combine as our new mode of cognition and break out from the moral constraints
> that contemporary classifications of experience have placed upon us. This can be in
> art or political action.... Surrealism would clear the way by attacking, lampooning
> or destroying all processes and mechanisms that created or perpetuated divisions
> within cognition and the social.[10]

L'Age d'Or participates in the destruction of social institutions through satire
(the lampooning of religion and politics), and it also gives us a new mode of
cognition based upon the imagination, the unconscious, and desire. The avant-
gardes of the 1920s (and, really, before then as well) were political in nature and
were aimed at heightening ideologically awareness of the social order. *L'Age
d'Or* is arguably a political/ideological film that takes a stance against established
forms of cognition and art by challenging our expectations regarding film art
and aesthetic creation. As Weiss surmises, "Surrealism attempted to constitute
one such set of sovereign, revolutionary laws, and utilized a perverse iconography to express its rebellious critique of culture. *L'Age d'Or* is a love story
which is organized according to such a transgressive mode of eroticism."[11]
Desire, and interrupted desire, can take away all sense of reason and blur the
boundaries between reality and the surreal.

Some of the other blasphemous or transgressive iconography in the film
includes the famous final sequence where a group of people engage in an orgy,
which Buñuel "borrowed" from the Marquis de Sade's *120 Days of Sodom*. The
film ends with a sequence of a cross in the snow and a figure explicitly resembling Christ. (The orgy itself, which has eight captive teenagers and four
immoral women, is recounted in voice-over.) The possible evocation of the
Marquis de Sade explains Buñuel's furthering the acts of transgression already
apparent in the film. According to Rob Stone, at the time of the production of
L'Age d'Or,

> Buñuel's enthusiasm for Surrealism was being subsumed into the even more liber-
> tarian doctrine that he had discovered in a copy of the Marquis de Sade's *120 Days
> of Sodom,* which recounts the abuse and degradation inflicted on selected young
> women by a quartet of degenerate noblemen. Here was sin, celebrated and exercised
> as the essence of freedom, as a potent antidote to the centuries of Catholic repression
> and indoctrination against which the schoolboy Buñuel had once rebelled. To sin
> by accident or uncontrollable instinct required repentance that earned forgiveness—
> but to sin on purpose! This was the means by which man became superior to bour-
> geois morality, religious doctrine and God, while any remnants of guilt only added
> to the delicious, erotic frisson.[12]

In the film, the figure of Christ emerges as the leader of the sadists, a blatant
image of surrealist subversion that characterizes many forms of avant-garde
art. That is, the idea of rebellion is fundamental to avant-garde art, and a film
such as *L'Age d'Or* that creates moments of rebellion surely is subverting the

traditions that have established "normalcy" for years. The metaphoric scorpion has indeed stung itself. The ending of the film also contains a cache of formidable surrealist images: a cow in the Woman's bed, a bishop tossed from a castle window, a giraffe and a flaming tree, and a man with a rock perched atop his head. Avant-garde films often rely upon the disassociation among images that seemingly have little meaning when juxtaposed onscreen through manipulative editing techniques. *L'Age d'Or* relishes such moments, making it one of the best-known and intensely erotic and political avant-garde features ever made. "Part brilliant social commentary, part rebellious schoolboy prank, the film leaves us no choice but to pick through the fragments left by its explosive power."[13]

L'Age d'Or is the perfect example of an avant-garde film that relies upon the historical moment; surrealism fueled its construction and therefore gives credence to its themes and messages. In its attack on tradition and the bourgeoisie, the film explicitly denounces any cultural, societal, religious, or political forms that deny people the freedom to explore their own pleasure. It is

> A poetic reverie with a structure somewhere between a narrative and a nightmare. It launches a savage attack on bourgeois values of propriety and decency and works to undermine our faith in the civic institutions of society, especially the church. The characters and events are fabricated, but they lack the coherence of a conventional narrative. Buñuel sets out to violate cinematic as well as social conventions.[14]

The film is full of rancor and shock, but its images are quite beautiful in their disturbing brilliance. While some of the outright attacks on religion may not be as shocking as they once were — and may not start riots— the film's effectiveness and strength also resides in its formal experimentation. The arrangement of the images and the way they are presented to us remain captivating. A sudden cut from a scorpion to bishops on a beach; the woman sucking toes; the Christ figure — all are placed in the narrative at places that continue to shock because of the way Buñuel has filmed them and the way he has edited them together. *L'Age d'Or* remains a supreme achievement in avant-garde filmmaking, a pure and passionate surrealist exercise that exploits and subverts reason and linearity, relies upon dream logic, and surprises through its anarchic spirit, dark humor, and disquieting and upsetting imagery.

The Blood of a Poet

Jean Cocteau's surrealist masterpiece *The Blood of a Poet* (1930) is one of the very first feature-length avant-garde films (along with *L'Age d'Or*), released at a time when the burgeoning Hollywood film was becoming the dominant mode of film production. An anathema to almost all types and genres of films, *The Blood of a Poet* is a dense, richly symbolic tale that transcends causal logic, spatial/temporal continuity, and narrative coherency to present a remarkably fresh take on the life of an artist. The film is presented as a series of vignettes that, arguably, could be traced as a kind of (allegorical) narrative about the development of the artist from a young age to adulthood, but the manner of its presentation and representational schema place it firmly in the realm of a symbolic order where meanings are derived from personal interpretation. A true cineaste's dream, the film also plays with tropes associated with fairy tales, mythological stories or allusions, and classical character and artistic creation. Cocteau shows us the interior life of the artists through images that are at once wondrous, bizarre, and astonishingly rich in connotation, creating a dream-like environment full of suggestive meanings, nuances, and subtexts that require an associative viewing experience predicated on the fact that the spectator must interpret while inferring.

The Blood of a Poet is quite extraordinary because it provokes contemplation throughout the viewing process, a deliberate tactic used in many avant-garde films. It is avant-garde, too, because it uses a full arsenal of surrealistic imagery and is completely uninhibited in its presentation of the visuality of the material. There is very little dialogue (or intertitles) throughout the film. Cocteau, a well-known artist in many fields—literature, film, theater, drawing—is clearly interested in altering perception through the visual poetics of the film. Indeed, *The Blood of a Poet* is often referred to as a "visual poem," a tag meant to evoke a certain kind of lyricism not found in mainstream cinema, as well as elevating the film (and other films) to a higher form of art. Ironically (perhaps), Cocteau maintained that *The Blood of a Poet* was not meant to be read as symbolic or allegorical, and not even as inspired by or associated with dream or dream logic. But he did insist that one could read the film subjectively, interpreting the poetry of its images as symbols, or, more appropriately, as allegory. He says:

> *The Blood of a Poet* draws nothing from either dreams or symbols. As far as the former are concerned, it initiates their mechanism, and by letting the mind relax, as in sleep, it lets memories intertwine, move and express themselves freely. As for the latter, it rejects them, and substitutes acts, or allegories of these acts, that the spectator can make symbols of if he wishes.[15]

This rather cryptic description *does* tell us that the film is full of dream-like imagery, symbol, and allegory—a heady mix of surrealism and poetry that makes it a unique kind of avant-garde film that relies upon memory as its narrative thread and theme.

The film is divided into four chapters or sequences, each detailing in some fashion the development, growth, or regression, perhaps, of the artist or the artist's perceived role in society. The film begins and ends with the same enigmatic image: a tall chimney tower that collapses into a cloud of smoke. After the initial shot of the tower as it begins collapsing, the film cuts to an artist's studio where the poet is drawing a charcoal sketch on a large white canvas. He draws a series of faces, and when he does not like the image, he smears it with his hand. Much to his dismay and horror, the mouth of the drawn picture appears in the palm of his hand, smiling and talking. This might be the first surrealist image in the film, and it is disarming. The poet then tries to get the mouth out of his hand (before kissing it — or kissing his hand) by rubbing it on a statue he has also been working on in the studio. The statue then comes to life. Again, the startling imagery evokes the surrealist idea of the dream-state, where anything can occur in an uncanny way. The eyes of the statue are both inviting and menacing, staring through holes carved into the all-white powdery face. The poet stumbles around the room a while before coming to a mirror. Standing before it, he contemplates the situation before falling through it. Again, the image is provocative: The mirror "splashes" as he falls through it, then he drifts through a dark nebulous place before landing at what appears to be a strange and mysterious hotel.

Once at the hotel, the poet crawls through the hallway and peeps through the keyholes of several rooms. He witnesses weird and fantastic scenes. In one room a child appears to levitate. In another a group of hermaphrodites convenes. In yet another a man is shot in slow motion, falls to the floor, and rises again as the film is reversed, then falls again. One cinematographic trick Cocteau uses in this sequence comes when the poet first falls through the mirror and lands in the hotel hallway. Apparently, the hallway was built on its side so that when the poet moves down it — he really appears to slide or crawl — it seems as if he is disjointed or disconnected from the spatial logic that creates actual walking. It is unsettling and really ahead of its time, in the sense of a surrealist style. The film's overall use of mechanized movement, and especially in these hallway scenes, is "evocative of a ballet, or even the exaggerated theatricality of pantomime. The poet's facial expressions, physical gyrations and general bodily movements are all very theatrical and dramatic, especially when he is being subjected to mental suffering or torture at the mysterious hotel."[16] I should note that Cocteau claimed *The Blood of a Poet* has nothing to do with surrealism, and in fact was made in direct opposition to it as an aesthetic movement. But surrealist imagery can be created through an unintentional or undirected set of incompatible images that rely less on logic than on associative meaning. Here Cocteau seems to be participating in the "logic" of surrealist texts simply because the meanings generated from the strange images onscreen occur precisely through their mysterious and dream-like presence. If the film does tap into the persistence of memory, as Cocteau did claim, then memory, too, is clouded — if not shaped — by reality and dream, which can result in surrealism. And it should be noted too that surrealism and lyricism found in poetic cinema are types of avant-garde filmmaking, housed together more so than being separated.

The next segment has the poet back in the studio where he smashes the statue with a sledgehammer. Because of this "creatively destructive" act, he becomes a statue and finds himself located in a snowy town square where a group of boys have a snowball fight. One of the boys is killed by a snowball and falls to the ground, where an aristocratic couple then lay a table over him and play a game of cards, which essentially is the final segment of the film. The woman tells the man he must locate the ace of hearts or he is doomed. He finds the card on the dead boy and then a black angel appears to take the dead boy and the ace of hearts card away. Losing the card, the man shoots himself. The woman transforms into the same unfinished statue from the poet's studio and slowly walks away. These final strange scenes illuminate a more important concern for Cocteau: the ever-presence of death. After the statue walks away, we see the tower from the beginning of the film complete its fall into dust. Death and destruction are an intimate process of creating art, as much as labor and love, and Cocteau aims to show us the dialectic involved in the process of aesthetic accomplishment.

So why is *The Blood of a Poet* avant-garde? It contains little narrative direction, though its story of the figurative and metaphoric life of an artist can be deciphered through its unusual imagery. It also is highly imaginative, personal, and, as mentioned, poetic, which really means that beyond the poetry of the imagery, the real poetic or lyricism comes from the manipulation of film language — the editing, cinematography, sound, or mise-en-scène. According to Bill Nichols, who calls almost all avant-garde film "poetic,"

> A poetic emphasis dominates films by the avant-garde. The goals of poetic work contrast sharply with the goals of logical discourse. Whereas logical discourse conveys information and presents the truth of a matter objectively, poetic works seek to create aesthetic patterns and speak to the heart of a matter subjectively. Poetic films draws attention to its forms as much or more than to what it refers to externally. The impact of poetic work is more expressive and emotional than rational.[17]

The Blood of a Poet can certainly be considered poetic based on these assumptions. Its dream-narrative, which relies upon metaphor, is intended to express poetically the mechanisms of creation and subsequently destruction. The film begins with an intertitle that reads, "Every film is a coat of arms: it must be deciphered." In this regard, the opening epigraph serves as an instruction to the spectator: In order to make any sense of the film to follow, you must abandon what you know and call upon another realm of interpretive devices that come directly from the seeming juxtapositions found in the film. The film is a masterful survey of the interior world of the imagination; depicting this interiority means using a cache of images that do not need to be explained through causal logic. Surrealist filmmaking, it should be noted, aims less for analyzation than for its pure and absolute experience of images. Cocteau blatantly denied the film's ties to surrealism, instead saying that it is in opposition to surrealist films, though being classified as such. But he also says, "At the time of *The Blood of a Poet*, I was the only one ... to avoid the deliberate manifestations of the unconscious in favor of a kind of half-sleep through which I wandered as though in a labyrinth."[18] I think that Cocteau, while divorcing himself from the "unconscious" desires that are often found in surrealist works of art, almost unintentionally aligns the film with another aspect of surrealist filmmaking, the dream-film, where "half-sleep" wanderings through labyrinths can be directly traced to the well-known trance films of Anger, Deren, or Brakhage. As Roy Armes says, "[*The Blood of a Poet*] uses some of the mechanics of the dream, not to explore social or psychological realities, but as ends in themselves. [Cocteau's] concern is less to analyze than simply to recreate a state of inner consciousness, a world preceding rational thought."[19]

The Blood of a Poet is adventurous filmmaking, where Cocteau-as-amateur (he claimed to know nothing about filmmaking when he made *The Blood of a Poet*) creates an other-world of lyrical abandon. Cocteau, I believe, is mostly interested in the concreteness of the images he gives us; as spectators, we can add our own subjectivity when deciding if they are symbolic, metaphoric, or surrealistic, let alone poetic or lyrical. This happens when one encounters avant-garde film; in essence, one must rely upon the exactness of the images to form an opinion about them. To this end, critic André Fraigneau says,

> What makes Cocteau's concept of cinema virtually unique is his persuasion that the cinema is ideally a poetic medium, different from verbal poetry but equally valid, flexible and expressive, an art of concrete visual images instead of symbolic or metaphorical ones.... The film appears as a means to make plastic poetry by transforming thoughts into images of greater immediacy and potency than verbal ones. If film is action by definition, it is poetry in action by implication.[20]

Cocteau's clever use of surrealist imagery, a non-linear progression of events, and the power of the imagination as depicted through the concrete forms of implied poetry, mark it as a revolutionary avant-garde film. Its thematic concerns of artistic struggle, death, and lust herald it as *different*; eschewing convention in style and theme, Cocteau transports us to an imaginative realm of psychological nuance and surrealist enterprise. As a surrealist film — keeping in mind Cocteau's attempts to distance himself from the movement — it participates in the surrealist ideas of irrationality, the combination of the dramatic with the psychological, and a nearly complete disregard for conventional storytelling. According to Rudolf Kuenzli, "The cinematic apparatus is used by Surrealist filmmakers as a powerful means to realistically portray the symbolic order, which they then disrupt with shocking, terrifying images."[21] The interesting point here is the seeming discrepancy between a realist/surrealist aesthetic; but Cocteau, I believe, does this remarkably well in *The Blood of a Poet*. The film *is* realistic in its depiction of the symbolic order of the artist's struggle, or it demonstrates "Cocteau's lucid classicism to surrealism's baroque mythopoeia."[22]

The Blood of a Poet is decidedly avant-garde also because of the way Cocteau uses film form. Throughout the film, Cocteau uses photographic tricks, like slow motion and reverse motion; splicing negative film with the final cut, which creates a ghostly effect; mattes; and turning off the camera to make objects or people seem to disappear. But Cocteau is no mere stylist; he is intensely interested in how images can convey a personal cinema, a hallmark of the avant-gardes. He says, in regards to *The Blood of a Poet*, "I was merely trying to express myself through a medium which in the past had been inaccessible to poets. So much so that without being aware of it I was portraying myself, which happens to all artists who use their models as mere pretexts."[23] In essence, the film becomes an autobiographical treatise of sorts on the potentials of the cinematic apparatus, of the poetic muse, and the desires that drive the artist. A.L. Rees concludes,

> Cocteau's film finally affirms the redemptive power of the classic tradition, but the dissolution of the hero's personal identity also undermines the Western fixation on stability and repetition, asserting that any modern version of classicism was to be determinedly "neo" rather than "post." It inaugurates a new genre in the avant-garde, the psychodrama, in which a central character undergoes a series of ritualized trials which typically end in either death or transfiguration.[24]

In this sense, the film again foreshadows the personal cinemas of the American avant-garde during the 1940s and 1960s. Cocteau's avant-garde film aptly demonstrates the capabilities associated with alternative cinematic practice — in both theory and practice — that address fundamental personal, subjective concerns, and where a combination of styles that evoke surrealism and classicism are mingled to great effect. The filmmaker-as-author is another attribute that Cocteau establishes as a method of critique, and in this sense his film also helps establish the auteurist criticism that would come to dominate film criticism in the 1960s and 1970s.

Dreams That Money Can Buy

Hans Richter is a well-known avant-garde filmmaker, having made several seminal short films during the 1920s and 1930s that established his formidable presence in abstract and surrealist film. His best known short, *Rhythmus 21* (1921), uses only shapes—squares and rectangles—to explore cinematic space and depth. In this film Richter is interested in exploring the rhythms generated through spatial movement, where shapes appear to move along the flat plane of the screen surface. It is decidedly an abstract film, one where form and rhythm combine into patterns that are fundamentally about perception, illusion, and the movement of images. Richter's film was influential on many levels and to many other filmmakers, so much so that when he made his first feature-length avant-garde film, he called upon his friends—luminaries in avant-garde art—to help him. The result, *Dreams That Money Can Buy* (1947), is an experimental narrative film that both harkens back to his early work but also forcefully looks ahead.

Dreams That Money Can Buy was the first American feature-length avant-garde film. It boasts a list of "who's who" in twentieth century avant-garde art: Both John Cage and Darius Milhaud worked on the musical score; Paul Bowles worked on some of the dialogue; and the film's dream sequences were written and choreographed by Marcel Duchamp, Fernand Léger, Max Ernst, Alexander Calder, Man Ray, and Richter himself. Despite this impressive pedigree, the film has remained obscure, or at least has not had as great an impact or lasting success as other feature-length avant-garde films like *The Blood of a Poet* or *L'Age d'Or*. It is often viewed as a failed experiment, an exercise in too many diverse styles that do not cohere in its weak narrative thread. The story revolves around a struggling artist (Joe) who discovers he has the ability to peer into the eyes of strangers and read their dreams after they fall asleep, almost hypnotized. For a price, he will also deliver a "big dream" to them while they sleep. People enter his office room, which really suggests a departure from the waking world to the dream-world; when patrons enter their dreams, what we get is a representation of unconscious states full of strange imagery and music. Despite the eccentricities of the plot, and specifically the weirdness of the dreams, each dream sequence is full of emotion — particularly the last, which is about Joe himself. This narrative structure gives Richter the chance to call upon his friends to create separate dream sequences, which are the real avant-garde moments of the film. The seeming incongruity of diverse artists lends a certain historical and aesthetic credence to the film; Richter "was not opposed to the industrial appropriation of avant-garde techniques, [and] was actively committed to ensuring the autonomy of independently produced 'poetic' films."[25] The dream sequences, which are all short films conceived by major artists, are exactly that — poetic films independently produced and used effectively to create a strong narrative avant-garde feature.

The film is a colorful narrative about dream-fulfillment, something akin to visualizing dream-states, also a projection of surrealist desire. It remains one of the most singular contributions to twentieth-century avant-garde film, mainly because it is so unorthodox, offering little commercial appeal (though it does liken itself to post-war *film noir*, although it parodies it just as it designs itself as *film noir*) but highly imaginative films-within-a-film. This approach really limits its appeal to spectators only interested in its novelty. *Dreams That Money Can Buy* was made shortly after World War II, a time when post-war anxiety, irrationality, and general malaise gripped the country. The Dada and surrealist-influenced films Richter made during the 1920s and 1930s were out of fashion (except for the practicing avant-garde filmmakers and amateurs), so the film might be read as a reflection of the unease that avant-garde artists felt at a moment of crisis in cinema culture and cinema history. Popular film — mainstream Hollywood production — was the dominant mode of film practice, and despite inroads into new forms and styles from the European nations that veered away from already established conventions, avant-garde filmmakers were not as viable or threatening, despite the call to arms by filmmakers like Jean-Isidore Isou (who I will discuss next) or the beginnings of the New American avant-garde, with people like Maya Deren and Kenneth Anger. Still, *Dreams That Money Can Buy* is a fascinating document that offers a stinging counterpoint to Hollywood's Dream Factory: seven surrealist dream sequences conceived and directed by prominent members of the avant-garde.

Dreams That Money Can Buy may best be described as a merging of image, music, and psychiatry. Richter (and the other co-contributors) plays with obscure psychical symbols that reflect dreams. (A more "mainstream" example of this very same idea occurs in Hitchcock's *Spellbound* [1944], which has a famous dream sequence conceived by Salvador Dalí.) Eerie, modern music accompanies the sequences to sometimes startling effect. It is experimental because it exists in the realm of the abstract, the subconscious, and the immaterial — areas traditionally confined to avant-garde film. Each dream sequence is unique, but some are more striking than others. The seven dreams, in order of appearance and their director, are as follows:

1. "Desire" — Max Ernst
2. "The Girl with the Prefabricated Heart" — Fernand Léger
3. "Ruth, Roses, and Revolvers" — Man Ray
4. "Discs" — Marcel Duchamp
5. "Ballet" — Alexander Calder
6. "Circus" — Alexander Calder
7. "Narcissus" — Hans Richter

Each dream is unique, and each is strange, surreal, or oddly affecting. The first concerns a bank clerk who watches a woman sleep; the second is about a woman who dreams she is a shop-window dummy who is pursued by a lovesick male mannequin; the third has a group of moviegoers in a theater who are instructed to mimic every action they see onscreen; the fourth follows a gangster who has poetic visions of a life outside of crime, but is really a filmed version of Duchamp's infamous "roto-reliefs," which become animated; Calder's segments are similar since he animates his famous mobiles, first billiard balls, then circus animals; and the seventh dream, Richter's own contribution, follows Joe, the dream provider, who turns blue and then proceeds to search for "himself" now that he has become alienated as a form of himself. At one point he stops himself from committing a murder, tosses down a bloody knife, and then realizes the knife continuously produces more blood the more he tries to wash it. In another nod to surrealist forbearers, Joe stops passers-by, asking for help; one's body opens to reveal a Magritte-like bird cage. Joe's dream is a total nightmare. As the dream-instigator, he perhaps feels guilty for what he can do and does for others and their wish-fulfillments. In his dream, Joe passes through a mirror and into a world that reflects his own nightmarish life. According to Richard Suchenski,

Richter's episode is the most allegorical and autobiographical.... With its soft color palette, expressive use of a subjective camera, deep-focus cinematography and enigmatic narrative, the "Narcissus" episode explicitly simulates the texture and flow of a dream, and it is unsurprising that Richter claims to have made it in a trance.[26]

Each of these segments has avant-garde motifs and techniques. For example, in Richter's Joe inexplicably sits on a large cake of ice; in Duchamp's there is a faint resemblance to his *Nude Descending a Staircase*, though now comprised of a prismatic focus and lumps of coal; and Léger's has animated dolls, something very important to the development of surrealist stop-motion animation as practiced by later filmmakers like Jan Svankmajer. The music for most segments also complements the avant-garde aesthetic of the entire film. Joe also fills his office with surrealist art and a large bust of Morpheus. I will briefly describe one dream in particular to highlight the film's overall surrealistic and experimental nature.

The first dream, Ernst's "Desire," is about a "methodical, exact" bank clerk accountant who reveals his inner sexual longings during his dream. His wife suggests to the artist/dream instigator (Joe) that she wants a dream for him "with practical values to widen his horizons, heighten ambitions, and maybe a raise in salary." In true surrealist avant-garde fashion (and a direct credit to the creativity of Max Ernst), the man's dream is a romantic, red-plushed reverie of desire, with motifs reminiscent of Ernst's collage work. The dream begins after the clerk shows Joe some clippings he has put in a folder; they include a man with an animal head, a woman reclining on a bed, a woman sitting on a man's lap, a red substance flowing with water, and a melting wax figure. Based on these, Joe conjures a dream. The dream contains people in classical costumes, a dense and painterly mise-en-scène, and a full chorus. Ernst himself plays a character named the President, who casts a watchful eye over the proceedings. The dream is completely surreal (and something David Lynch would be proud of): Leaves fall beside a red curtain where a woman reclines on a red four-poster bed while a small golden ball rises and falls from her mouth as she breathes. At one point the red curtains mesh and become her red dress. She swallows the ball, smiles, and falls asleep. A man appears behind bars, watching her sleep. We see her dreams—of calf-footed nightingales—and the man telephones her to ask her what she is dreaming about. She drops the telephone, which falls to the floor in a plume of smoke that envelopes her bed. The hallucinatory atmosphere of this segment and its particular dense (and potentially symbolic) mise-en-scène have remained highly influential. As A.L. Rees asserts, "Ernst's episode eroticizes the face and body in extreme close-up and rich color, looking ahead to toady's 'cinema of the body' in experimental film and video."[27] This type of focus for more recent avant-garde films has a strong tradition in experiments like Richter's *Dreams That Money Can Buy*.

Clearly, Ernst is visualizing one of his famous paintings (*Girl Menaced by a Nightingale*), which suggests both Richter's appreciation for others' art and also the unification of the similarities among all of the artists included in the film. In other words, each dream sequence stems from a historical and cultural grounding in 1920s Dada and surrealism. Richter was one of the founding members of the Zurich Dada, and his interest in abstract forms that can create dialectic interplay between shapes and emotions is also present in *Dreams That Money Can Buy*. (Each dream sequence has objects that take on particular significance when they are either used or animated.) But the film is more than an exercise in individual short films that can be read separately or concurrently; it also helped usher in the "acceptance" of new forms of film that would influence the longer formal exercises of the 1960s underground and the oneiric experimental films of contemporary avant-garde artists. In summing up the film and some of the sequences in it as influential to modern avant-garde cinema, Rees concludes, "Regarded at the time as 'archaic,' *Dreams* now seems uncannily prescient of a contemporary post-modernist sensibility. David Lynch selected extras from it, along with films by Vertov and Cocteau, for his 1986 BBC *Arena* film profile."[28] Richter's influence cannot be overestimated. His work in the 1920s is still remarkably fresh, and his other feature-length avant-garde films (*8 x 8*, 1957, and *Dadascape*, 1961) are just as intriguing as *Dreams That Money Can Buy*. These features, and particularly *Dreams That Money Can Buy*, "emphasized the revelatory potential of the irrational and the subconscious depths of the human psyche."[29] Many films can lay claim to portraying the inner life of people, but Richter's accomplishment in this particular feature-length avant-garde film remains one of the best examples of the kind of cinema that has been co-opted by mainstream cinema. Dreams and dream-like worlds flourish in many contemporary films. But *Dreams That Money Can Buy* is unique because it is a realistic portrait of the oneiric. Given its historical setting, it is indeed way ahead of its time.

Venom and Eternity

Venom and Eternity (1951) is a French experimental film directed by Jean-Isidore Isou, founder of the Letterist (or Lettrist) movement, an aesthetic and political group primarily interested in overturning tradition through active deconstruction of film norms and by establishing an arsenal of filmic techniques antithetical to what had come previously. *Venom and Eternity* is one of the first film-essays: It is presented as a text that one must "read" in order to grasp its thesis and other supporting ideas. The film aims for extreme provocation and innovation; Isou offers philosophical, aesthetic, political, and critical evaluations of all things pure or traditional: society, art, and especially the way films have been made and the way they should be constructed. Isou evokes the names of filmmakers (in voice-over) who have approached cinema differently: Chaplin, von Stroheim, Griffith, Cocteau — all people who altered perception in some form through stylistic or thematic breaks with tradition, exactly Isou's goal with his stubborn film project. *Venom and Eternity* is a film that attacks pretentious cinema — that is, cinema without a center, without hope, without function. Isou's brand of filmmaking is completely anathema to any that came before it, and as a result, he has left a resounding influence on filmmakers as diverse as Jean-Luc Godard, Chris Marker, and Stan Brakhage.

Like *L'Age d'Or*, *Venom and Eternity* (which has also been translated as *A Treatise on Drool and Eternity* and *A Treatise on Slime and Eternity*) caused a riot at its premiere at the Cannes film festival in 1951, and the police had to turn fire hoses on the spectators to squelch it. Such a reaction stems from intense and excessive provocation, which is a good thing for avant-garde cinema to engage in, according to Isou. Isou even evokes *L'Age d'Or* in the film, citing the reaction spectators had at its premiere as something he "loves." The plot, if it may have one, revolves around a young poet-philosopher (played by Isou) who wanders around the Latin Quarter spouting his theories and poems on a non-synchronized soundtrack. Isou uses some formal innovation: He scratches the filmstrip and colors several frames, and also shows shots that are upside-down. The film begins with Isou walking through the streets reciting his own poetry, then moves into an impassioned theoretical debate over the cinema, then evolves into a quasi-love story. All sounds and dialogue are presented offscreen in voice-over. In this manner the formal experimentation provides a disjointed effect. The barrage of words, juxtaposed with the simplicity of the imagery — of a walk through the Left Bank — gives an unsettling feeling. *Venom and Eternity* is one of the first films about revolutionary filmmaking; instead of a written manifesto, Isou declares war on tradition through images and voices. It is an angry manifesto, a passionate assault on all types of cinematic convention, from narrative to editing to music. Early in the film, Isou as protagonist outlaw declares in voice-over:

> Let people come out of a movie with a headache. There are so many movies from which one emerges as stupid as one entered. I'd rather give you a migraine than nothing at all. I'm not paid by an optometrist to bring him clients, but I should rather ruin your eyes than leave them indifferent.

This diatribe, coupled with the formal innovations (scratched film surfaces, inverted images), combine to give the spectator a visual and aural assault on the senses.

Lettrism is based upon the principles of Dada and Surrealism, and Isou's film bears hallmarks of each antithetical movement. But Isou wants to carry the tradition farther; he sees cinema, at the time of his film, to be dead and in need of serious revitalization. As Bret Wood notes, "Lettrism privileged the new and original in art above all else, and attacked anything perceived to be the least bit conventional with a vengeance."[30] Isou used the metaphor of "chiseling" away at the already-decaying cinematic tropes he saw ruining cinema in order to rebuild them anew. In a voice-over during *Venom and Eternity*, he states:

I believe firstly that the cinema is too rich. It is obese. It has reached its limits, its maximum. With the first movement of widening which it will outline, the cinema will burst! Under the blow of a congestion, this greased pig will tear into a thousand pieces. I announce the destruction of the cinema, the first apocalyptic sign of disjunction, of rupture, of this corpulent and bloated organization which calls itself film.

Isou's agenda seems clear, and though he may come across as overly ambitious (or pretentious), he is ardent in his belief. In order to create something new, the old ways must be destroyed. Any film that declares as much — that really wears its heart on its sleeve — is avant-garde. The film is indeed avant-garde based on all the formal innovations and cinematographic tricks Isou creates, but it also follows the tradition of Dada and Surrealism because it is overtly political or ideological as well. The Lettriste group was one that was essentially an assault on culture. According to A.L. Rees,

> [The Lettriste Group's] attacks on meaning and value look back to Rimbaud, Nietzsche and Dada, and anticipate William Burroughs. Among their tactics of "*detournement*," or subversion, Isou and Maurice Lemaitre cut commercial found footage literally to pieces, scratching and painting the film surface and frame, adding texts and soundtracks to further dislocate its original meaning. These often very long works joined a Lettriste armory of collage-poems, manifestos and provocations.[31]

Lettrist films like *Venom and Eternity* are known for their experimentation as well as their appropriation. This appropriation may include language or images. Isou uses both, especially the borrowing of language to form his essay-film (something Godard does as well). Lettrist films also utilize Brechtian distanciation, a method of involving the spectator in the performance. With *Venom and Eternity*, this means that the spectator has to be fully engaged with the debates and issues Isou addresses. At one point in the film, Isou-as-narrator says, "I hope you will quietly watch the screening of this film which at least has the virtue of being different." A film-essay is personal and often autobiographical (like may literary essays), where subjectivity often trumps the more standard kind of objective film fund in mainstream cinema. Like *L'Age d'Or*, *Venom and Eternity* also is transgressive; "transgression is a characteristic that the essay film shares with the literary essay, which is also frequently described as a protean form."[32] Essentially, an essay-film is one that develops a line of argument that purposefully engages and challenges the viewer, just as a written essay might. In this regard, what Isou and other Lettrist filmmakers were doing was creating a new cinematic style, one couched in an avant-garde attitude, yet also one that developed an avant-garde style. This would profoundly influence future filmmakers.

Lettrist film also subscribed to two basic principles of innovation. The first was the idea of chiseling away at the film. This was meant metaphorically (breaking down the norms of cinema) and literally (scratching and painting the film strip). The second was a technique called "discrepant" cinema, where the image track and the sound track were non-synched so that each would tell its own particular story, often crossing, merging, yet remaining apart. In the film, Isou-as-narrator says, "The break between speech and image shall form discrepant cinema. I am launching the manifesto of Discrepant Cinema." This abstract form signifies a divergent path for film history, one that was arguably started in the 1920s by the German avant-garde abstract filmmakers (like Richter), and later used by the likes of Brakhage. In the art-house sector, Godard, Chantal Akerman, Bruce Conner and Su Friedrich used similar tactics. In addition to the chiseling and discrepant inventions, Isou uses a variety of jump-cuts, image insertions, and bleached celluloid. Additionally, Isou keeps things static, then dynamic. For instance, he films empty streets, empty apartments, or cafés. But these shots are almost always accompanied by speeches from the audio track. In its audacity, *Venom and Eternity* continuously examines and re-examines the very nature of film form. Isou uses a multitude of avant-garde techniques that disrupt narrative and stylistic convention: As mentioned, he uses scratched white lines or black dots over the images; intertitles appear throughout, sometimes completely over the images; titles appear in the middle of the film; images frequently appear upside-down; people's heads are bleached out of images; and an animated arrow is shown alongside an image of a traveling motorcycle. Stock footage, a Star of David, and a plus sign punctuate certain images, giving them an abstract quality.

Venom and Eternity is a strange mix of fiction and nonfiction, of documentary-like footage and fictional interlude. We follow the protagonist (named Daniel), who comes across as a self-centered narcissist and poetry-spewing womanizer, as he expounds poetically (and didactically) on the cinema. The film is divided into three parts: "The Principle," "The Development," and "The Proof," which all could be interpreted as the organizational structure of a formal essay. Cinema, for Isou, should be rooted in language. (A semiotician would most likely have a field day with this film.) As such, mistakes in communication and meaning occur, which is also important to Lettrist filmmaking. Throughout "The Principle" Isou offers commentary on the cinema. We also see famous poet friends of Isou (including Cocteau) and various buildings and streets where he wanders. He often looks directly into the camera as he speaks or, more interestingly and terrifyingly, remains silent.

"The Development" ostensibly switches to the love story of the film, though the entire story is told in voice-over, again adding to the disarming effect of juxtaposition between sound and image. After Eve is introduced, Daniel makes absurd comments about the need for slavery, Communism, and violent death. In one scene, while Eve and Daniel dance, images of an upside-down ship, a statue, and a man running are intercut with their movement. This odd juxtaposition and irrational narrative hints at surrealism in addition to the Lettrism Isou practices. Also, when Daniel talks about Eve in both condescending and flattering terms (he says at one point she has the "haughtiness of movie stars"), the film inserts footage of skiers going downhill and a fisherman on a boat, as well as water flowing from a shower. Daniel is deceptive, and basically fools Eve into loving him, not for his ideals but for his own haughtiness, though she tells him flatly that if she were to spend her life with him, "My life would mean nothing." After a weird upside-down image of men walking backwards, Daniel reminisces about his old girlfriend Denise, someone he wants to both "pleasure" and then "break her heart." Denise wants him to "grow up" and take responsibility. Many times during the "scenes" with Denise, the screen remains black. All we hear are their voice-overs and an occasional shot of something disjointed from their speech (like, for example, boats in a harbor). Daniel is completely self-serving and arrogant; he tells Denise he does not want to have a "happy ending like in movies" because such things do not exist. He later says that "only systems where form goes beyond story are of interest to me." He also says of couples who grow old together, "Each has been a witness to the other's downfall." In essence, Isou seems to be chiseling away at the tropes of the typical romantic movie, something he clearly abhors. Despite his meanness, he and Denise copulate violently (which the narrator describes in voice-over). The worst claim Daniel/Isou makes during Part II is in a final intertitle that denounces traditional film style and theme. It reads:

> The author of this chapter, Jean-Isidore Isou, wrote this chapter during a spell of poisonous tenderness resembling that of the girls who emerge from his room with an "I love you" meant for no one and bursting with desire like a fruit into which no one will ever bite ... so monstrous does it seem at a distance. But upon reading these lines over, on a day of love-super-saturation he found this entire chapter insipid.

Isou's rant might be very off-putting to many viewers, and his misogyny will certainly appear offensive. But the point seems to be one of vitriolic refusal to compromise.

"The Proof" is a culmination of theory and practice. In a title, Isou indicates it contains Lettrist poems that have little significance to the film. The poems are recited onstage, and Daniel and Eve listen in the audience. Isou rants against traditional poetry, surrealist poetry, and American jazz, claiming all are not "authentic" and that they conspire in "phony primitivism." "Real" primitivism, we are told, stems from the body itself in the form of language, the pure and essential doctrine of Lettrism. In a self-reflexive move (which occurs regularly throughout the film), someone protests that using found footage is old hat. Isou responds by invoking the surrealist idea of juxtaposing discrepant images "to drown in the ooze leaking out of the comparison." Eve then protests the editing of the film and Daniel's/Isou's creation of it; after a discussion, Eve concludes, "All images are equally indifferent. I know that others before you have already destroyed the image. But you are the first to understand this destruction." Eventually, after more self-congratulation, Isou/Daniel claims, "I know that my film is above all existing films today." After further haranguing, which includes an explanation of the title of the film (derived from Nietzsche), the film ends with the following direct address to the audience: "Ask yourself on the way out whether or not this film possesses at least the value of a gangster film or a love story — or any 'realistic' film which critics consider acceptable." Isou's declaration is all too clear: People have been duped for far too long about value and meaning, so *Venom and Eternity* erases that and supplants it with something new and different.

In many ways, then, *Venom and Eternity* is a film that is an exercise in pure negation, or at least in denial, repudiation, and denunciation. It contradicts as it proclaims; it teaches as it performs; and it slaps as it tickles. In true avant-garde fashion, it becomes something beyond itself. In as much as it is a formal exercise in filmmaking, it is a cinematic treatise on art, normalcy, society, and culture. Not all feature-length avant-garde films are as involved as *Venom and Eternity* is in this endeavor, but on the whole, this film — like other avant-garde films— exposes the weaknesses of others while it reveals its own strengths. Isou is testing our capacities as spectators to become fully engaged in a cinematic practice based on language first, then image. (Derek Jarman would do something similar with *Blue*, where the audio becomes the center of attention.) He is also forcing us to see beyond the surface value of images, something he believes clearly does not occur in mainstream film. The film takes a huge risk, but that is what is needed to rejuvenate commonplace filmmaking. The avant-garde seems rightly suited for such an undertaking, and Isou, far from wanting to satisfy the demands of convention, does so with *Venom and Eternity*.

PART II

THE *REAL* AVANT-GARDE

Much has been written about the filmmakers who are considered to be the most important, influential, and personal avant-gardists of the twentieth century. These include such seminal people as Maya Deren, Kenneth Anger, Stan Brakhage, Gregory Markopoulos, James Broughton, Hollis Frampton, Ken Jacobs, Marie Menken, Michael Snow, Carolee Schneeman, Joyce Wieland, Jonas, Mekas, Jordan Belson, Harry Smith, Andy Warhol, Ernie Gehr, and Peter Kubelka. This is a fairly short list and can be expanded considerably, and almost all of the artists lived and worked in the United States (though some in Europe as well). The works of these filmmakers have been documented extensively (from P. Adams Sitney to Scott MacDonald, Paul Arthur and Jeffrey Skoller, William Wees to Michael O'Pray, just to name a few scholars who have detailed the "canonical" avant-gardes), so I will give only a quick overview of their contributions to the contemporary feature-length avant-garde film. Typically, when one thinks of avant-garde film, these figures come to mind, and rightfully so: Their works are better known, they are (but not all) archived, and they are used in classes devoted to avant-garde film. Still, the main difference among all of these filmmakers and the contemporary directors and films that I will detail more extensively in Part III of this book is that the majority of their films are of short length. Except for a few of these directors— Warhol, for example — the ways to investigating the canonical avant-garde is through the short films of these and others artists. But some of these filmmakers did indeed make longer films, and it is here in this section that I devote some attention to them. First, though, some clarification of the canonical avant-garde filmmakers and their films.

§ **Chapter 4** §

Some Considerations of the Influence of the *Real* Avant-Garde

As outlined in chapter two, the historical avant-gardes of the 1940s through the 1960s marks the period in American film history and culture best known for instigating a new form of personal filmmaking. The avant-garde filmmakers from this era ultimately were creating works that were so new, so different, and so individualistic — though traces of similarities can be made among them — that it is impossible to consider the state of contemporary avant-garde filmmaking without taking into account the relevance of some of their stylistic and thematic concerns that either directly or indirectly found their way into other types of filmmaking. Perhaps the best-known and still relevant type of filmmaking that began in the 1940s and extends through today's avant-garde is the highly personal, subjective films known alternatively as "poetic," "trance," or "lyrical." These types of films constitute a larger body of cinematic practice that demonstrated a new way of presenting interiority, focusing on a combination of narrative construction and abstract imagery. Painterly and literary influences helped establish a more subjective, first-person cinema that was more synaesthetic: creating worlds where everything from light/shadow, editing, or point of view focused our attention matters of style and theme.

The most vocal proponent of the "trance" film, and indeed the person who coined the phrase, is P. Adams Sitney, whose groundbreaking (and already mentioned) study in avant-garde cinema, *Visionary Film: The American Avant-Garde*, is still considered the best introduction to the theory and practice of avant-garde cinema. Sitney details the major figures in avant-garde film, offering insightful commentary on individual films as well as giving labels to certain types of films he notices have similarities. The poetic trance film, or "psychodrama," is one such category that remains influential. Sitney delineates several key characteristics of the trance film by first describing Maya Deren's canonical *Meshes of the Afternoon* (1943). He suggests of this film and others like it that they contain "a fluid linear space," that they evoke "the dream state," and that the "filmmaker use herself or himself [as the] protagonist."[1] He continues, saying the origins of the American avant-garde is based on the fact that "film becomes a process of self-realization," and that the "erotic and irrational imagery that we encounter in many of these earlier films evokes the raw quality of the dream itself."[2] The focus on the dream-like states of the people in such films has ties to surrealism, but these new avant-garde films focused more on the filmmaker him/herself as sole transmitter of knowledge and creation. These types of films also eschew distinct interpretation, something very important when considering feature-length avant-garde films; their complexity generates multiple plausible responses. Elsewhere, Sitney claims of trance films:

> They deal with visionary experience. Its protagonists are somnambulists, priests, initiates of rituals, and the possessed, whose stylized movements the camera, with its slow and fast motions, can re-create aptly.... Here is the classic trance film: the protagonist who passes invisibly among people; the dramatic landscape; the climactic confrontation with one's self and one's past.[3]

Some contemporary feature-length avant-garde films arguably have similar structures, from *Eraserhead* to *Conspirators of Pleasure* to *Careful* to *The Last Rite*. Perhaps in a more succinct description, A.L. Rees describes the new American trance film as

> [M]odeled on dream, lyric verse and contemporary dance. Typically it enacts the personal conflicts of a central subject or protagonist. A scenario of desire and loss, seen from the point of view of a single guiding consciousness, ends either in redemption or death. Against the grain of realism, montage editing evokes swift transitions in space and time. The subjective, fluid camera is more often a participant in the action than its neutral recording agent.[4]

Here Rees describes not just thematic concerns but stylistic ones as well, which do indeed creep into particular modes of expression found in longer avant-garde films. The most important thing to remember, I think, when considering these earlier and well-known short trance films is the focus on the highly subjective perspective and the hallucinatory or dream-like scenario of them. It seems that many avant-garde films follow suit, and longer films experiment with form and style while maintaining a semblance of narrative to detail the particular viewpoint of either the director or protagonist of the picture.

The canonical American avant-garde filmmakers of the 1940s and 1950s (Anger, Deren, and Brakhage, to name the best known) used "mythical themes and images" in their recreations of inner states, where the "poetry of private passions" found articulation through carefully nuanced films, and where imagination was the strongest contributor to a new film form.[5] Brakhage, of course, would venture into very different territory with his explorations of the ontology of the image itself, but for the most part the (American) films of this era helped establish a new kind of filmmaking that influenced both the underground movement of the 1960s, and more recently, video installation projects from a new generation of avant-garde filmmakers whose personal vision and display of the self (think Matthew Barney) harkens back to this earlier time. Abstract expressionism would become an important aesthetic touchstone for these and other avant-garde filmmakers as well. The style of the avant-garde film often rested upon "the manipulation of time and space [and was] equally a property of film form, so editing could undermine the surface realism of cinematography to create a new language that was film's alone."[6] Such stylistic tendencies are important to remember when thinking about contemporary feature films, where form dictates style, such as with abstraction or associative filmmaking. Many patterns that revolve around shapes, colors, or even characters or ideas can be found in feature-length avant-garde films. Such films (like Peter Greenaway's *The Falls*) involve spectators on perceptual and conceptual levels. Sounds, edits, or certain kinds of mise-en-scène may create a more associative type of experimental or avant-garde film, where patterns develop based on the juxtaposition of images (or sounds or objects). Collage films, from Bruce Conner's famous short *A Movie* (1958) to Craig Baldwin's *Spectres of the Spectrum* (1999), are based on this idea. The lyricism found in abstract collages is also important to note in more contemporary films like Godfrey Reggio's *Koyaanisqatsi* (1982), a latter form of the city symphony film.

Further experimentation came with the freeing of the camera, as evidenced in Marie Menken's films (*Geography of the Body*, 1943), or the stasis of the camera, best shown in Warhol's films (like *Empire*, 1964). Such diverse use of cinematography (and editing) is seen in contemporary avant-garde features like the overly frenetic *Tetsuo: The Iron Man*, the detailed close-ups and jumps in *Conspirators of Pleasure*, or the calm placidity in *Sàtàntàngo*. These developments helped solidify a new form of filmmaking, which has influenced filmmakers, from the French New Wave to video experimentalists. Still other means of expression come from a new kind of realism, one that offers entirely individualistic ways of interpreting society, culture, or history. The future of American independent cinema, as well as the primacy of subjective realism — the kind filtered through modernism or through the filmmaker's individualistic/idiosyncratic perspective — is linked to such techniques. According to Jonas Mekas, the "godfather" of the American avant-garde, writing in 1961,

> Whereas the experimentalists such as Maya Deren, Willard Maas, Hans Richter, and Sidney Peterson were concerned with the exploration of the subconscious, with the development of a universal, abstracted film poetry, free from time and place, this other group of filmmakers were interested in exploring their world in a more prosaic and realistic manner, right here and now.[7]

Although Mekas is speaking of a very particular kind of filmmaker, I think what he says is applicable to many feature films that follow. As mentioned, any kind of filmic practice can be interpreted as a way of seeing, and avant-garde film is certainly the exception and the better avenue to use when considering how to view the world differently. Hence, even dream-like trance films, surrealist films, or even abstract films may be considered ways of looking at the material world in particularly unique ways. Mekas eventually concludes that there are complete poets (Breer, Brakhage and Menken in particular) working in cinema, which "thematically and formally, represent ... the best of the tradition of experimental and poetic cinema." He continues:

> Freely, beautifully they sing the physical world, its textures, its colors, its movements; or they speak in little bursts of memories, reflections, meditations. Unlike the early avant-garde films, these films are not burdened by Greek or Freudian mythology and symbolism, their meaning is more immediate, more visual, suggestive. Stylistically and formally their work represents the highest and purest creation achieved in the poetic cinema.[8]

Mekas makes a clear distinction between the surrealism of the 1920s avant-gardes and the more realistic films of pure poetry, even though Breer and Brakhage are concerned with forms antithetical to "real" objects (Breer works in animation; Brakhage in hand-painted and scratched films). But both strands, I think, are present in even the films Mekas designates as "poetic," and both are present (perhaps in dialectical fashion?) in many feature-length avant-garde films.

There are many other types of avant-garde films made during the second great wave of avant-garde filmmaking during the 1940s through the 1960s. From trance to lyric, collage to structuralism, surrealism to realism, non-narrative to narrative, the short films produced by both American and European artists of the post-war years radically altered avant-garde filmmaking. Their history has been detailed critically and objectively in various texts; hence I offer no detailed examination of the already well-chronicled films and filmmakers from this time frame. Besides, I am focusing on a rarely explored area of film culture, the avant-garde feature film, which, as I have suggested, has direct links to the practices of the early avant-gardes, even when they are entirely original enterprises. The final point I would like to stress, then, is that in order to consider the contexts and intertexts for contemporary avant-garde feature films, we must remain cognizant of the varying types of films created during this highly prolific and fundamentally aesthetic and ideological era. Knowing this past helps elucidate the features and the tropes found in them, or at least the associations we can make with other kinds of avant-garde films. The following case studies will, hopefully, expand on and illustrate some of the ideas mentioned in this brief chapter.

∮ Chapter 5 ∮

Case Studies

Heaven and Earth Magic

Harry Smith was an extraordinary purveyor of art in many areas: film, musicology, anthropology, and painting. He epitomized the amateur do-it-yourself approach in his films, creating works that were seemingly primitive in construction yet full of startling images, thematic concerns, and formal innovation. *Heaven and Earth Magic* (1957–1962) is probably his best known film, an hour-long feature animation work that evokes mysticism, poetry, and a formal structuring that highlights his fascination with ephemera, objects, and the inner workings of the mind. The film is a surrealist exercise in bringing the unconsciousness to light: "The film employs everyday metaphors about states of consciousness as sources of imagery," which in turn underscore how the unconscious mingles freely with the consciousness of anyone, and at the same time accentuates the enigmatic nature of this mingling itself.[1]

Heaven and Earth Magic consists of cut-outs and objects animated through stop-motion photography. Though not the earliest form of animated film, it is one of the most original examples of this kind of painstaking filmmaking process because of its ambiguous narrative, which is only one of the reasons it is avant-garde. The feature is also complicated because it presents us with a slightly absurd yet elaborate and ultimately deeply metaphorical, symbolic, and mythic narrative. The narrative of the film is recognizable enough: A woman chases after a dog that has stolen her watermelon, and then she goes to a dentist who puts her under with a strong anesthesia, after which she travels to heaven and experiences a series of powerful oneiric interludes. Here is Smith describing the plot:

> The first part depicts the heroine's toothache consequent to the loss of a very valuable watermelon, her dentistry and transportation to heaven. Next follows an elaborate exposition of the heavenly land in terms of Israel, Montreal and the second part depicts the return to earth from being eaten by Max Muller on the day Edward the Seventh dedicated the Great Sewer of London.[2]

This scenario gives rise to a whole set of ambiguous and thought-provoking images, all unusual because they are the product of a collage approach. Collage films, which I will detail a bit more when discussing *Lyrical Nitrate* in Part III, are traditionally avant-garde because they appropriate images/words/texts/objects—anything really—and reuses them in ways that subvert or get rid of their intentional meanings. It may appear primitive simply because Smith is moving around cut-outs, but the final aim of this film (and others like it) is both to draw us nearer to its aesthetic process and to its possible deeper metaphysical concerns, albeit in a more subjective fashion since each spectator may garner what he or she will from the film. *Heaven and Earth Magic* "uses cutout animation to produce a mysterious world of alchemical transformations in which objects suggest a multitude of possibilities."[3] The film presents an extension of the surrealist technique of dis-assemblage and re-assemblage to create meaning (a juxtaposition of ideas/images) out of recognizable images, and transpositions them through alchemy—itself a characteristic of animated films, and especially the work of Jan Svankmajer, who I will discuss more fully in Part III. Smith also uses language from the Kabala, Freud, and experimental psychology. Additionally, the film is full of objects that take on symbolic meanings: brooms, cats, eyes, hollowed heads, boxes (á la Joseph Cornell), horses, eggs, bells, skeletons, umbrellas, and eels, to name a few. The feature is also accompanied by a soundtrack that mimics movements and gestures onscreen (e.g., we see the woman's head get hit and hear a "thunk"; when a bell rings, we hear a screech; we hear a "moo" when we see a horse; and there are random bouts of applause that have little to do with synchronicity), as well as offering animal sounds, crashes, and flowing water. It is truly an amazing mix of the audio-visual, and signifies a distinct type of film in avant-garde feature filmmaking.

Smith described the film as a process of automation or of creating and extending the "automatic"—regular, repeated, and mechanical occurrences that suggest different meanings and create rhythmic patterns and formal designs. He described it as such:

> I tried as much as possible to make the whole thing automatic, the production automatic rather than any kind of logical process ... [so] I proceeded on that basis: Try to remove things as much as possible from the unconsciousness or whatever you want to call it so that the manual processes could be employed entirely in moving things around. As much as I was able, I made it automatic.[4]

This process of creation through automatic positioning is what in part creates the surrealistic imagery and patterns in the film. The automatic process also allows for the associative relationships between objects in the film and the relationship between film and spectator. The film's dominant motif is that of transformation—throughout we see various objects become others or the woman transform herself. As Noel Carroll points out, "The surrealist use of transformation as a means of identification" structures the film.[5] Smith, I believe, is interested in the magical transportations that occur through the mind. The emphasis on imagination and what the mind can do and where it can take us is the thematic unity in *Heaven and Earth Magic*. Its seeming primitivism belies a larger concern about the magical/alchemical powers of the imagination. We graphically see this when Smith several times shows a large head where we can see machines turning and grinding, a continual and repetitive process of generating thought and imagination; "At times, the insides of the heroine's head are portrayed as a set of springing gears, with a jack hammer and other machine noises synchronized on the sound track."[6] Heads appear in boxes for our scrutiny and fascination, where we can see, quite literally, how the mind operates. It is why Sitney says the film is "among the very highest achievements of the American avant-garde cinema and one of the central texts of its mythopoeia phase."[7] Indeed, Carroll sees the entire film as a representation of the mind itself, calling it the cinema of mind. He suggests, "The narrative serves as a pretext for the almost autonomous proliferation of imagery — a rapid, energetic succession following its own principles. These principles derive from a conception of cinema not based on narrative models like the epic poem, or the short story, or the novel: they model cinema on the mind."[8] Elsewhere, he contends, "[The] film presents itself as an image, or better, as a set of images of consciousness, of the mind itself"; and "[the] film is a series of poses, identifying with this or that metaphor of mind, trying on different and not always evidently harmonious images of thought as the basis for the genesis of imagery."[9] This heady conclusion does point to the fact that Smith was interested in something beyond merely animating cutouts. In true avant-garde fashion, he has constructed a feature film that dares examine the way the mind operates on cognitive and imaginative levels through the use of stop-motion animation. Through spatial alignments and disorientations, *Heaven and Earth Magic* shows how the methods of construction are as important as the styles and themes it generates, from surrealism to philosophy to psychology to metaphysics, which again reiterates it as a film open to interpretation (and Smith's own descriptions of the plot do not do much but obfuscate his meanings and allusions).

The journey of the woman protagonist through the film is alternately violent and humorous, scatological and determined. For example, objects give rise to other things: an egg hatches a hammer that turns into a machine that produces liquid, which ends up in the images with the woman. The giant head of Max Muller (a nineteenth-century philologist and book editor) is used as a magician conjuring and casting spells, and later in the film he eats the woman and other characters. The woman is dismembered and reconstructed. Smith clearly has antecedents in Max Ernst and Joseph Cornell, and *Heaven and Earth Magic* also recalls surrealist Exquisite Corpse exercises of the 1920s. The entire film is structured like a dream, or perhaps a nightmare. As Carroll points out, "There are constant references to the fragmentation of the self through visual images of persons splitting apart, through visions of dismemberment, and through images of glass shattering and splintering," a possible means of interpreting the film as a disintegration of the self.[10] The sheer amalgamation of images works in an associative manner, a very specific detail of avant-garde spectatorship, where meanings are not as directly based, in this case, on the process of increasing composition. Despite a highly formal composition, the disparate objects that fill the film defy a straightforward logic, which again is why the film is avant-garde. According to Carroll, the film's enigmatic structuring, and its focus on the unconscious, is akin to the surrealist films and creations that preceded it. In part, he says,

> [It] was essential to the surrealist project that its display of the operations of the unconscious remain partly inscrutable. Through the hermeticism of *Heaven and Earth Magic*, Smith engenders this provocative inscrutability, intimating sense through the presence of unconscious expressive processes, thereby making the unconscious manifest, eliciting its recognition by displaying its universal modes in such a way that the audience gasps as a mirror is held up to its repressed mental life.[11]

The audience gasps, but it also enjoys the challenge, the process of discovering meaning or aspects of themselves through the meticulous nature of the film's construction and presentation. It is indeed mythical, and demonstrates Smith's "quest for a magical center that all arts, and all consciousnesses, share."[12] The references in the film are obscure and arcane, but that adds to its power of enchantment and surrealistic exploration of the unconscious mind. The objects that are on display eventually yield a narrative — or metaphor — about how the mind operates, since they are a composite of *something* that Smith wants to articulate.

Sleep

Andy Warhol's contributions to twentieth century art are undeniably highly influential, given his work in several mediums, and his output has been documented considerably. Given this, I will limit my brief discussion to one of his better known feature films, *Sleep* (1963), a movie that creates as it destroys, critiques as it knowingly winks at tradition, all while forming a very new and specific kind of avant-garde film. In other words, Warhol is deliberately playing with the tropes of cinematic form, imbuing this film with a stubbornness based on the way signs/signifiers are, essentially, meaningless, mainly because *Sleep*, like several of his other films (*Empire, Eat, Blow Job*, for example), are basically one long take without editing or any kind of post-production manipulation. His films are revered and despised, enjoyable and excruciating, formal and *in*formal, but rarely forgettable. The codes he creates through the extreme long take, which is the primary characteristic of most of his films, including *Sleep*, suggests a reductionism and subversion, an exercise in stasis, durability, duration, materialism, and (non)narrative structuring that suggests the "idea of a filmmaker filming an object over a lengthy period of time without any attempt

at film construction or story or even drama was anathema" to any kind of traditional form or style of filmmaking.[13]

One of the "myths" surrounding *Sleep* is that it is indeed one interrupted
take that is looped to create the final six-and-a-half-hour film. The films does
have at least a dozen shots, but the camera's positioning remains ostensibly the
same; the images may shift to other places in the frame (e.g., a shot of the face,
the stomach, or full figure), but overall, the film is structured like one long take.
Even though there are edits, repeated loops and freeze frames—which makes
it what might be called fragmented — the film is based on repetition and duration. *Sleep* is ostensibly a movie about sleeping: Warhol films his then-lover
John Giorno at night while he sleeps. Several critics see this as an inversion of
the dream or trance film that had dominated much avant-garde filmmaking in
the United States. Warhol, unlike Deren or Anger or Brakhage, does not reveal
the dream through his film. Instead, Sleep "sums his attack on film as dream
and metaphor. Warhol parodies the trance film: we see a man sleeping for six
hours, but not his dreams."[14] This "monumental inversion of the dream tradition" allowed Warhol to explode "the myth of compression and the myth of
the filmmaker."[15] He focused almost exclusively on the material aspects of the
film — namely, how it (the film) could capture a moment of elongated and
uninterrupted action or, better, direct representation. In its minimalism, *Sleep*
(which was shown at 16 fps instead of the customary 24 fps, slowing it down
even more) demonstrates that a film's avant-gardism can come from both the
approach and the execution, traits common in avant-garde film practice, but
ones really turned on their head by Warhol. Warhol does not use a shot as the
essence of constructing film; the camera confronts what it films directly and
forces us to fix our gaze rather than move it. In other words, watching the film
requires a completely new kind of viewing process that was antithetical to both
mainstream and other avant-garde films. The complete objectivity of the film —
the sleeping body on display—forces a new perspective or subjective scrutiny.
The way the film manipulates time — the extremity of the shot, combined with
looping and freezing—creates a form of filmmaking that, in essence, was not
in existence before Warhol. According to Sitney,

> [The] latent mechanisms [of non-editing] must have suggested other conscious and
> deliberate extensions: that is, he must have inspired, by opening up and leaving
> unclaimed so much ontological territory, a cinema actively engaged in generating
> metaphors for the viewing, or rather the perceiving, experience.[16]

Warhol's focus on the long take, in other words, makes us reconsider the nature
of film's ability to capture, re-create, and show us reality. *Sleep* makes us keenly
aware of the relationship between film and reality in ways other mainstream
films cannot, ironically making us active viewers to the passive world of the
film's subject matter.

By never really moving the frame, or moving it only slightly, and by making a film of extreme duration, Warhol's *Sleep* really was a watershed in avant-garde filmmaking. By simply turning on the camera and letting it record, Warhol's reductionism of cinematic tropes was similar to his deconstruction of classical art. In part, Pop Art's aim was "to paint something so obvious no on had noticed it, something that therefore demanded acknowledgement."[17] For Warhol and a film like *Sleep*, this meant showing something as common-place, ordinary, and routine as a man sleeping. And, as Thom Anderson notes, "Pop Art wasn't so much about the turning low culture into high culture as it was about turning the mundane into the representable, and sleeping is even more mundane than a can of soup."[18] *Sleep* does indeed create a film where the sign/signifier relationship is displaced or undermined. And even though there are numerous edits in the film (but mainly unobservable because they are pri-marily looped), Warhol's focus on repetition is what makes the film unique and unheralded for its time. There was "shocked incredulity that such a work could even be considered art ... [a] response [that] had much to do with how film had always been understood."[19] Warhol was the "first filmmaker to try and make films which would outlast a viewer's initial state of perception."[20] In some regards, Warhol seems to be suggesting that a film without a plot or narrative, and therefore one without a true beginning or ending, is as important in under-standing the relationship between image/reality as any other. Avant-garde films quite often take charge against realistic forms of representation, though they engage in alternative or extreme forms of representing reality. Warhol's six-hour *Sleep* persistently asks us to question the subject as well as the object of filming; he wants us to understand the self-referential structure of film as much as he wants to test our limits of patience.

Warhol places the body (Giorno) almost in the center of the frame and uses a light source from the right and behind the sleeping body. This creates an intricate shadow-pattern over the face, chest, and torso that, if one is willing to search or study, seems to create patterns of light/shadow that seem carefully constructed and organized. There are similar patterns on the pillow and sheets. Giorno's head also switches from side to side as he sleeps, and occasionally, when a reel runs out, his head moves from a jump cut. So even though the film tests the duration of a film's capacity to record, and the duration of the spectator to attend, it does have moments of small editing that can either refocus or reawaken our gaze. Michael O'Pray describes the body as "classical," due in part to Giorno's looks, but more so to the composition and patterns created within the frame based either on stillness or movement. And while there is a certain exaggeration to this description, it nevertheless suggests a way to "read" the film. Here is O'Pray describing a "scene" from the film:

> Another shot is a profile close-up of the right hand side of Giorno's head, which lies with the chin towards the right side of the frame.... This shot abruptly changes to a more intense close-up during which Giorno moves in his sleep, throwing his arm above his head. The latter part of this movement is repeated before the shot changes

to a slightly differently angled one in which the chiaroscuro light falls over much of
the shot and the sleeper once again settles himself in a sighing movement. The
sleeper's movements are reflected in the slight changes of shots in this section. Of
course, in such a film of intense stasis, the slightest movement of shot sets up a quite
different patter of light and shadow on the figure.[21]

This description outlines a "narrative," but one that does not follow any
rules of narrative construction. The static camera, the long take, the looping —
all avoid a direct involvement in the narrative (of a man sleeping) because
Warhol directs our attention (and attention spans) to both the deconstruction
of the narrative (its inversion or subversion) and the materialism of the film.
The syntax Warhol creates enables a certain type of avant-garde film (structuralist) that is more about its spatial and temporal qualities than it is about
its subject, though the way the subject is treated is important. Sitney says there
are four characteristics of the structural film: "a fixed camera position, the
flicker effect, loop printing, and rephotography off of a screen."[22] Sitney sees
Warhol employing three of these characteristics in *Sleep*:

> He made famous the fixed-frame in *Sleep* (1963), in which a half dozen shots are
> seen for over six hours. In order to attain that elongation, he used both loop printing
> of whole one-hundred-foot takes (2¾ minutes) and, in the end, the freezing of a
> still image of the sleeper's head. That freeze process emphasizes the grain and flatness
> the image precisely as rephotography off the screen.[23]

Structural films, like *Sleep*, are about the process of creating and watching, of
the material aspects of construction and the immediate awareness of viewing.
As the name indicates, we are interested in film's structuring possibilities,
"wherein the shape of the whole film is predetermined and simplified."[24]

What kind of person would want to sit through *Sleep*? It is difficult and
requires discipline — not unlike other avant-garde feature films. Warhol's films
are certainly non-traditional; he wants to prevent a formalist experience of
editing, instead allowing the camera to do the revealing. Writing about the film
in 1964, Henry Geldzahler says the film "must be infuriating to the impatient
or the nervous or to those so busy they cannot allow the eye and the mind to
adjust to a quieter, flowing sense of time."[25] He adds, "The movie is not so
much about sleep as it is about our capacity to see possibilities of an aspect of
film carried to its logical conclusion —*reductio ad absurdum* to some, indicating
a new awareness to others."[26] It is precisely this attitude toward a film that is
so intensely difficult that makes it compelling. It *does* indicate a new awareness
about the possibilities of filmmaking, which makes it avant-garde even when
it eschews the tendencies of avant-garde filmmaking that have come before it.
The ceaseless, incessant stare of the camera at its object ushered in a type of
film that was cutting-edge and innovative. As Sitney also says, "By sheer dint
of waiting, the persistent viewer would alter his experience before the sameness
of the cinematic image."[27] Without narrative concerns, the spectator experiences
the slow passing of time. There is a fixed view of the object that corresponds

to the viewer's fixed perspective, since the camera does not move. Watching *Sleep* is challenging, and "the great challenge of the structural film became how to orchestrate duration; how to permit the wandering attention that triggered ontological awareness while watching Warhol films and at the same time guide that awareness to a goal."[28] In essence, *Sleep* compels us to rethink the characteristics of film construction, and it is precisely for this reason it is avant-garde. As a feature film, it also forces us to view images differently over an extended period of time, an avant-garde tactic or device, and an essential quality to the experience generated by the avant-garde feature film.

Diaries, Notes, & Sketches: Walden

The influence of Jonas Mekas on the American avant-garde cannot be over-estimated. He was one of the first persons to champion alternative forms of filmmaking in the 1950s by establishing film showings for directors who had no other outlet for their films. He was the founder of Anthology Film Archives, started the Filmmakers' Cooperative, and founded and wrote for *Film Culture* magazine. He wrote tirelessly for and about avant-garde cinema during the 1960s, a time when many different forms or types of avant-garde film emerged, including underground, cult, and experimental narrative. Mekas himself made films, and he is best known for instigating a particular avant-garde film type, the diary film, which would be practiced in avant-garde cinema since his work was first shown in the 1960s. *Diaries, Notes, & Sketches: Walden* (1969) is a monumental diary film. A diary film is a very specific form of avant-garde filmmaking. A diary film lacks a cast or crew, a producer or script, or really any kind of plan or agenda, and is based solely on the director's filming of everyday quotidian life and events. The director of the diary film, here Mekas, shoots the raw material of reality: natural events, perfunctory encounters with others (and *Walden*, as it is generally known, is full of famous people that Mekas meets), city life (of New York) and actions, which are all then presented as a rhythmic collage. *Walden* is, in Scott MacDonald's description, "An epic chronicle of Mekas's personal experiences, of the daily life and seasonal cycle of New York City, and of the cultural scene as Mekas observed it from 1964 to 1968."[29] Mekas's personal observations— through the camera lens and his own voice-over — structure *Walden*. The telling details of the filming of seemingly random things— a flower, a wedding, a circus, for instance — offer a deeply poeticized view of empirical reality. *Walden* is a three-hour film that shows us how *real* real life is.

Walden is avant-garde because of its very starting point for subject matter, which essentially means it has no specific subject matter since Mekas points his camera and films, and because of its distinct style. Most of the film is composed of hand-held shots, creating an erratic, even jerky, focalization of the objects and people he films. But he discovers a kind of poetry through this method. Almost the entire film is naturally lit and offers elliptical narration and different forms of music (from folk to classical to Mekas himself singing). The chronology of the film is occasionally mixed for some dramatic effect, though Mekas is interested in letting the images speak for themselves. And it is also avant-garde because he uses superimposition, sped-up sequences, and double exposures, which often transforms the perception we have of the natural phenomena he films. The section on the circus "Notes on the Circus," for example, contains hyper-fast images and superimpositions that force us to see the performers and animals in new ways— a heightened sense of seeing and experiencing that otherwise seems normal until seen through Mekas's filming. In many ways, *Walden* is about the authorship of new perspective (something akin to Thoreau, who provides the impetus for the film's basic motifs) because Mekas invents a kind of film practice that stems from and forms anew individual consciousness, which is why it is a "diary." Like a written diary, *Walden* is a collection of observations, thoughts, perspectives, and comments on and about life; it is a personal look at the world as seen through one person's life, especially in its frequent moments of simplicity and universality.

Walden is a socio-cultural scrapbook of the 1960s, a diary of events and happenings, of people and places, that matter first to Mekas and then to his larger audience. Like any diary, the central figure becomes Mekas himself as watcher and listener, and eventually as craftsman. Mekas is interested in establishing a new film form that is antithetical to mainstream cinema, and, in some regards, to typical experimental or avant-garde film. Critic David James has perhaps best articulated Mekas's process of creating the diary film more than others. In describing how a diary film comes into being, he states:

> Swinging across the pun on "film" itself as designating alternatively a medium of activity and a completed artifact, the metamorphosis of Mekas's film diary into his diary films is summary of the conditions by which an antibourgeois cultural practice negotiates its context in bourgeois society. Just as much as a written one, a diary made in film privileges the author, the process and moment of composition, and the inorganic assembly of disarticulate, heterogeneous parts rather than any aesthetic whole.[30]

In other words, Mekas has transformed his film diary — the recording of many dissimilar things— into a diary film proper, which means it has undergone a process of aesthetic creation (and editing and embellishment). The finished film is therefore a filtering of Mekas's thoughts. It is here, perhaps, that Mekas has a string analogue with Thoreau, the namesake for which he called his film, a literal and metaphoric announcement of a certain attitude and compositional strategy. P. Adams Sitney describes Mekas's process of composition and ties to Thoreau in this way:

> Thoreau's *Walden* was an account of an experiment, a new life; the description of an isolated place as scenery for the acts of the self; the mediations of an obsessive

journal keeper in one different but well-contained essay. Mekas's film follows its namesake metaphorically in chronicling the author's daily life, making New York (and emblematically its Central Park) the focus of observations for an isolato lodged in a simple room at the Chelsea Hotel, and recasting the diary form as an essay on life as art, identifying just enough of the events and the characters to keep the roiling superabundance of what remains unnamed an issue.[31]

Sitney here designates an important aspect of the diary film — namely, that it is shot in public and recollected in isolation. Walden as a metaphor suggests an isolated place, hence Mekas's evocation of it, wherein his film becomes an "essay on life as art." Mekas has said in various interviews that Walden, for him, can be found anywhere. For example, in an interview with Scott Mac-Donald, he says, "To me Walden exists throughout the city. You can reduce the city to your own very small world that others may never see."[32] And elsewhere he reiterates this, saying, "In general I would say that I feel there will always be a Walden for those who really want it. Each of us live on a small island, in a very small circle of reality, which is our own reality."[33] This idea of living in and having one's own reality is specifically a part of the diary film practice. *Walden* is Mekas's own lived reality, his ode to the self and its reality. Thoreau's book is full of descriptions of things that only he loves; likewise, Mekas, in many voice-overs throughout the film, explains himself simply by stating he is "celebrating what he sees," and that "I am searching for nothing — I am happy."

Walden as diary film is a kind of avant-garde feature film that takes its cues from a highly personal viewpoint that cinema need not be constructed beforehand but during the process. Inasmuch as Mekas is filming his self/reality, he is finally making claims about the aesthetic possibilities of filming the everyday, and then transforming it through avant-garde techniques. The personal view of the director is important to almost any avant-garde film, since many are based on an alternative perspective of reality and how that reality may be reshaped. In *Walden*, Mekas takes the raw footage of life, as it were, and transpositions it as automatic, authentic, and indisputably personal and idealized. In a sense, by re-appropriating his film diary into a diary film, and by adding intertitles, non-synchronous sounds and music, and forms of narration, Mekas has formed an amalgam of personal ephemera into a whole, a finalized film product that becomes both autobiography and postmodern pastiche. It is a primal, observational film, where the diary form dictates content, style, and attitude. Diary films are essentially narrative, but Mekas adds the avant-garde touches of juxtaposition (with sound/image) and superimposition and double exposure to form a specific kind of diarist film form. The syntax of the diary film is somewhat akin to home movies in that the seeming unprofessionalism of its style and method produces great moments of beauty discovered in light, staging, or simply the spontaneity of real life. As MacDonald notes, "*Walden* announces what had become Mekas's credo: 'I make home movies— therefore I live. I live — therefore I make home movies.' For Mekas, 'Walden' is a state of mind open to the inevitability of natural process, regardless of where or how one experiences it."[34] Walden-as-idea is important to understanding Mekas's film, especially in terms of its relative simplicity. Likewise, Sitney says, "If Walden is a name for a home, and for what you see, it is a state of mind, an investment in the present moment just as it is undergoing revaluation under the threat of destruction. In later volumes of the film diary, [Mekas] will sometimes call this state paradise."[35]

Walden offers a compendium of places and people who populated the cultural, political, social and ideological landscape of the 1960s. Among those who appear in the film are Stan Brakhage, Andy Warhol, Tony Conrad, P. Adams Sitney, John Lennon and Yoko Ono, Carl Th. Dreyer, Timothy Leary, Baba Ram Dass, Gregory Markopoulos, Allen Ginsberg, Jack Smith, Nico and the Velvet Underground, Ken Jacobs, Hans Richter, Standish D. Lawder, Adolfas Mekas, Shirley Clarke, Peter Kubelka, and Michael Snow. All of these figures are a veritable "who's who" of a specific cultural milieu that consists primarily of fringe, alternative, avant-garde or outsider artists and thinkers. Mekas is able to present these people as part of the counter-cultural zeitgeist, but he also is able to make them part of his unique subjectivity. *Walden* appeared at a crucial time in avant-garde film production and also in the specific historical moment. James suggests that "coinciding with the disintegration of the oppositional countercultures and the underground films they had sustained, [*Walden*] reflects the industrialization of social aspirations, yet it afforded a means of mobilizing subjectivity."[36] In other words, the film presents an encapsulation of the socio-historical moment captured through a highly personal and personalized form, the diary film. Mekas created a film that was really new; a diary film was not something typically practiced in cinema. In interviews, Mekas has mentioned that the diary film for him emerged after World War II, mainly because people "got tired of invented stories. All that we could still do was to turn to real life, and look around us, and try and understand what was going on, what was real in our own story."[37] For Mekas, turning the camera on "real life" meant eschewing the escapist fare of Hollywood film (even though film noir, arguably, was also created as a reaction to the horrors of the war and post-war society). Mekas continues, discussing the post-war climate that generated his diary film impulses, "Everything else seemed senseless, escapist, unreal. That's at least my personal interpretation of why I chose the diary form."[38] James also says:

> Mekas was the first fully to articulate this combination of imperatives—the need to respond immediately with the camera *to* and *in* the present, and the need to subjectivize that recording—as the essential conditions of the film diary, and the first fully to turn them to advantage, and eventually to invest filmic attention to daily life with religious significance.[39]

In many ways *Walden* is a retroactive film practice couched in the primitivism of early silent cinema, as well as in a form conditioned by the "religion" of the everyday, a nod again to Thoreau. The film is dedicated to Lumiere, we are told at the beginning, which shows Mekas's denouncement of the conventions of narrative cinema and also his alignment with early cinematic practice. There is also a simple piousness in the revelation of the everyday. The poeticism of the (non-famous) figures and the mundane objects that appear in *Walden* suggest this, while the jarring camerawork and editing and the musical accompaniment and ambient noises all suggest a higher sense of recognition and self-identity, as Mekas reveals himself as much as he does the things around him. It is why Sitney can conclude that

> [O]bservation, fragmentation, and revelation ... go to the core of Mekas's enterprise. The effort to mold the cinematic material into some kind of conformity with experience initiates a dialectic of self-analysis. Starting off in ignorance of his own intentions, he transforms the image and its context to make it both more interesting and more his own.[40]

In short, *Walden* aspires to be something truly original, an avant-garde feature that is a strikingly original enterprise and a blueprint for the diary film in general.

Walden's influence cannot be exaggerated enough — it really does create a new film form of highly personal, investigative, and reflective cinema. The area that it most directly affects is the personal-essay film, which is, in all regards, a diary film as well, and one that is especially prominent in women's experimental and avant-garde filmmaking. I will detail some of these films in Part III, but for now it can be said that Mekas's grand enterprise is without peer. Only his other long diary films compare. The diary film is a hetroglossaic text, one that engages in a dialogic and often discursive relationship with its ties to writing (the diary as literature), the past (as in a reflection on the recordings of the self), and the present, both in terms of the self-on-display and the engagement with the larger social and cultural context from which it stems. It is why James concludes, "Where the pure visual practice of the film diary privileged a single sense and a single textual system, the diary film subjects the original images to sounds and disjunct visual material."[41] Mekas's style — the abrasive cinematography that orchestrates abrupt changes — establishes a rhythm of daily life through images manipulated to some degree through the mechanisms of cinema. Mekas turns the subjectivity of the film diary into a diary film. The constant stream of disparate or complementary images — from a dog to a park, to a foot or legs, to faces or close-up of a face — creates a euphoric feeling of genuine pleasure at the rediscovery of real life. Finding beauty in the observational is crucial to developing an understanding of *Walden*, and also for the formal avant-garde techniques it employs. As James suggests, "The short bursts of photography and especially the single-framing by which Mekas takes note(s) of the loveliness of daily life characteristically involve swift modulations of focus and exposure that transform the colors and contours of a natural object or scene."[42] Through Mekas's obsessive Vertovian kino-eye, we get to perceive anew our world, and that is ultimately a very beneficial thing to learn from the type of avant-garde film he creates, the naturalistic diary film, where vision is altered through the objectivity of the images and through the subjectivity of the filmmaker's technique. For that reason alone, *Walden* anticipates many contemporary feature-length avant-garde films.

Zorns Lemma

Hollis Frampton's *Zorns Lemma* (1970) is one of the best-known avant-garde films, and I include it here because I believe it is one of the best *instructional* avant-garde films ever made. That is, watching it becomes an exercise in *how* to watch avant-garde/experimental films. Its entire structure is a kind of basic introduction on movie watching. It has received much critical appraisal, so I will limit myself to only a brief discussion of its structure and thematic concerns. It has traditionally been called a "structural" film, and while structural films are extremely important to the canonical avant-gardes, their influence on the kinds of features I describe in Part III is minimal. I include it here because it is a fine example of the avant-garde feature film as practiced *in extremis*— it demands (and commands) careful spectatorship and intellectualism, and it points to a decidedly "perfect" form that enables a deeper appreciation of film language.

Zorns Lemma is divided into three sections, each unique but linked narratively through images and words/sounds that complement a specific thematic concern about letters or the alphabet, recitation and repetition, and the formal considerations of thought-construction, which positions the viewer in a distinctive cognitive receptive mode. The first section contains a dark screen and a woman reciting *The Bay State Primer*, an early American textbook of grammar that focuses on how to learn letters of the alphabet through connecting them to the Bible. The second long silent section contains various images that correspond to a twenty-four-letter alphabet that gradually gains momentum through loop printing and rapid montage. The final section is one long take of a man and a woman and a dog crossing a snowy field, while different voices narrate one word at a time from an eleventh-century text, *On Light, or the Ingression of Forms*. This structure emphasizes the progression of time, the process of learning, and the instruction of viewing. The entire film really is about the process of perception, on how the mind operates when seeing. According to Mark Segal, "What Frampton is doing is not audience manipulation, something he said he eschews. It is, rather, an expansion of the field of perceptual possibilities available to the viewer."[43] In this regard, it is best perhaps to think of *Zorns Lemma* as a film that continuously draws attention to itself as a structure of cinema (its structural form), while also dictating a particular kind of viewing or perceptual process that provokes audiences to participate via cognitive reinforcement of conceptual strategies. In other words, the film creates for us a basic text on film viewing: It starts in blackness, proceeds to quickened pacing and image looping, and ends with light. By heightening its structural framework, *Zorns Lemma* also reminds us of the power of oral language, of visual language and of thought processes derived from interpretation of language precepts, finally leading to a more logical examination of its mathematically-inspired and highly calculated formal elements.

Structural film is predicated on repetition and duration, and *Zorns Lemma* is the kind of film that uses these basic ideas to construct its "narrative." The entire second section of the film, for example, reproduces one-second shots of images corresponding to alphabetic letters. A structural film's content directs our attention to its cinematic techniques, but they also help is construct a narrative. *Zorns Lemma* does ostensibly "tell a story" about learning. Scott Mac-Donald sees the film as presenting stages of intellectual and physical development, an almost literal aging process. He says:

> The most fruitful approach to the progression, however, is to see it as a narrative mapping of human intellectual development. This approach accounts not only for the film's particular imagery and sound, but for the unusual experience the film creates for viewers.... Frampton places the viewer in relationships to imagery and sound that are analogous to the successive phases of development.[44]

The film's structure enables such a reading of the film's themes, and it is not incorrect to see *Zorns Lemma* as a process of development. It is structured as a continuation (darkness to light), and as one that follows the developmental process of growth and understanding. Structural film was first described and popularized by P. Adams Sitney. They are "static, epistemologically oriented films in which duration and structure determine, rather than follow, content."[45] Structural cinema "depends upon the viewer's ability to grasp the total order of the film — its shape — and the principles which generate it while he is viewing it."[46] Sitney also emphasizes the way structural films have a participatory nature: "[Formal] constructions have approached the form of mediation — the structural film — in order to evoke more directly states of consciousness and reflexes of the imagination in the viewer."[47] He goes on to say, "Hollis Frampton was presenting montage as a logical function and cinematic construction in general as a system of thought in his film *Zorns Lemma*."[48] Finally, Sitney suggests, "In the structural cinema, however, apperceptive strategies come to the fore. It is cinema of the mind rather than the eye."[49] These reasons are why I think *Zorns Lemma* serves as a primer of avant-garde film viewing: It teaches us how to think about form and content. As Peter Gidal suggests, "The mental activity of the viewer is necessary for the procedure of the [structural] film's existence. Each film is not only structural but also structuring."[50]

The title of the film also hints at its precise structure. Zorn's lemma is a mathematical equation theorized by mathematician Max Zorn. According to

Scott MacDonald, this connection makes Frampton's film both opaque — in the sense that it is hard to decipher because of its assumption that people "get" the title — and structural, but only in terms of its analogy to a set, rigid formula like a mathematical equation. He states:

> [Frampton's] fascination with mathematics, and in particular with set theory ... is the source of the title *Zorns Lemma*. Mathematician Max Zorn's "lemma," the eleventh axiom of set theory, proposes that, given a set of sets, there is a further set composed of a representative item from each set. *Zorns Lemma* doesn't exactly demonstrate Zorn's lemma, but Frampton's allusion to the "existential axiom" is appropriate, given his use of a set of sets to structure the film.[51]

As mentioned, the film's structure creates both its formal construction and thematic awareness. The first section of the film, the reading of *The Bay State Primer*, instigates the set axiom of the alphabet, and then the 45-minute second section starts another kind of ordering: Letters of the alphabet "fall" in one-second intervals and are replaced by an image (e.g., G is replaced by the washing of hands; B becomes a bird flapping its wings). Finally, in the third section, with the recitation by six women of the *Ingression* text, the voices themselves — the audio — become phrases of one second apiece. This mathematical set structuring is also what involves the viewer in meaning-making. As Sitney says, "The units of one second each, the alphabets, and the replacement images are ordered sets within the film. Our perception of the film is a participation in the discovery of the ordering."[52] Watching *Zorns Lemma* is decidedly an intellectual adventure; it provides a template for discovering the multiple ways films can communicate, a particularly important characteristic of avant-garde films, and especially ones that are structured in longer forms (as features). The film explores "some of the many new possibilities inherent in the film-perceiving situation," which is part of the general characteristics of structural film.[53] Structural films rely on formal elements that create the structural concepts present in the overall narrative presentation of the film. For Frampton, the concept of the alphabet as a mathematical arrangement or axiomatic set of sets provides the spatio-temporal structuring of *Zorns Lemma*. Frampton utilizes both the image and the sound to present this idea, which in turn "structures" the film as a whole, creating what MacDonald calls "a phantasmagoria of environmental language."[54] It is environmental because it encompasses both the visual and the aural. And in the process of its creation, a structural film places emphasis on the image as creator of meaning: Its relationship to the construction of the film (literally each individual shot) can be read as a deconstruction of the representational power of the filmic image since its structure produces meaning, rather than its representational aspects. Mark Segal addresses this idea, to some extent, suggesting,

> In film, what has come under attack is the concept that a film is built up by balancing shot against shot, scene against scene, with different parts carrying different relative weights, and with decisions about where to cut and what to juxtapose being made

on an intuitive, arbitrary basis. Hollis Frampton has rejected this method of making a film by formulating "a priori" systems which, once devised, determine the structure of the work automatically…. But by removing his decisions from the actual making process, by confining them to an "a priori" status, Frampton provides his films with a solid internal logic and a structural necessity which few contemporary films share.[55]

Zorns Lemma is a film based almost entirely on its preconception of form-as-structure, and it must be perceived as such.

Structural film has been, and continues to be, a very specific kind of avant-garde film. Rarely are there feature-length structural films, but *Zorns Lemma* proves that when a specific idea is approached from a more distinct and imaginative perspective, which Frampton certainly does, a longer work may result. Structural films exist far outside mainstream films; the feature-length avant-garde films that I will focus on as case studies do not share similar formal/structural techniques. But *Zorns Lemma* still fascinates and perplexes, and its thematic influence resonates in many films: the discrepancies between unity/disunity, similarity/difference, logic/interpretation — all ideas that can become the basis for any film really, but more so, perhaps, for those wanting to experiment by creating more specific approaches to subject matter that demand viewer interaction. A film like *Zorns Lemma* also makes one question the nature of reality because it radically alters our perceptions of everyday phenomena, most clearly articulated in section two of the film. And that is why it is inexplicably one the finest avant-garde features ever made.

Part III

The Contemporary Avant-Garde Feature Film

The contemporary avant-garde feature film exists in a cinema culture dominated by mainstream production, distribution, and exhibition. But they do not exist in a vacuum, and for that reason they can be sought out, discovered, and viewed. Still, there remain many experimental and avant-garde films that float on the peripheries of cultural, historical, and cinematic society, where only a small contingent of ardent film scholars or cineastes finds them. Barring a few examples, the majority of the films that I will discuss in this section are the ones available for viewing. There are a couple of important reasons for this. First, many short avant-garde films cannot be (readily or easily) seen; they are either in the hands of their creators, museums, or rentals through cooperatives (a wonderful thing), which limits their circulation. Second, since I am focusing on longer films, I describe certain avant-garde films based on my own assumptions of their inherent qualifications for inclusion in the genre/type of avant-garde cinema. In other words, many of the films I discuss were actually released for commercial intent. Cult films, for example, were not necessarily created solely for the inclusive market of midnight movie-houses or relegated to one-time showings that perhaps solidified their significance in cult enthusiast circles. Also, many of the films I describe may not be considered avant-garde by others; but, as I have argued so far, an avant-garde feature film may be one that is recognizable based upon its thematic or stylistic relationship to the films that came before it. Before detailing specific types of avant-garde films, however, it is necessary to outline some of the further developments in film history/culture that helped shape the contemporary avant-garde feature film.

The Contexts for Change

Film culture from the late 1950s to the early 1970s changed dramatically due to new aesthetic approaches to cinema, the political and sociological environment, and the radically different filmmakers themselves who both embraced the new and reflected upon the past through critique, homage, and outright deconstruction. These moments in the history of film have been documented exhaustively; my purpose here is to suggest a particular contextual alignment between some of the ways in which film altered during this period and the relations, connections, overlaps or, even counterpointedly, gaps that occurred which ultimately shaped aesthetic practices within the burgeoning avant-garde and underground movements of the 1960s, and subsequently the development of particular individual visions that established a new form of the contemporary avant-garde feature film.

Film histories can easily be structured based on periodization, and while this is in many ways a redundant practice — let alone a slippery one — it dominates traditional histories of cinema (national cinemas in particular) and ultimately can provide a constructive framework for considering general film practice. In other words, to perhaps contextualize contemporary avant-garde films means developing a trajectory versus a teleological path, where developments help elucidate patterns based on a nexus of activity, including theory, culture, history, practice, industrial relations and spectatorship. Movements and moments do help us make sense of film history as a whole, isolated as they may be. The general development of film as an art, which has traditionally been associated with experimental and avant-garde cinema based upon the assumptions that they are not commercial-driven or studio-supported, found correspondence with the New Waves that emerged on a global basis after World War II. Instead of detailing all of these cinemas, which has been done extensively, I will only address some important characteristics of the new "art cinema" that can help form a critical framework for understanding contemporary feature-length avant-garde films. These films that I focus on in the last part of the book can also be termed "art-house," and they can also be interpreted based on the qualities associated with art cinema in general. Additionally, I will consider the shaping influence of modernism/modernity as an aesthetic category, a mode of representation, and as historical occurrence, and how the term(s) connote certain characteristics that have been aligned with avant-garde film and also have been placed in opposition to it.

Art Cinema and the Art-House Film

Art cinema is one of the most important concepts (or genres, or mode of production, or ambiguously defined grey area of film production...) in film studies, and its significance stems from post-war European (and other world) cinema. Something new and radical was occurring in many films throughout parts of the world, but many of the films that transformed the way film is discussed and criticized came from Europe. Art cinema has routinely been described as one that is aesthetically challenging and intellectually appealing, is (typically) non-commercial and narratively ambiguous, and is serious in its treatment of "adult" issues. Moreover, art cinema is characterized by its constant and conflicting relationship with the mainstream film industry, which has helped shaped its status as a viable outlet for alternative forms of film production and consumption. European art cinema, from Italian Neorealism to the New German Cinema, influenced spectators' understanding of what cinema is and, more importantly, what it can do. The same idea can be applied to avant-garde film; avant-garde filmmakers are those who ruin expectations by presenting alternative forms of representation, requiring a new way of seeing. Similarly, the art cinemas that flourished during the 1960s offered alternative viewpoints on society, culture, politics and *real life*. Though I am certainly not equating the two, there are similar characteristics between art cinema and avant-garde film. For instance, the terms themselves are flexible and connote different moments in time and also different types of filmmaking practice. Also, art films deliberately positioned themselves as reactionary to mainstream film, much like avant-garde film. Art cinema also works tangentially to mainstream film, often intersecting but never fully merging with it. Like avant-garde films, art films eschew classical narrative storytelling in favor of temporal/spatial dislocation, ambiguity, and perhaps metaphoric/symbolic relations. One major — and crucial — difference for the original art films of the late 1950s to 1960s was that they did indeed receive distribution, and sometimes to larger markets. Avant-garde films and their exhibition often remained "underground" at museums, colleges, or private screenings. As Barbara Wilinsky notes, "[The] extent to which art films — as opposed to purely modernist cinema or avant-garde/experimental films, which mainly played for private film societies — could offer an alternative to Hollywood cinema was limited by censorship and economic interests."[1] Art films in this sense welcomed critical attention far more so than avant-garde films, which remained "private." Still, as I will detail later, the more contemporary feature-length avant-garde films that I discuss all have received critical attention, a credit to the changing parameters of film culture and the definitions (as articulated in Part I of this book) of avant-garde cinema that have indeed evolved over time — which, again, does not mean that the films I discuss are received by everyone as avant-garde (but for my purpose, they do).

I will reiterate again: I am not equating avant-garde film with art cinema; the two are vastly different. However, in the cultural (and film) climate of the 1960s, there was an increasing desire on both the part of the filmmakers and that of the spectator to *discover something new*. This idea fueled both art cinema and avant-garde film. Art films have been defined and described in many ways, somewhat similar to how avant-garde films are categorized. Art films are characterized, according to Geoffrey Nowell-Smith, by their "superior (or at any rate distinctive) artistic qualities," their "openness to a variety of experiences and their sexual frankness."[2] Art films are "challenging and open to multiple interpretations"[3]; they "are seen to be more loosely structured, working against the primacy of cause and effect in Hollywood films"; and they "foreground the artistry of the auteur and navigate between the subjectivity of the auteur and an aesthetic of realism, resulting in ambiguous causal linkages and motivations."[4] Finally, in the most straightforward sense, art cinema "describes feature-length narrative films at the margins of mainstream cinema, located somewhere between fully experimental films and overtly commercial products."[5] Further distinctions (and overlaps) of clarity come in extended enunciations of "art cinema" as a specific category (or genre) with noticeable features. Angela Ndalianis writes:

> Art cinema adopts a looser narrative form that breaks up linearity and causality through the use of techniques such as ellipsis (which creates narrative gaps); "dead time" (action that has little or no effect on narrative progression); episodic sequences paralleled by drifting, aimless protagonists; and an open-ended structure. Influenced by modernist practices, art cinema directors prioritize style and cinematic image over narrative exposition, and are frequently associated with notions of "artistic vision."[6]

Many feature-length avant-garde films have similar qualities. Unlike the known short avant-garde films of the canon of experimental cinema, the longer films tend to have a more recognizable structure.

A final clarification and description of art cinema comes from (or continues with) Rosalind Galt and Karl Schoonover, who suggest:

> Typical (but not necessary) features [of art cinema] include foreign production, overt engagement of the aesthetic, unrestrained formalism, and a mode of narration that is pleasurable but loosened from classical structures and distanced from its representations. By classical standards, the art film might be seen as too low or excessive in its visual style, use of color, or characterization.[7]

Many of the avant-garde features I will describe have similar traits; they are concerned with film's formal characteristics and openly display them; they have a distinct visual style; they have "loose" narratives; and they offer unique perspectives of representative reality. I would add, too, a fundamental aspect of avant-garde cinema in its relation to the spectator. Spectators do have to "work" while watching an avant-garde film. But they also have to be aware of what it *does*, of what it *makes appear*.

If there are indeed some correlations or corresponding traits between avant-garde film and art cinema, then it shows how two strands of cinema can maintain an oppositional status; however, the avant-garde remains in the outer limits, unlike art cinema. More recently, art cinema has become recognizable through festivals and critical assessments, which, as mentioned, directly relates to my observations of the feature-length avant-garde film: Most of these films are shown in art theaters or at festivals, and receive attention based on the director's name or the prestige bestowed upon the films by critics. Here is where I believe the films I will devote attention to in Chapter 8 fall: as both avant-garde feature films and as art films. But I will focus on their inherent qualities as avant-garde or experimental films, and not necessarily on their status as art films.

Modernism and the Avant-Garde

Modernist sensibilities have affected film practices in numerous ways, but the idea of a "modernist" cinema has remained a somewhat contentious notion. Modernism denotes a conscious impulse to be new; modernist artists take an innovative approach to their subject matter, sometime rendering the end product obsolete in terms of its association with aesthetic realism. Modernism also denotes a particular emphasis on form and the content of the art object as a formal construction (either as subjective or as objectively "real"). Modernity, which, in essence, is a term used to denote a period (or periods) of modernism or of modernization, or even as a term interchangeable with modernism (for some), implies progress, change, speed and interrogation — a thoroughly critical line of investigation that confronts reality, knowledge, consciousness, and art on many levels. Avant-garde cinema has been called a form of modernism — and likewise disassociated from it as well — but the idea of a constant need for change predicated on overturning the established ways of communicating through art is at the base of much modernist art. As Matei Calinescu suggests, "Modernity has opened the path to the rebellious avant-gardes."[8] He continues:

> Modernity in the broadest sense, as it has asserted itself historically, is reflected in the irreconcilable opposition between the sets of vales corresponding to (1) the objectified, socially measurable time of capitalist civilization ... and (2) the personal, subjective, imaginative *durèe*, the private time created by the unfolding of the "self." The latter identity of *time* and *self* constitutes the foundation of modernist culture.[9]

The point made here can be applicable to contemporary avant-garde feature films because what essentially is at stake is a (potential) dialectic between the director's subjective vision and the more acceptable notion of objective reality. The films under discussion in Chapter 8 will elucidate this a bit more, but the idea of the way films are created (subjectively), projected (objectively), and consumed (subjectively) is important in understanding the appeal of avant-garde film in general. Modernism is in many ways a reaction to modernity; the artists of the early twentieth century (the time of modernity and the time of the first modernisms) reflected upon (and against) the onslaught of advancement.

The modernist movement of the early twentieth century — which extended well into the latter half of the twentieth century — was seen in many ways as a cultural, aesthetic, technological, and intellectual evolution, one that deliberately and forcefully sought new forms of representation through film, literature, painting, sculpture, architecture, and music. Still, there can never be a direct break from the past and its influence, which is why some critics of avant-garde film see similarities or traditions among early spectacles and "attractions" and the overt display of film form found in recent avant-garde cinema. According to influential art critic Clement Greenburg, modernism is essentially about aesthetic self-reflection, which, I think, overtly suggests how avant-garde film is a medium meant for revelation: in style, form, theme, or quality.[10] He also believes "modernism is an artistic movement capable of authentically expressing the experience of the modern world."[11] Modernism engages in a dialogic relation with other forms of art, with history, and with culture in general. In this regard, modernist art works—and film is often described as such—participates in the attempt of representing the modern world, of reflecting actuality. Modernism

> [in] all its forms preached the sovereignty of artistic construction, of truth to materials. It glorified in experimentation in new processes of signification, because it believed that the task of art is to liberate us from our preconceptions by forcibly rearranging our very ways of processing meaning.[12]

In this regard, avant-garde film, as a modernist aesthetic practice, is an attempt at representing objects and subjects that are at once familiar and destabilized in order to create a viable form of cinema. As Andras Balint Kovacs suggests, "Early avant-garde film was an initiative to make cinema accepted as a practice of full aesthetic value."[13] Art cinema does something similarly (with tradition)—it breaks free in order to create, but also to allow a recognition of the intrinsic nature of the medium. But art cinema is also based on narrative filmmaking, whereas the avant-garde (or at least the traditional avant-gardes) is not. However, the contemporary feature-length avant-garde film has ties to modernism's strong avowal for newness, and art cinema's condemnation of current practice (ca. 1950s–1960s).

Modernism is typically considered an aesthetic category of artistic production. Its ties to modernity are solely or primarily based on the historical time frame of each, generally considered (in the twentieth century) to be the 1910s to 1920s, although the reach of modernity extends back two hundred years and also stretches forward by several more decades (until rendered asunder by postmodernism). While the terms modernism and modernity are not interchangeable, they are interrelated. As Ben Singer points out,

> While some critics perceive some kind of relationship between social modernity and aesthetic modernism, characterizations of that relationship cover the spectrum: modernism as a celebration of modernity; as a sanctuary from modernity; as a radical attack on modernity; as a mirror of the chaos of modernity; as an expression of the rationalistic order of modernity, and so on.[14]

Many of the artists of the 1920s (and these include filmmakers), attempted to capture the burgeoning sense of displacement, mass industrialization (and alienation), and ways to represent reality. Modernism's aesthetic stems from the idea that with progress comes liberty, or, put more presciently, with new filmmaking techniques and styles comes new ways of liberating the camera, the spectator, and the image. Avant-garde film is a manifestation of this idea that arguably is a "result" of modernity. As Calinescu points out,

> Insofar as the idea of modernity implies both a radical criticism of the past and a definite commitment to change and the values of the future, it is not difficult to understand why, especially during the last two centuries, the moderns favored the application of the agnostic metaphor of the "avant-garde" (or "advanced guard," or "vanguard") to various domains, including literature, the arts, and politics.[15]

While Calinescu is not necessarily developing a teleological history of "avant-garde" art, he does suggest that with modernity a more "modern" form of art develops. Ironically — or paradoxically or dialectically — the avant-garde of the 1960s favored a kind of primitivism that perhaps does not associate itself with modernism or modernity. But the international cinemas that constitute art cinema were seen by some as a continuation of modernist aesthetics. In this sense the contemporary avant-garde feature films I focus on can be considered both modern (that is, as a progression or development) and a critical commentary on modernity (that is, as social critiques of the ways in which vision is clouded through modernity and therefore requires the restoration of sight). The avant-garde returns us, in many ways, to a *sight unseen*. The feature films that can be considered avant-garde are all ones that allow for a way of perceiving phenomena anew, like modernity, but also like a time before modernism. Hence, they are different films altogether. The typical historical avant-gardes detailed in Part II can also be seen in this light. But for my purpose here, it is best left to think about how feature-length avant-garde films perhaps both reflect modernity and modernism while also delicately side-stepping each through their own individualistic, internal agendas.

* * *

The social and cultural climate of the 1960s gave rise to new kinds of cinematic practice, including underground film, cult cinema, and experimental film. All of these have been discussed as variations of avant-garde cinema. In some ways this is true because the different cinemas that emerged participated in alternative forms of representation, whether subversive (e.g., *Flaming Creatures*), essayistic (e.g., Godard's experiments like *2 or 3 Things I Know About Her* or *Le Gai Savoir*), or blatantly experimental-structural (e.g., *Wavelength*). In the next chapter I will discuss some of the characteristics of the types of films that also influenced the contemporary feature-length avant-garde film. To understand the significance of underground or cult cinema on contemporary avant-garde film, for instance, is perhaps to draw links among practices that not only show the influence of the earlier avant-gardes, but also how the 1960s, in all its variant manifestations of protest and aesthetic (de)construction, enabled certain filmmakers to establish unique styles based on those films that altered the foundations of cinema.

↻ Chapter 6 ↺

Underground Film
and the Avant-Garde

One of the most important areas of inquiry for avant-garde film remains the significance of the diversity ensconced within the Underground film movement(s) of the 1960s. The most noteworthy and considerable changes that occurred were in New York, though various "undergrounds" can be traced to San Francisco and London (and other European cities). But the climate in New York during the late 1950s and throughout the 1960s favored *newness* and *change*. The Underground films produced during the 1960s were diverse, astringent, and, in some cases, fashionable. Avant-garde film in the 1960s became in many ways *noticeable*, due to a large extent by the increasing popularity of the filmic underground. Underground cinema was a part of the cultural matrix that gave rise to changes in politics, music, media, and socio-cultural entities; "further enhancing the impact of the New York film underground throughout the 1960s was the fact that it fit into a much broader counterculture scene that encompassed many art forms."[1] This expanded scene was endemic of the 1960s counter-culture, when film intersected with other forms of art to become more than just a fringe cinema, more than just an avant-garde, and more than just a rag-tag group of experimentalists. Instead, the avant-gardes became subsumed to some degree by the new Underground. Underground cinema is a form of experimental film, but it encompasses a wide range of styles, forms, objectives, and subject matter. Its relationship to more contemporary avant-garde feature films is important, mainly because many filmmakers who created feature-length avant-garde films emerged from the 1960s. Some of these include Dusan Makavejev, Sergei Paradjanov, Peter Greenaway, and Yvonne Rainer, just to name a few. More importantly, what the underground cinema of the 1960s gave rise to was the increasing popularity of cult films, widely divergent and new types of avant-garde films, and a new sense of, on the one hand, the institutionalization of avant-garde cinema, and on the other, the increased knowledge of avant-garde cinema as a legitimate form of film practice (which can also be attributed to the popularity of the art film).

100

First, what exactly is Underground film? In many regards, Underground cinema represents a conflation of avant-garde and experimental film as it had been traditionally known. This means that different strands of avant-garde film practice — from surrealism to structuralism to trance film to personalized amateurism — all were or still can be considered underground. The term itself is also of importance. Avant-garde designates the "advanced guard"; likewise, the "underground" stems from a military term — those who defied authority by literally and symbolically going underground, which in artistic creation signifies another defiance of tradition and the norm. A.L. Rees traces the historical and social change of avant-gardism to the Underground, saying,

> The 1950s institutionalization of modern art under its newly acquired name ("Modernism") bred a reaction from disestablished or oppositional artists. Aiming to keep art outside the museum and its rules, they looked back to earlier times (especially to Dada) when its "negative moment" — art as a critique of reality — was more heightened. This movement later became the "counterculture" or, more popularly, "the Underground." The shift of emphasis is telling; one military term — an "advanced guard" scouting ahead of the pack — is replaced by another which reflects clandestine resistance, tunneling rather than charging, to echo a post-war identification with partisans and prisoners.[2]

This brief historical account is telling because it points to one of the more important aspects of contemporary feature-length avant-garde films: the goal, aim, or critique of a heightened sense of reality. In many ways the underground avant-garde cinema of the 1960s helped define the more regularly practiced aesthetic of subjectivity; cameras captured the essence of life, even though the means by which reality is portrayed can be intuitive, creative, surreal, or highly symbolic. In other words, it becomes radically altered as a form of avant-garde film practice. Phrased in another way by film historian and theorist Parker Tyler, who was writing during the 1960s,

> The main strength of the Underground Film per se (not simply as a variety of avant-garde film) is currently to use the camera as the self-sufficient reporter of vital activity. It is as if to say: The technique and the form do not matter, only the message matters. And yet here the message is what makes the medium look easy — *that* is the ultimate message: The Underground has enshrined the camera as a wild, willful, inquisitive eye, disposed to give graphic publicity to everything that has remained taboo in the realm of popular commercial films, even the most serious and artistic among them.[3]

If this is true, and indeed it *was* true for many of the types of Underground film produced during the 1960s, then it suggests that the goal of many filmmakers was to represent the unrepresentable, and, when doing so, to do it in a highly personalized and "inquisitive" manner. In their book *Midnight Movies*, Jonathan Rosenbaum and J. Hoberman also point to the taboo-shattering nature of the Underground film. They say, "Underground movies — the very term was redolent of danger, secrecy, subversion, resistance, liberation; not to mention perversity, alienation, even madness."[4] And, in discussing the filmmakers themselves and their films, they suggest the films of the Underground were a "combination of willful primitivism, taboo-breaking sexuality, and obsessive ambivalence toward American popular culture (namely Hollywood)."[5] These goals of the underground point to the various styles and films that emerge in contemporary avant-garde filmmaking, particularly the way many features eschew standards, critique the status quo, or attempt a total annihilation of acceptance through a reconfiguring of taboos or other transgressive acts. Of course, not all avant-garde films have acts of transgression, nor do they address taboo themes. Some do, but many — including the majority I focus on in the next section — are better known for their stylistic creativity than their interesting subject matter.

The Underground films of the 1960s showed a diverse array of styles. Many filmmakers used different techniques that became "standard" in both the mainstream and independent film worlds from the 1970s to the present. These include hand-held cameras, scratched film surfaces, fragmentation of images, spatial/temporal dislocation, light flares, and low-budget films with realistic subject matter and naturalistic locations. Still, the vast majority of films that were avant-garde remained radical, innovative, and decidedly uncommercial. As Lauren Rabinovitz notes, "Although avant-garde film expressivism of the 1960s overlapped with that of other art forms — jazz, experimental theater, Beat poetry, modern dance, vanguard painting — the production and reception of avant-garde cinema has largely been understood within the social networks that encompass the other avant-gardes."[6] In other words, most of the "traditional" avant-garde films that emerged from the 1960s still, in some fashion, can be measured against other epochs of avant-garde filmmaking. The Underground film movement was one that increased the recognition of particular filmmakers who were either experimenting or reacting against the staid world of the status quo. The young filmmakers of the 1960s who were part of the Underground — and they could range from Andy Warhol to Kenneth Anger to Hollis Frampton — were, in some regards, reacting to their exclusion from culture, so they created and nurtured their own in Underground Film. In turn, they created "fascinating, vital and effective strategies to resist and subvert bourgeois culture"[7] in order to becomes its own culture, a "community and a way of life [and] a sensibility that could realize the secret subtext of utopian liberations in popular culture.[8] This kind of rhetoric is well-known to historians of the counter-culture movements of the 1960s; filmmakers, too, were involved with the total revolution of the arts and the cultural mainstream. Some of this "utopian" rhetoric can be found in the writings of Jonas Mekas, one of the strongest and most vocal proponents of avant-garde film during the 1960s. In part, Mekas said:

> The artist is beginning to express his [sic] anxiety and discontent in a more open and direct manner. He is searching for a freer form, one which allows him a larger scale of emotional and intellectual statements, explosions of truths, outcries of warn-

ings, accumulations of images— not to carry out an amusing story but to fully express the tremblings of man's unconscious, to confront us eye-to-eye with the soul of modern man. The new artist is not interested in entertaining the viewer: he is making personal statements about the world today.[9]

Avant-garde films have always, in some ways, been part of a larger network of subverting the traditions of art, so the idea of seeking a "freer form" or "making personal statements" makes sense. But Mekas generally is describing a certain kind of film practice that does not include all forms of avant-garde filmmaking. Contemporary feature-length avant-garde films do use a free-form style, or they are marked by their creator's personal visions, but they may not be engaged in a startling utopian form of recreating art. Mekas further said that the new filmmaker is "not interested in public acceptance"; that he [sic] must "encourage his sense of rebellion, his sense of disobedience, even at the cost of open anarchy and nihilism"; and finally, the new filmmakers must doubt and attack "all public ideologies, values, and ways of life."[10] Perhaps there are some feature-length avant-garde films that are similar to Mekas's descriptions; Makavejev's *W.R. Mysteries of the Organism* or *Sweet Movie*, Jarman's reconceptualizations of history and culture through a queer and avant-garde lens, or Carlos Atanes's underground films can be seen as anarchic. But many contemporary avant-garde feature films are marked by their very distinctiveness from any other films inasmuch as they may have some influence from their antecedents. The films of the 1960s were also, of course, very diverse; as Wheeler Winston Dixon notes, "One of the key aspects of the American Experimental cinema during the 1960s remains the uniqueness of each individual artist's vision."[11] So while it may be argued that there were plenty of similarities among filmmakers, there was also a radial difference among them as well, particularly in subject matter, style, and ambition.

The Underground film of the 1960s was in part a cultural manifestation of the increasing anxiety regarding authority, which was generated, arguably, in the 1950s by youth films, Elvis Presley, Beat poetry, and jazz. Additionally, the experiments that were occurring in Europe, which included avant-garde filmmaking as well as the New Waves, influenced the attitudes and styles of the Underground cinema. Walter Metz notes, "The American avant-garde was at its most provocative and challenging in the early years of [the 1960s], when its daring and radical alternative vision of human logic, sex, drugs, and cinema stood out so expressively against the background of a still quiescent mainstream culture."[12] In Europe, experimental films (and New Wave films) were made by cultural and political dissidents who were hostile to "tradition." The post-war European avant-garde was "both formally innovative and often politically radical," where "the autonomy of the artist from the art and state institutions was central to its concerns."[13] Rees, too, suggests that "the American underground was broader than the European and less easily defined."[14] The Underground was concerned with testing the limits and capabilities of the medium itself, of expanding perception through a variety of styles and themes, and of questioning the dominant modes of representation that permeated mainstream film. Arguably, it was this new mode of representation that influenced — even triggered — the contemporary avant-garde feature film. Independent film practice, which can constitute certain areas of art cinema as well as avant-garde cinema, is a broad intertextual and discursive realm of practice and theory, couched in historical exigencies and cultural contestations. Ideas and issues that stem from the everyday (reality) as well as from the illogical (surrealism, dream) find room for aesthetic exploration in avant-garde feature films. The new cinemas of the 1960s "embraced the transalterity of those for whom there [had] previously been no effective agency; it sought to escape the tyranny of history, and the commodification of the future in the mainstream cultural industry, through the abdication of all conventional standards of photographic representationalism."[15] In this regard, the Underground cinema of the 1960s could be considered the foundational textual area for creating a more nuanced type of avant-garde film practice, where such drastic change signified a lasting impression, enough so to cause future filmmakers to follow divergent and similar paths to heightened subjectivity. Even though its ongoing cultural impact may be questionable, since it was a movement of its time, the cultural impact of the Underground cannot be denied.

Avant-garde films tend to focus on the formal properties of the medium itself — an investigation *of* the medium — and on presenting subjects to us in new ways that require a more careful viewing experience. They demand an appreciation for the interiority of the filmic landscape and the creativity of the filmmaker, along with a willing acceptance of the presentation of the exterior world. Parker Tyler uses an analogy to early film to describe something similar about the focus of avant-garde film on perception. He says:

> [The] existence of the camera eye implies *an optical omniscience which nothing can be concealed*, since it is able to reproduce both microscopic and telescopic effects, with the result that all barriers between spectator and spectacle necessarily seem arbitrary and artificial — a mere matter of "stage illusion." Naturally, then, a classic function of all independent films, avant-garde and other, has been to provide "peephole excitement."[16]

The aesthetic character of avant-garde film positions it as a form of enlightenment through audio-visual stimuli predicated on the notion of change, newness, and "spectacle," but only in the sense of a distinct manifestation of *vision* that cerates a certain vantage point (the "peephole") that stimulates pleasure and exhilaration ("excitement"). Contemporary avant-garde feature films rely on the same tactic. They are aggressive in their aesthetic and textual practices, and individualistic and iconoclastic in their representational strategies. In this sense, many contemporary avant-garde features share certain tendencies with the Underground of the 1960s. In characterizing the contemporary (ca. 2002) Underground film scene in the United States, Mendik and Schneider suggest that it is "a vibrant domain that defies the broad classification of mainstream cinema," where critics, filmgoers, theorists, and practitioners alike "view the underground film scene as a space where art-house stands shoulder to shoulder with spectacle-based atrocity, and where experimentation is a regular feature of exploitation."[17] While this conflation is not entirely accurate for all types of avant-garde film (or underground), it does suggest how the divergent strands of filmmaking, from art-house to experimental to underground, all help position the current avant-garde feature film as being unique, though informed by its lineage. O'Pray sees the current avant-garde scene as being in many ways ontological. He suggests, "More broadly, it may be argued that there was a shift from asceticism [of the underground and avant-garde] to aestheticism. In an Oedipal reaction, the young filmmakers embraced what had been anathema to their elders—subject matter."[18] Again, this has not occurred across the board, and we must remember that the majority of the criticism of avant-garde film (like O'Pray) still focuses on short(er) films. But it is perhaps true that pure experimentation, where there may *appear* to be a lack of "subject matter," has given way to films with a more recognizable subject, which certainly is true of the avant-garde features I will discuss. But then again, some of the films I discuss may not be considered avant-garde at all by others, though in my analyses of the films, I hope to explain exactly why they are.

One final consideration should be the cult film. Cult films became exceedingly popular during the 1970s and remain so to the present. Cult films were part of the cultural zeitgeist upheaval of the 1960s, but they can be films from any era of film history. Cult films are those that acquire a rabid following because they are retrieved from history, they are so transgressive that they can only be shown/seen at particular venues at particular moments, or they offer such antithetical stories to mainstream film that they create specific areas of production and consumption that label them factious/offbeat/unordinary. According to Ernest Mathijs and Xavier Mendik:

> A Cult film is a film with an active and lively communal following. Highly committed and rebellious in its appreciation, its audience regularly finds itself at odds with the prevailing cultural mores, displaying a preference for strange topics and allegorical themes that rule against cultural sensitivities and resist dominant politics.[19]

This definition aligns cult films with the underground, and the description is also somewhat apt for avant-garde films. The relationship between the avant-garde and cult films is based primarily on the attitude one has toward them. That is, a keen moviegoer who likes cult films already has an established taste for the unusual; likewise, someone interested in avant-garde film enjoys the status of it as belonging to a group outside the mainstream where "rules" mean very little. Cult films are innovative and often technically inferior (though some *appear* superior) to mainstream films, and offer narratives that can be exploitative, subversive, deviant, gross, tasteless, bad, derivative, satiric, surreal, experimental, or amateurish. Mathijs and Mendik offer a list of terms/ideas/issues that surround and describe cult films. Some include well-worn terms associated with cult films like "innovation, badness, transgression, strangeness, or gore," while they also offer more critical terms, areas for inquiry that allow a more open access to discussing the relationship between cult films and other types (including avant-garde): "genre, intertextuality, commitment, rebellion, nostalgia, and cultural sensitivities."[20] Such terms tell us about the wide range of films within the cult genre (similar to avant-garde films), and they also suggest ways in which to discuss them more accurately, including on an ontological and phenomenological level, where "ontological approaches to cult cinema are usually essentialist [and] objectivist," and "phenomenological approaches shift the attention from the text to its appearance in the cultural contexts in which it is produced and received."[21] Such approaches indicate the seriousness by which one may understand cult films, and it also suggests a broader intertextual network among cult films, underground films, avant-garde films, and art-house films. One final point that Mathijs and Mendik make that is worth mentioning is the way one perceives a cult film. They suggest, "Cult films challenge traditional means of watching films— either because they are weird, or because they evoke certain responses. Therefore the concept of perception (how one physically and psychologically perceives an object in its appearances) becomes pivotal for studying cult cinema."[22] They go on to suggest that both psychoanalytical and cognitive theories of perception can be applied nicely and neatly to the perceiving of cult film. Likewise, as I suggested earlier, watching an avant-garde film requires a very dedicated mental cognition, one that requires a conceptual and perceptual framework for identifying and observing the phenomena within the world of the film. Some of the avant-garde features I will describe in Chapter 8 can also be considered cult films. And like cult films, many avant-garde films and filmmakers have rabid followers. Films that have radical potential to provoke spectators into certain viewing positions is anathema to most mainstream film practice, but the avant-garde feature, like the cult film and the films of the Underground, do so, even when considering the array of diversity among them.

The avant-garde films produced within the Underground cinema of the 1960s existed within a larger nexus of cultural activity. Many of the films from the era are rightfully forgotten, but there are some that continue to inspire — mainly those of the canonical avant-gardes. The broad appeal of these films also helped create a new audience for avant-garde films, which is vital for their continued "popularity" among cineastes. Narrative, anti-narrative, ambiguous, transgressive and subversive — the films of the avant-garde have much in common with labels placed upon the Underground and the Art-House film. Self-reflexive, modernist, the formal structuring and textual openness, the spatial and temporal schemes, the enigmatic characterizations or lack of characters— avant-garde features share such traits with their forebears, and create viewing experiences that are rewarding because they (often) resist fixed meanings and invite continued viewings. Duncan Reekie has suggested there is a contemporary "new" Underground cinema, one that is "chaotic and indiscrete, and [one that] still rages with the unresolved tensions of its hybrid development."[23] Perhaps this is the broad appeal of such challenging films as the avant-garde feature. However, Reekie also suggests that "it is possible to identify a repertoire of radical subversion against the bourgeois state in both its official cultural system (Art) and its industrial structure."[24] The cataloguing of the items that fit into his repertoire include "convivial, consensual, illegitimate, profane, subversive, resilient, montage, variation, improvisation, anonymity, indiscretion, mongrel, marvelous, simultaneous, collective, illiterate, [and] commercial...."[25] While it might be tempting to place films into such categories, or locate filmmakers who use such tactics, it is probably best left to say that if there is indeed a far-ranging list of tropes associated with the new underground, then it again helps identify a radical alternative to the mainstream. As Reekie concludes, "The new Underground cinema already deploys most of these cultural strategies but now it must understand their meaning and begin to dictate them to a revolutionary experimental purpose."[26] Perhaps, but it is noteworthy to indicate that toady's avant-garde filmmakers—who can possibly be considered part of the new Underground—have an awareness of their aims, goals, and various ideological purposes as existing outside and alongside the mainstream. As we shall see, many avant-garde filmmakers also understand the relevance of various cultural strategies that inform their films.

❦ Chapter 7 ❦

Types of Avant-Garde
Feature Films

As indicated in the first part of this book, calling avant-garde cinema its own genre creates limitations and restrictions as well as opportunities for expansion and revision. There are so many varying types of avant-garde films, and the means that different critics use to define them enable generic conventions while at the same time making such generic tropes destabilizing. In other words, what I think might serve as a better means of understanding the "genre" of avant-garde film is to consider some of the types of feature films we may call avant-garde, based on the ideas I have suggested in Part I and also based on their production, distribution, exhibition, and reception. Avant-garde films can take many forms and utilize many styles, methods of presentation, modes of representation, and means of communication. Since I am focusing on contemporary avant-garde feature films, I will limit my discussion to certain types that are linked to earlier traditions in avant-garde cinema but also cross new boundaries, creating works that are both recognizable (as avant-garde films) but also are different, mainly because they participate in forms of discourse that (often) bridge historical eras, multiple genres, or styles. Contemporary avant-garde films are often intertwined in discourses about art cinema, modernism, postmodernism, video technology, digital filmmaking, economic practices, and cultural commodities, but the uniting factor for almost all of them is that they present something recognizably different. Of course, there are many types of film that do this, challenging hegemony or taste, but avant-garde films (or experimental films) can be considered antithetical because their styles, forms, and themes make them so.

Jeffrey Skoller touches upon these ideas in formulating a way of recognizing, defining, and delineating avant-garde films and practices in contemporary (and historical) forms. He suggests:

> The complicated definition of avant-garde practice as it emerged as a modernist stance refers to an art that aspires to be an implicit or explicit critique of, and resistance to, the pervasiveness of dominant cultural forms and ideologies. In one aspect, such a critique is structured by the notion of withdrawal from the dominant social

order with the ideal of developing institutional autonomy and counter-hegemonic discourses that exist as a parallel to mainstream culture. As counterculture, this offers an alternative to dominant aesthetic and political assumptions about the nature of art and its role in the production of consciousness in society.[1]

In the attempt at creating a counterculture, avant-garde film succeeds because it does not subscribe to understood notions of cinematic form, nor does it aspire to be a part of the dominant social order. So many contemporary feature films that are also avant-garde are defined by their cultural resistance, cultural critique, or cultural ideology. But these films also are different from canonical avant-garde films because many have (recognizable) narratives, character development, and established spatial and temporal zones of activity. In fact, many of the films that are experimental in terms of narrative or manner of representation can (and do) exist in other genres, from cult film to art film to documentary film. Hence, there is a multitude of avant-garde films that exist today as I have defined them; but they still require the same kind of intense, active viewing and acceptance of their alternativeness. In many ways the enduring value of the term itself — "avant-garde" — establishes a way of critiquing film form or style, cultural representation, aesthetic practice across different arts, and especially the film medium itself. For this reason there can really be *many types* of avant-garde films. I shall limit myself to three categories.

The Essay Film, or the Theoretical-Dialectic Film

The Essay film is such a specific kind of avant-garde film that it is often discussed as its own genre, one that has been around for many years in the history of cinema. Essay Films are literary, philosophical, and filmic in their intentions and formations, making them, in some cases, "hybrid" films, although they are essentially engaged with *ideas*. Perhaps one of the best articulated notions on the Essay film comes from Alexander Astruc's celebrated essay "The Birth of the New Avant-Garde: The Camera-Stylo" (1948), where he announces the essayistic potential of film as one of the most important advancements in modern film and media history:

> The cinema is quite simply becoming a means of expression, just as all the other arts have been before it.... After having been successively a fairground attraction, an amusement analogous to boulevard theatre, or the means of preserving the images of an era, it is gradually becoming a language. By language, I mean a form in which and by which an artist can express his thoughts, however abstract they may be, or translate his obsessions exactly as he does in the contemporary essay or novel.[2]

Astruc argued that filmmaking was becoming analogous to the novel or painting; any filmmaker could potentially claim "I" like a novelist or painter. "The 'camera-pen' formula valorized the act of filmmaking," Robert Stam says, surmising Astruc. "The director was no longer merely the servant of a preexisting text (novel, screenplay) but a creative artist in his/her own right."[3] The idea of a "film author" is very important in film studies (as the *auteur* theory), and, as I suggested previously, it is helpful in distinguishing avant-garde filmmakers from their contemporaries who exist in the mainstream. But what Astruc suggests, and what is critical in understanding the avant-garde Film Essay, is that these films are essentially *structured* like an essay. According to Timothy Corrigan (drawing an analogy between the written form and the film form of an essay):

> Essays describe and provoke an activity of public thought, and the public nature of that subjective experience highlights and even exaggerates the participations of their audience, readers, and viewers in a dialogue of ideas. More than other literary or representational practices, even the most personal of essays speak to a listener who will validate or trouble that personal essayistic voice, and the more immersed that voice is in its exterior world the more urgent the essay becomes in embedding and dispersing itself within the public experience and activity it desires.... In this sense, one of the chief defining features of the essay film and its history becomes an active intellectual response to the questions and provocations that an unsettled subjectivity directs at its public.[4]

The essay film is the kind of avant-garde film, then, that engages the viewer through several lines of discourse. It is meant to provoke and instigate thought and reflection. I also offer the idea of a theoretical-dialectical model of the film essay as one whose very form and thematic content suggest a more nuanced type of film essay.

The Essay film is can be considered avant-garde in terms of its deliberately dialectical narrative structure and style. Therefore, a more apt name for the avant-garde essay film may be a "theoretical-dialectic film." Typically, this kind of film constructs its narrative around a single premise, or thesis/theory, and the film then debates, criticizes, deconstructs, or explains the tensions inherent within the thesis/theory itself, thus creating the dialectic. Because of this, the theoretical-dialectic film is very personal and idiosyncratic, as it often plays upon viewer expectations and emotions, presents subject matter as it also represents certain themes, and, despite its structure, still manages to have a narrative and style unique to the filmmaker. An essay film is one that is "based on a specific point of view and purport a given interpretation of the world."[5] Essays, and the essay film in particular, engage in critical thinking, and they often may be constructed from a subjective viewpoint. If a film is essayistic and also theoretical, it offers a means of explaining, of theorizing its subject matter in a way that forces us to believe its theory. When any theory is proposed, it is done so to persuade people. But just as much, there are competing and conflicting theories about the same subject matter, which is one of the reasons the Essay film enters into a broader intertextual discourse with different representations of the subject or theme of the film, whether a historical document or text, a biography, a documentary, or simply a separate (written) essay articulating a separate theory. In discussing the goals of documentary film, which relates to my point, Bill Nichols says:

Engaging the viewer in a distinct perspective emotionally or persuading the viewer of a particular perspective intellectually go hand in hand in documentary, even though different films vary the balance between these two goals. Both goals take precedence over narrative emphasis on telling an engaging story or the avant-garde stress on the form of the work itself.[6]

Though talking only about documentary films and their particular modes of engagement, the point stressed that seems suitable to theoretical-dialectic essay films is the focus on persuasion and form. Avant-garde Essay films strive to articulate their persuasive agendas in different ways, and they are often self-reflexive exercises in form. According to Laura Rascaroli, these types of essay-istic films, which rely on "their foregrounding of autobiography and their expression of authorial subjectivity, position them in between three traditions: that of the personal cinemas of the avant-gardes; that of auteur and art cinema; and that of the first-person documentary."[7] What sets these films apart from straightforward documentaries with a subjective or autobiographical compo-nent (e.g., Michael Moore's films) is their manner of presentation; the style and form are heightened, the representation of the subject matter is often exper-imental, and they are consciously outside generic tropes of documentary or fictional narrative. In some way or another, "However diverse its shapes and interests, essays have shared a constellation of motifs about glancing contin-gencies, the folding movements of historical experience, and the necessity for the relentless and provisional pressure of conceptualization and thought," Cor-rigan notes, so that "filmmakers have increasingly engaged modernist concerns with spatial fragmentation and temporal motions as zones where subjective expression and interpretation could reshape traditional realist transparencies as ideas in motion."[8] The concept of an "idea in motion" serves as a metaphor not only for the cinema, but, more particularly, for the cinematic essay. Essays aim to present and preserve the process of cognition, and theoretical-dialectic film essays extend this by including visual and/or audio metaphors or markers as further ways of stressing reflection. In discussing Montaigne's inherent and overriding significance to the essay as a literary form, Rascaroli states, "Indeed, the most important stamp that Montaigne left on the genre, and which derives from classical philosophical traditions, consists in the skeptical evaluation of the subject matter, which self-reflexively includes the evaluation of the author's same conclusions."[9] For the theoretical-dialectic essay film, this suggests the ongoing deliberation the film's subject matter creates for the spectator as well as the filmmaker, whose presentation of the subject matter is decisive but not always entirely convincing, which, as an essay, is its purpose: to provoke con-templation. In other words, the filmmaker may take a skeptical stance, but his or her stance is almost always recognizable, forthright, defended, and issued as a way to thinking.

The film essays of Hans-Jürgen Syberberg, Chris Marker, Jean-Luc Godard, and Su Friedrich are all prototypical examples of the kind of theoretical-dialectic essay films that are deliberately constructed and presented as means of shaping thought through contemplation. They are also well-known directors of experimental or avant-garde cinema, so I have chosen them intentionally because they represent the essayistic form excellently, and they also are all staunch practitioners of personal cinema.

HITLER, A FILM FROM GERMANY

Hans-Jürgen Syberberg's ambitious masterpiece, *Hitler, a Film from Germany* (1977), is a truly radical avant-garde film that challenges spectators to consider its thesis/theory during the course of viewing, while also defying characteristics of traditional cinema in general. In categorizing Syberberg's film this way, I am assuming it falls under certain stylistic, formal, and thematic tropes characteristic of the type of avant-garde film I am calling "theoretical-dialectic." The theoretical-dialectic film foregrounds its form only in the sense that we can recognize how the film is constructed. Like an essay film, it has a central concern (or sometimes it has several concerns or issues), a "thesis," which the film revolves around. Syberberg's film form is about the artificial construction of film space and the artifice of that very construction. Formalist concerns also deal with associative interpretation based upon, for example, the theatricality of the mise-en-scène. Syberberg creates a very unusual and extremely personal style with this film (and with his other features, for that matter, which can also be considered essayistic). He favors intricate and elaborate stages upon which the actors recite more than act; in this way his films, and especially *Hitler*, resemble plays. It is arguable whether or not Syberberg is interested in Brechtian distanciation (though I think he is), but the film certainly is meant to provoke the spectator — its very subject matter, Hitler, demands it.

Syberberg's film is theoretical because it examines Hitler as both a literal figure and as a concept — specifically, as a *film* to be projected. The title of the film indicates this, and Syberberg wants to persuade us to believe that the film Hitler is crucial as the person Hitler in an effort to understand how he penetrated national and individual psyches. In focusing on Hitler in such a way, the movie serves as an essay on the nature of image-making, both through the rise and fall of Hitler, and in more cinematic ways, such as the filtering of the imagistic Hitler through time and space. Through his own idiosyncratic and subjective aesthetics, which includes theatrical staging, rear-projection, and a multitude of puppets and performers, and coupled with his own critical analysis of Germany and his own interpretation of German history, Syberberg creates a dialectic around notions of identity and art through the twentieth-century's most vital *film*, Hitler. *Hitler, a Film from Germany* is a highly innovative film essay: it is structured like a huge theatrical production (Wagner is continually evoked), where the players enter the stage and recite long speeches, rarely interacting with one another. Hitler is portrayed as a puppet, as Chaplin's Tramp, Frankenstein's Monster, Lang's child killer in *M*, and a house painter. It emphasizes active interpretation on the part of the spectator. Syberberg places the audience in an uncomfortable position — he asks spectators to study themselves through close scrutiny and questioning of the terrible/terrific subject matter, Hitler, and the requisite mourning involved, and to discover the reasons why Hitler is presented and re-presented *as a film*. The task of Syberberg, as author of the film essay, is to question the logic (or illogic), or the rational (or the irrational) ways Hitler is perpetuated — that is, how he affects national and personal psyches. Provoking the audience is normal in theoretical-dialectic avant-garde films. Syberberg's elaborately filled mise-en-scène, which resembles at times circus rings, though it is predominately a stage setting, allows him to use cinema as a form of essay: almost all the lines are uttered as monologues. He uses static cameras to record the "action"; uses tableaux, rear-projection, actual radio broadcasts of Hitler and others in the Third Reich; and combines them in layers to subject the viewer to his thesis. Syberberg often may seem overly discursive or excessively didactic, but, as an essay that is built upon a theoretical idea which results in a dialectic (over Hitler the person and Hitler the "film"), it is *meant* to be. If we are to accept Syberberg's themes, we must be subjected to a radical, subjective analysis that is abstract and personal. Avant-garde cinema has the capacity to amend representation in such a way, and Syberberg clearly suggests these representations of Hitler are what haunt spectators through their perpetual projection. Using multiple representations of Hitler (from Tramp to Napoleon to puppet to stuffed animal) reinforces this notion. Syberberg himself says, "All these techniques used with the marionettes elucidate the fact that it is we who have given life and movement to Hitler."[10]

As an essayist, Syberberg's goal is to author a film that will make us think and respond in particular ways. Syberberg is known for his grandiose, Wagnerian cinematic endeavors, and *Hitler, a Film from Germany* is the epitome of a kind of gross excess—like Hitler. The cluttered stage, multiple sounds, and various images all yield a massive essay built upon a theory of Hitler and how we are to respond to him. As Syberberg points out, "Film is the most important art form that the democratic twentieth century has produced. Film should register a few things about the condition of the general will of a country and its current situation."[11] Ironically, the century also produced the world's most discomforting film, Hitler himself. This estimation also points toward Syberberg's proposal that cinema serves as the best medium to project and re-project images and ideas in essay form. For Syberberg, the investigation of Hitler-as-person and Hitler-as-film is an intellectual opportunity, both because he takes risks with his experimental approach and because he theorizes Hitler as one big spectacle, a mass entertainment projected and consumed. As Susan Sontag notes, Syberberg "offers a spectacle about spectacle: evoking the 'big show' called history in a variety of dramatic modes—fairytale, circus, morality play, allegorical pageant, magic ceremony, philosophical dialogue."[12] All of these representational modes allow Syberberg to author the film essay, creating a conflicting emotional position for the spectator (another means of dialectic) because though we loath the subject, we demand it. Another reason that as spectators we are complicit, or at least have our subjectivity displaced, is because the film has an associative plot without a clear or strict chronology, which is characteristic of avant-garde film, but here also allows for Syberberg's argumentative theory to unfold. There is a dialectic involved when viewing the film because as spectators we search for narratives where little exist, but are also in full engagement with the images and the monologues. Both visually and verbally, the movie demands that the audience find its own place in a text which indeed *belongs* to the audience yet which is concomitantly too much for it. The film constantly provokes through a continuous flow of words and images and overwrought theatrics. Syberberg's is a decidedly intellectual cinema where rich imagery never overpowers language; illusion remains subordinate to enlightenment; and theory supplants narrative. Syberberg's confidence in his aesthetic choices as adequate to his immense subject matter draws from his idea of cinema as a way of knowing, of discussing the human condition, through theory and discourse, which ultimately invites speculation resulting from the "reading" of the film (both Syberberg's film *and* Hitler-as-film) to take a self-reflexive turn, a tactic associated with the Film Essay that other directors like Jean-Luc Godard, Chris Marker, or Su Friedrich employ in their metatextual cinema. Syberberg, in other words, has presented us with a thought-provoking essay on the lingering effects of the twentieth century's most despicable individual, as well as the twentieth century's most enormous film — Hitler.

Le Gai Savoir

There are any number of Jean-Luc Godard films that can be considered a theoretical-dialectic Essay Film, and Godard himself proclaimed he was indeed an essayist first and filmmaker second: "I consider myself an essayist; I do essays in the form of novels and novels in the form of essays: Simply I film them instead of writing them."[13] If this is the case, then Godard is really a master of a kind of critical cinema that, as Peter Wollen has demonstrated, is a kind of avant-garde film practice that is "neo–Brechtian," in that it is "in the spirit of Brechtian epic theatre, [where] such film practices work to confront the audience with the historical significance of the specific social and political conditions of a film's existence."[14] Like reading an essay, this type of cinema encourages the spectator to take action to better understand his or her world. Critical thinking and reflection is the key. Put another way,

> Of all the features that are most frequently identified in the essay form, both literary and filmic, two stand out as specific, essential and characteristic: reflectiveness and subjectivity. Jean-Luc Godard, for instance, who is widely considered to be an essayistic director, has suggested in his *Historie(s) du cinema* that cinema is a "form that thinks" as well as "thought that forms"; elsewhere, he defined himself as an essayist,

and specified: "As a critic, I thought of myself as a filmmaker. Today I still think of myself as a critic.... Instead of writing criticism, I make a film, but the critical dimension is subsumed." ... In both quotes, Godard stresses the importance of the reflective component of the essay form.[15]

Godard has long been considered a radical, experimental filmmaker, and he has received a lot of critical speculation, but almost all of it suggests that he is making films that are akin to a type of theoretical undertaking about the nature of cinematic representation and cinematic form. *Le Gai Savoir* (1969) is one of his film essays, an avant-garde work that is both reflective and subjective, but also dialectical because of its structure and subject matter.

Le Gai Savoir makes little pretense of having a narrative; in it, a young man and young woman meet at a television studio so they can make a television film (as Godard was doing), but instead engage in long conversations on the meaning of language. In the course of their discursive discourse, they address how language structures individuals, how language positions itself as "an enemy," and how language both creates and destroys. There is no action that takes place, and outside of seeing (really, listening to) the two talk, there are a few images of city life and a couple of interviews with children and an older man. *Le Gai Savoir* is a very good example of cinematic intellectual discourse rendered through words and images (because Godard does have a lot of images filter throughout the film, despite the focus on language). It really is an essay, one that is complex in its thematic content yet presented simplistically, since two figures occupy a black, blank space for most of the film; it confounds as it reveals. The film offers a direct confrontation with its subject: language. The two characters argue throughout the film over the primacy and function of language; hence, we are invited to "converse" with them. The simple mise-en-scène is done in dialectical fashion to "normal" cinema (i.e., elaborate or purposeful), as well as to theorize the idea of continual direct address: Godard's characters speak, but *he* does as well (in a whispered voice-over), so the language bombardment hardly ever stops. Godard not only questions language but the urgency and agency of cinema as well. So it ultimately is highly self-reflexive (a characteristic of the essay), probes deep meaning through its analysis of its subject matter, offers a theory on language (and, by extension, spectatorship), and distinguishes itself politically, ideologically, and culturally as a social product constructed of verbal montage. Like in Brechtian theater, Godard wants us to link the cinematic experience to the social forces that give rise to its formation as an experimental essay film and as an exploration of themes that resonate precisely because they are perceptive. *Le Gai Savoir*'s "interrogation of the signifying and representational bases of cinema" makes it a radical form of the theoretical-dialectic essay film.[16]

Because *Le Gai Savoir* is structured like an essay and full of critical discourse, it can be off-putting to many, appealing to some. Its fragmentary style and lack of narrative ask the audience to interrogate its subject just as much as the subject interrogates us, which is to say it is a cerebral undertaking. At one point Emile, the male character, reaches toward the camera as a gesture of acknowledgement of us and to further the exteriority of language. The desire to force the film and the mental processes into a more physical connection with reality (in this case political action) is central to Godard's film, and it helps justify why Godard is interested in breaking down the semantics of film language while drawing attention to the semantics of language itself. The film is political (shot in 1967 and edited after the May 1968 uprising), and there are images of several revolutionaries, from Mao to Che. In many ways his essay film is about how to deal with politics and culture through image-making and word-making. According to James Monaco,

> Godard experiments with two theories in this respect in *Le Gai Savoir*. First, he "stops down" the materials—sounds, images, characters, ideas—of the film, limiting himself so that he can *know* what he is producing. Second, he forcibly distanciates the film: "We are on TV," Émile and Patricia continually remind us. Totally black sections of leader punctuate the film, further forcing the point.[17]

This theoretical undertaking is demonstrated in the continual flow of words and images, and is punctuated by sounds as well. The whole film has the background sound of radio static. There is a constant buzz or hum or bleep, and while Godard's voice-overs underscore the characters' thoughts, the sounds add additional layers of ambiguity *and* meaning; its themes are obscure at some instances, lucid at others. But that seems to be the point: Its structure demands a dialectic because it constructs one. Kaja Silverman notes, in relating the nature of the way images construct (or connote/denote) meaning as much as words— the ostensible "theme" of the film — how, based on Patricia's (the female character) creative words that she tells us to define ("nylon images," "reflex images," "virtual images," "book images"), "after encouraging us to focus upon the image's subjective effects, *Gay Knowledge* [sic] invites us to think about its materiality. To think about an image in its materiality is to allow it to appear as such, distinct from ourselves; it is to grasp the image as signifier."[18] Herein lies the theory of the film, reiterated in a different way, yet carrying the same weight — that semiotics, whether through words or images, is reflexive and possesses a material essence, and forces us to contemplate "meaning plays," a term used during the film to increase awareness (that is, language) because of our film viewing.

One final aspect of *Le Gai Savoir* makes it an avant-garde essay film: its focus on the performance of the actor-character, on Godard, and the performative nature of the images and words used in the film. What this means is that it *presents* itself as performance; it foregrounds its visual and aural presentation instead of couching them in narrative. As Rascaroli notes, this is something particular to the essay film and to Godard more specifically: "Because of its hybridism and experimentalism, and its generic instability, the essay film, in fact, foregrounds and problematizes issues of performance; and, on account of its openness and reflexivity, it articulates its concerns in an eminently performative manner."[19] For *Le Gai Savoir*, this is demonstrated through the repetitive nature of the foregrounded meetings and conversations between Emile and Patricia, the montage of images, the cacophony of sounds, and the voice of Godard himself. The film's style is its content. Its essayistic nature is its form. And its message — the construction and deconstruction of language — provides Godard with rich material upon which to base his theory, create the dialectic, and bemuse and baffle his audience.

A GRIN WITHOUT A CAT

Chris Marker's *A Grin Without a Cat* (1977) is an epic film essay about political upheaval around the world during the 1960s and 1970s, focusing on Vietnam, Bolivia, Prague, Chile, May '68, and the New Left. Its enormity is justified through its collage-like assemblage of global images that serve as time markers (historical documents) in the continual evolution (or devolution) of political strife. The film is an impassioned examination of the way film (and other images) document history, time, memory, and reality; it uses found footage, old newsreels, television clips, news reportage, and voice-over narration to scrutinize the events of nearly two and a half decades (Marker recut the film in 1993 after the fall of the USSR). Taken as a historical document and a film essay, Marker's film suggests the way images can evoke or recall and ultimately distort and contrast; memory becomes displayed in front of us. Someone who is highly self-reflexive and utilizes unconventional methods of filmmaking, or who is critical of empirical data, could be considered a postmodern filmmaker, but the term implies much more. Historian Robert Rosenstone suggests that "postmodern history," which Marker practices in his daunting movie, engages the spectator in a number of rhetorical and theoretical ways. These types of histories, and in this case Marker's essay film,

> foreground their own construction; tell the past self-reflexively and from a multiplicity of viewpoints; forsake normal story development, or problematize the stories they recount; utilize humor, parody, and absurdist modes of presenting the past; refuse to insist on a coherent or single meaning of events; indulge in fragmentary or poetic knowledge; and never forget that the present moment is the site of all past representation.[20]

Marker's objective is to use collage aesthetics to give some kind of voice to the left-leaning political activism and disturbances that shaped social and cultural activity, inasmuch as it did history. While it may be that he is postmodern by Rosenstone's definition, he is more experimental and typically avant-garde in the way the material is presented to us. Its historical premise is perhaps why critic David Sterritt can reasonably conclude that *A Grin Without a Cat* is "not a lesson in history but a lesson in how history is dismembered and remembered by every generation in its own way." He also adds, "The film is like a dream gradually coming into focus, or rather, a dream having its last bursts of energy as it gives way to newer but equally skewed patterns of cognition, imagination, and wishful fantasy."[21] The film is therefore very much in the vein of the avant-garde film essay, where experimentation dictates style and form as well as the representation of the thematic content and its theoretical positioning.

A Grin Without a Cat opens with a startling use of montage that immediately sets the mood for the film. Marker uses the famous Odessa Steps sequence from Eisenstein's *Battleship Potemkin* and intercuts it with shots of street marchers and protestors, revolutionary signs and banners, speeches, and shots of Stalin. Then he cuts to an American pilot in Vietnam describing dropping napalm on the Vietnamese below ("... we can see people running everywhere! Fantastic!"). After the ludicrousness of this sequence, we see the results of such action: the burned victims being treated in a hospital. It is a startling and imaginative collage, one that uses film footage, archival news footage, and incisive, scathing commentary to immediately put us on edge and force us to reckon with the essay's self-reflexive means of getting us involved. By and large, the film has no narrative structure other than having two separate parts with chapters in each section, but it uses the images to articulate levels of importance that create meanings through their association, ultimately finding ground in the overall arrangement as a masterful film essay.

Marker is concerned with how images and media representation interact with memory, forcing us to reexamine the past through a subjective lens. In shaping *A Grin Without a Cat* as a film essay, Marker is inviting speculation about the very idea of past/present/memory. The avant-garde film essay is often constructed as a type of self-reflexive exercise about subjectivity, and Marker's film is no different:

> Due to its decidedly self-reflexive nature and its metacritical attitude, the essay film is particularly inclined to explore the relationship between image and reality, between film and document, between audiovisual record and historical event. Essay films, in fact, often include archival material and found footage, and many of them are collage films.... As a consequence, essay films pose searching questions about the cinema as repository of memory, as museum and as archive. These questions ... are also, as widely accepted, central to Chris Marker's work.[22]

Marker is interested in employing formal theoretical concepts in his works, and *A Grin Without a Cat* is an essay that theorizes as it creates meaning through its juxtaposition of images. The title of the film is a reference to Lewis Carroll's Cheshire Cat, "celebrating the promise of socialist ideas (the grin) while realizing that the brave new world they envision (the cat) remains elusive and intangible as its twentieth-century trial runs slip farther into the past."[23] Realizing this, perhaps, Marker laces the voice-over commentary (spoken primarily by actress Simone Signoret) with satirical edge, ambiguity, and heightened subjectivity.

A Grin Without a Cat is an impressionistic essay involving a collage-like collection of significant images of the recent past. It presents these images (and words) in ways that make them connected (street riots, Castro speeches, Chilean uprisings), thus forming both its theoretical stance and its dialectical construct — that such massive turmoil resulted in very little, though ambitious in magnitude and spirit. The rise and fall of the New Left, the film's subject matter, which we see in its many manifestations globally, is shown through the found footage and montages of images to great effect; it creates a type of poetry, a lyricism that highlights the film's ambitious undertaking. Its visual style (Marker often tints images different hues, from red to blue to green) also heightens its poeticism, making *A Grin Without a Cat* a huge artistic tapestry, one woven with such startling grace and aesthetic sensibility that it has the potential to overwhelm the spectator. But that is part of the point of the theoretical-dialectic film essay — to prompt reflection as it reveals itself.

The last essay film I will discuss is also a poetic meditation on memory and it also will serve as a bridge to the next (extremely important) type of avant-garde film and filmmaking practice, women's experimental cinema.

Women's Experimental Cinema

A second type of avant-garde film that has become an essential aspect of film culture and film history is women's experimental cinema, and I place it here as a "type," though it could be considered its own genre. But I do think as a category of avant-garde film practice, women's experimental film is extraordinarily diverse and particularly significant in terms of representation, spectatorship, and voice. Unlike mainstream films by women directors, avant-garde films by women are often social or political in nature, and many were influenced by feminist theory that emerged in the 1960s and particularly the 1970s. According to Jean Petrolle and Virginia Wright Wexman,

> Women's experimental film practice often challenges masculinist avant-garde aesthetic dogmas by juxtaposing narrativity and non-narrativity, deploying narrative pleasure alongside narrative disruption, providing viewers with identification as well as critical distance, and so on. Adhering to such a definition allows ... women's formal innovation to encompass an array of non-mainstream film practices ... [including] hybrid forms that combine genres and mix filmic modes.[24]

This definition aligns women's experimental and avant-garde film with traditional definitions, but it also singles out the ways in which certain women's avant-garde films differ, thus creating the specific and unique type of film covered in this brief section. There are a number of different and very good texts on women's experimental film and avant-garde practice, so I will limit my succinct introduction here to a few remarks about the issues raised by such films — mostly their styles, and more importantly, thematic content.

Tracing the lineage of women's experimental and avant-garde cinema from Maya Deren to Marie Menken to the present typically yields an alternative history; it is often revisionary, exclusive, or culturally motivated. Many of the films associated with the group of films known as contemporary women's experimental cinema are autobiographical, documentary-like, and diarist in form. Hence, many such films open up lines of theoretical discourse about the diary film or the documentary film, since the structure of these films is often intertextual or formally experimental. Crossing and re-crossing these boundaries — diary, documentary, autobiography — creates a very specific type of film. According to Robin Blaetz, "The most perilous but popular focus in these films is the female body itself," where many women directors "have blurred the line between performer and observer in their work as a means of investigating thorny issues surrounding the representation of the female body."[25] The presence of the filmmaker in these types of films is very recognizable, much like essay films (which are prevalent in women's avant-garde cinema) and also even in narrative features, which suggests "the interrogation of the body's status as a cultural or linguistic sign, rather than a natural object, is pervasive and constant" in theory and practice.[26] This type of recognition has theoretical implications, as these types of films challenge preconceived notions about identity, subjectivity, and cultural and social signification. Some critics even suggest that "women who direct experimental films respond to a patriarchal context fraught with voices and images that describe the world from a masculinist perspective."[27] While this may be true for many of these specific types of avant-garde film, I would suggest that many more are concerned with *the personal* — the ways by which the filmmaker herself can communicate meaning through cinematic texts that may or may not be a direct confrontation with patriarchy. It is why, then, one may conclude:

> Experimental filmmaking by women undertakes to discover, among other things, formerly unknown principles at work in the lives and psyches of women. It further aims to explore these principles, test them, and improvise alternatives. One defining feature of an experimental film, therefore, is the spirit of discovery, inquiry, and innovation that animates such a project.[28]

In essence, these types of films engage in personal explorations of the self and representations of the female self through exploratory, innovative, and experimental means. These types of films are in many ways cultural, political, and social forces that necessitates a consideration of their form and style as much as their themes, which, as mentioned, may not be sympathetic to feminist concerns, but rather are interested in avant-garde form as a means of critique, structure, and counterpoint to mainstream narrative film.

Women's experimental film shares many formal and stylistic traits: fragmentation, documentation, collage, surrealism, and impressionism; hand-held cameras, static positioning of the camera, montage, long takes, first-person subjectivity, omniscience, seriousness and humor, superimpositions and distortions, visual effects and animation, close-ups, pans, swishes, or incorporating video. All these techniques inform avant-garde filmmaking to some extent, but the way they are employed in women's experimental cinema is usually overtly tied to the subject matter. In assessing avant-garde film practice and the ways to interpret and analyze them, Bill Nichols suggests that a "dual analysis" of form and social reality may be the best method of discovering their significance: "Formal innovations can be situated within a larger social context involving other arts and changing social conditions, and political engagement can be understood in terms of its fresh, cinematic techniques."[29] Though not always this simplified, the examination of women's experimental film through its status as social product, avant-garde aesthetic, and ideological perspective does help us recognize some of the concerns that are shared but ultimately presented differently by each individual filmmaker. Such is the case with Su Friedrich, whose work crosses several boundaries: avant-garde film, documentary film, diary film. Her films typically examine women's roles in society, how these roles are shaped, and the social/sexual relationships between women.

THE TIES THAT BIND

Su Friedrich's "personal" cinema has manifested itself in different forms, including the essay and documentary format, but it is her collage approach that has made her works more experimental in nature. *The Ties That Bind* (1984) is a lyrical examination of her past, specifically that of her mother's past (in Germany in the 1930s and 1940s), and how what shaped her mother helped shape her. It essentially chronicles the past and how it is often ever-present. Most of the film is structured like an interview, but we never hear the questions, just the mother's answers. Occasionally the questions appeared scratched on the surface of the film, but for the most part the only thing we hear is the mother's voice, solemnly and sometimes humorously reflecting. *The Ties That Bind* also uses found footage in the form of old family movies, but there is an ostensible rhetorical emphasis in the way Friedrich re-uses old home movies, documentary, travelogue, interviews, and narrative. But the film is not a documentary portrait of her mother, nor one of someone remembering fascist Germany and the subsequent relocation to the United States (as Friedrich's parents did). In Janet Cutler's summation, there is a tension that stems from the dialectical nature of the image-word-sound collage created by Friedrich, though the primary conflict is Friedrich's own concern about how her mother *feels* about the past. Cutler says:

> [W]hile Friedrich's mother speaks on the sound track, the accompanying images rarely correspond to her words. Instead, the film presents a rich mix of material: various nonsynchronous images of the mother; footage Friedrich shot on a trip to Ulm, Germany, to see where her mother grew up; archival footage of the war; home movie footage taken after the war; an early cinema single-shot film of a woman dancing while holding an American flag; and footage of Friedrich participating in political protests in the present.[30]

The film's contrasting rhetorical strategies make it experimental in its form. It mixes the poetic with the theoretical or argumentative, resulting in a hybrid avant-garde film where Friedrich re-examines home movies by offering present-day commentary, and re-evaluates her past based on the interviews with her mother. In a way, Friedrich has revealed the everyday as a site of hidden meaning, where images and words clash for separate significance.

The Ties That Bind is experimenting with traditional forms of avant-garde film — namely, the experimental narrative, collage technique, and autobiographical essay. It is a hybrid of different techniques, which gives Friedrich her true voice, that of personal and social commitment, sociological and cultural discourse, and a thorough experimental mix of unconventional film rhetoric. Despite the amount of sources present in *The Ties That Bind*, Friedrich has made them come together through the remarkable editing, "which develops a range of thematic and formal 'ties' between the various visual and auditory strands of the film."[31] For instance, at one point we see home movies of Friedrich swimming as a child, an ostensibly happy moment in the filmmaker's childhood. But her commentary deconstructs the scene: She felt the need to perform well for her father. The images and words clash, and the result is more than just a reminiscence of a past event, but, more strikingly, how the event plays out in the future, which is now the present. This form of collage is an avant-garde technique and aesthetic choice. This also makes *The Ties That Bind* both an emotional and intellectual exercise: It is a personal film that provokes thought because it is about the past and present, memory and meaning. Her own personal experience becomes the thematic tie that binds the film (and most of her other films as well) and elucidates the merging of avant-garde experimentalism and more straightforward generic forms, like the documentary. In *The Ties That Bind*, Friedrich uses found footage filmmaking, a very specific form of avant-garde practice, and entwines incongruent or even dissimilar fragments (sounds, images, texts) into a unified film essay. In this way, too, the film form itself becomes a kind of structuring of memory — a blending of things; so, again, the subject matter informs the way the film is made. But what makes the film unique is its harrowing narrative (of her mother's experience in Nazi Germany) and her method of approaching the subject as both daughter and filmmaker, a personal/public mix that also makes the film resonate emotionally with viewers. In an interview Friedrich said:

> I'm known as a "personal filmmaker," known for making work that's often autobiographical, and that's true; I do tend to speak from my own experience.... Perhaps I could explain this more easily by saying that I do believe the feminist motto: "The personal is political." I don't see any break between inside and out; my experiences are shared by millions of other people, and what I/we experience is a mirror, or a microscopic version, of the things that unfold on the largest possible scale. And because of that, it makes perfect sense to me to have my films confront the most local (personal) issues through the filter of the global, and vice versa.[32]

This kind of awareness creates a self-reflexive film style that is avant-garde and unlike traditional forms of representation through documentary or even the "replaying" of old home movies. *The Ties That Bind* is about the past and the incongruent ways memory is used in creating meaning, which mirrors the way the film is formed. A vast multitude of external stimuli affects memory just as much as watching home movies can, interviewing your mother can, or simply trying to unravel the way the mind processes information. It is a serious undertaking, and the experimental collage method proves admirable in the attempt to present the themes that concern her the most.

Friedrich's film is an intricate portrait of the artist's mother, and by association, the artist herself. The home-movie feel of the film only contributes to its aesthetic appeal and recognition as a work that really has "ties" to us all. Describing Friedrich's overall experimental style — that is, the way she constructs most of her films — Cutler offers an inventory of tropes and themes that are directly applicable to *The Ties That Bind*, and how the films affect us as spectators to her unique world and working methods:

> Friedrich's personal, provocative films are finely woven tapestries of disparate materials: text scratched into film stock, intertitles, black-and-white leader, still photographs, home movies, found footage, television broadcasts, and original images; ambient sound, spoken word, popular music, and silence. Seen and heard together, Friedrich's juxtapositions of images, words, and music lend her films great intensity and power. Watching Friedrich's films is like watching a person's mind working: you can sense the filmmaker thinking through the possible ways to proceed, drawing parallels and making connections between otherwise unrelated images and sounds, encouraging the viewer to follow a line of thought to the point at which a new idea or a new understanding emerges.[33]

This description is elaborate and complex, but it rightly situates Friedrich's work in an avant-garde milieu, and *The Ties That Bind* is also accurately a type of avant-garde film that bridges experimental narrative and personal autobiography. In an interview, Friedrich said, "I always want my films to be very sensuous. I want the rhythm and the images to be gratifying."[34] What this film ultimately accomplishes is a lyrical rhythm, a candid portrait of personal history and memory formed through social and cultural mediation and experience. It is an analytical film, questioning form and theme through idiosyncratic personal representation.

JE TU IL ELLE

Chantal Akerman's most celebrated film is *Jeanne Dielman, 23 quai du Commerce, 1080 Bruxelles* (1975), a searing cinematic portrait of existential void and hypnotic simplicity. It has been written about at considerable length, so instead of another brief overview of it, I will discus another Akerman film that is equally experimental in its treatment of the subject — female self and society — and its formal structure. *Je Tu Il Elle* (1974) is an intense examination of self-identity created through self-reflection, self-denial, and self-fulfillment. It is easily the kind of film that can draw many distracters; it may be called self-indulgent as well (Akerman plays the lead character, the "I" of the title), and it could very well be considered an autobiographical experiment in desperation. However, I would suggest that despite its overt ambiguity, and it is ambiguous only because it offers no explanations, it is more about the demystification of loneliness and romance, and its realism belies its experimental nature. Moreover, the film is about the fragmentation of the self, which is presented through the experimental form that shapes its narrative and style. Described as a "brooding, minimalist, visually drab meditation on late-adolescent sexuality," *Je Tu Il Elle* is much more about the way spaces create memory and nurture behavior.[35] While its minimalism is part of its experimental framework, the overall tone of the film — melancholic, sorrowful — contributes to its ambiguity.

The plot is rather straightforward: Taking place over two days, the film follows a woman (Akerman) who in the first third of the film remains in her starkly bare room, rearranging furniture, painting the walls, and eating only sugar, and apparently writing a love letter that she often arranges in sheets of paper on the floor around her. In the second part she leaves her flat and hitches a ride with a truck driver; at his bequest, she provides a sexual encounter (a hand job). The third part of the film has her arrive at the home of her lover, a woman, and after small bickering and voracious eating, they engage in frantic lovemaking before the film simply ends. The bareness of each segment highlights the performance of the character, here taking on a duality of meaning or representation, as Akerman plays the title character. (The title, *Je Tu Il Elle*, translates to "I, You, He She," wherein the "you" is ostensibly us, the spectator, and the "Il" is the male and the "Elle" is her lover.) But the film is an experiment in disjunctive representation, more so than a paean to ill-suited carnality.

One avant-garde technique Akerman uses is the discrepancy between word and image. The first part of the film that takes place in her apartment highlights the unusual way that the voice-over counterpoints what we see. The voice-overs often come before what we see — or after — disrupting the temporality and spatial unity. Akerman uses such aural cues to suggest the woman's growing alienation and psychic rupture, which culminates in the trysts. None of the voice-over correlates to the onscreen images we see, creating a diegetic/non-diegetic gap that also suggests the disintegration of the self and thus the attempt to find meaning or stability later. Akerman is an observational filmmaker, a personal filmmaker, an avant-garde filmmaker, and a theoretical one; her films engage semiotics, feminism, and existentialism, and discovering *Je Tu Il Elle* as a modernist work about these issues — presented in style and theme — makes it more relevant because it is about the search for self-worth, a point anyone can relate to. Assessing Akerman's work overall, Jonathan Rosenbaum makes a point that is quite suitable to understanding the merging of theme and form in her work. He says:

Virtually all of her films, regardless of genre, come across as melancholy, narcissistic meditations charged with feelings of loneliness and anxiety; and nearly all of them have the same hard-edged painterly presence and monumentality, the same precise sense of framing, locations, and empty space. Most of them are fundamentally concerned with the discomfort of bodies in rooms.[36]

This last point, the "discomfort" one finds in rooms, is central to *Je Tu Il Elle*. The opening is a powerhouse exercise in the representation of uneasiness and anxiety that stems from being in a solitary space, with little or no *room* for exit or solace (after she moves to the final room with her lover). Akerman's film is conceptual and structural in that it offers a more intellectual yet corporeal means by which to understand the phenomenology of consciousness and the unconscious desires that filter into reality. Again, the opening demonstrates this idea. It is fragmented and disassociated from any context or frame, and the woman participates in self-inflicted mundane rituals: rearranging furniture, painting, and writing copious amounts of stream-of-conscious items and tidbits of information about herself and a presumed lover. The grimness, indeed the very unencumbered realness of the scene, strikes as avant-garde. Critic Ivone Margulies says that "given the hyperbolic quality of Akerman's referentiality, her work doesn't need to be defended from being co-opted by realism. On the contrary, the alienating force of the work's hyperrealism is enough to place it alongside other progressive currents of realist cinema."[37] The isolation rendered through the static camera, the positioning of the woman in the mise-en-scène, and the obsessive behavior reiterate the arbitrariness of her situation. Formally, this scene is structural because of the way it is filmed. The indecisive nature of the woman's activity further highlights the theme of dispossession, as she recites things that never quite match the activity we see onscreen.

In discussing three of Akerman's later films, Jerry White mentions that "each film centralizes a subjective voice, makes it clear in each frame that this subjectivity is female, and maintains an uneasy — and very Barthesian — tension between textual pleasure and critical distance."[38] He further concludes, "Akerman's versatility — her ability to facilitate an active, Barthesian textual pleasure across a wide range of historical and generic forms— makes her avant-garde in the truest sense."[39] While focusing on later films, these remarks ring true for *Je Tu Il Elle*. The seeming duplicitous nature of *Je Tu Il Elle* (the "Barthesian" subversion of certain narrative elements to others, or the gaps in narratives) comes from the tension between its austere realism and its (paradoxical) alienating effect. To this effect, the film's bluntness makes it a certain kind of experimental film that is noticeably associated with performance, feminism, and subjectivity, elements that make some women's experimental film more recognizable as both theoretical and ideological, especially when the film is as *realistic* as this one. What makes this premise of realism, really the *literalness* of the representation, is the thematic tie of the instability of subjectivity, made most clear during the incongruous narration and mismatched imagery. *Je Tu Il Elle* is thus about the search for the authentic self, but Akerman does not provide the way to discover such an individual. And while this rings true of some feminist works, Akerman's method is quite different. As Margulies argues,

> The images [in *Je Tu Il Elle*] don't cancel representation; they reveal scene and character starkly. But referentiality is imploded, for though reality is entirely apparent, even naked, it is represented as simultaneously faltering and excessive, discontinuous and repetitive, circular and nontotalizing. Overt display creates an aporia of evidence — we see all of the room, all of the character, all of the love-making — yet this "all," this totality, is denied, through the sparseness of the visual elements, the cleansing of anecdotal events and, most important, the resolute assertion of particularities.[40]

It may be, then, for Akerman (and especially *Je Tu Il Elle*) that form converges with theme or subject, but never in a didactic manner: "Always open ended, her political engagement with the presentation and re-presentation of feminine subjectivity avoids pedagogy or propaganda. She toys with her viewers, invoking recognized forms only to radically revise them. In such textual deceptions, however, subversion and pleasure meet."[41] *Je Tu Il Elle* is the kind of film that offers up many arguments but no solutions. Instead, it sets up a problematic (whether about illusionism and reality, narrative and non-narrative), radical departure from mainstream cinema. Never one to present someone who is easy to read, Akerman's heroines (like Julie, the woman of *Je Tu Il Elle*) are oblique and transitory. We get glimpses of their lives, and in the case of *Je Tu Il Elle*, we see how identity formation is a constant and ongoing crisis, where the idea of "self" is confounding and elusive and always shifting, just as the parameters of filmmaking are shattered through experimentation and avant-garde techniques.

*   *   *

The experimental women's film is a thriving area of film culture and practice. While there are those who work in the mainstream, the type of films produced in the margins — whether in the avant-garde, independent, or video sector — are all far more adventurous, personal, and aesthetically and thematically innovative. The sense of "otherness" that situates women's experimental and avant-garde film alongside and far outside the mainstream is both an apt and often misleading label; it suits because theirs is literally an "other" kind of cinema, and it is ambiguous or deceptive because it may imply a deliberate ideological or political position which is not always the case. Filmmakers like Friedrich and Akerman express a consciousness of the "history and theory of the medium that influenced their styles of filmmaking, which is to suggest that they know the work of like-minded women filmmakers while decidedly creating works that are individualistic."[42] Simply put, in terms of avant-garde feature films, there may not be a richer, more diverse range of experimental films than those made by ground-breaking women directors and their contemporaries.

The Modern City Symphony

One final example of a type of contemporary feature-length avant-garde film is the modern city symphony. Peter von Bagh's *Helsinki, Forever* (2008) follows a long tradition in avant-garde cinema, the "city symphony film," a particular kind of film that takes its inspiration from the city itself that is being documented or captured through its imagistic history. These kinds of films present a vivid depiction of a particular city, using various techniques, like fast/slow motion, superimposition, collage, and image-text-audio juxtaposition, to create a portrait of the (given) city. Most avant-garde city films create "a 'New Realist' montage of the city's contradictions. The contradictory social forces and conditions visualized in the film are accepted as endemic to urban life."[43] While *Helsinki, Forever* does not necessarily fit this trend (of contradictions), it still manages to create introspection through its amalgam of images and voices. City films are often highly stylized pseudo-documentaries and are avant-garde because they typically shun a recognizable narrative, though there are often guiding motifs that construct their linearity or themes. Vertov's *The Man with a Movie Camera* (1929) and Ruttman's *Berlin: Symphony of a Great City* (1928) are two of the best-known examples of this type of avant-garde feature film. *Helsinki, Forever* is a bit different from these because von Bagh has fashioned his portrait mostly out of old movie clips; Vertov and Ruttman take their cameras to the streets and document the immediacy, the modernity of city life occurring in the moment. They create senses of rhythm and abstraction based on movements of people, cars, trains, and the like, and through shots of architecture, focusing on angles, cubes, patterns, and light and shadow. The avant-garde city film typically shows the city as a vibrant entity unto itself. We are invited to speculate on the images, rhythms, and movements created through montage, crosscutting, shape-shifts, or inventive cinematography. City symphony films are a type of avant-garde film because they do not have traditional characters that enact cause-effect plots, nor do they appear as outright documentaries. Instead, they present an associative collage of a particular place that is not tied to any spatial or temporal rules; von Bagh's film traces Helsinki over nearly a century. Ultimately, what the city symphony film does is allow us to see the city anew; it alters our preconceived ideas about the place and therefore establishes new modes of cognition and perception based on the images and the way they are selected and arranged. Peter von Bagh's remarkably cinematic and captivating city symphony film *Helsinki, Forever* is an extraordinary encapsulation of the city as shown through old films, architecture, sociological and cultural statistics, historical data, and Finnish pop music. The film's collage technique is reminiscent of other films of the genre, but von Bagh illuminates Helsinki like never before; if your only glimpse of Finnish cinema is through Aki Kaurismaki (a fantastic way, as it were), then *Helsinki, Forever* not only suggests the rich history of Finnish film, but also Helsinki's preeminence in European history.

The film opens with a stunningly surreal and beautiful scene: an old, massive ship enters the frozen city harbor of Helsinki. The ship breaks through the ice as it slowly *crunches* forward. Then we see a small boy walking next to the ship, smiling, unfazed by the ship's progress and proximity. Other city dwellers watch as well — men, women, and even a car that crosses the ship's path — a time capsule of the people and a moment that informs the entire film: cold, shadowy, effervescent, stark, and magical. The clever beginning, where progress collides with fate (ship vs. ice), and people's smiling (or some serious) faces observe, positions the city as an interesting and wondrous place. Helsinki, relegated to being Europe's outer, upper "other" city, becomes a place of surprise and seriousness, a place that, as it turns out, has as much of a unique cinematic history and cultural past as anywhere else. The entire film revolves around the revealing of the city through its archives.

One of the remarkable things about *Helsinki, Forever* is its collage-like construction, its essayistic tone (which also adds to its formal production), and its ample use of old and new texts, including verbal, audio, and image. Following the tradition of city symphony films, *Helsinki, Forever* is about the city as an art form, an aesthetic *thing* unto itself that is revealed in multiple layers. Through three separate (and often competing and complementary) voice-overs (two male and one female), the city's history is shown through its film archive (both fiction and documentary), and through the images and readings of them that the three narrators detail in often scatological or fragmentary fashion. The fragmenting of the city is often a stylistic device used in city symphony films; the collage of images shows how vibrant and diverse any city can be. Each narrator in the film recounts moments in Finnish (film) history in poetic and essayistic form. (The theoretical-dialectic film, women's experimental film, and the city symphony all share the fundamental aspic of being a form of the essay, making them all, in some form or another, avant-garde essay films.) In some essays films there is the potential for either a dialectic or self-congratulatory tone, but *Helsinki, Forever* never seems either; its images speak, making it lyrical (like a Marker film) and personal (like a Friedrich travelogue — part fiction, mostly docu-essay). The juxtaposition of images and sounds aligns *Helsinki, Forever* with experimental collages of city life — everything from Marie Menken's *Go! Go! Go!* to more experiential city symphony (or "world") films like Ron Fricke's *Baraka* (1992) or Godfrey Reggio's *Koyaanisqatsi* (1982), all, incidentally, avant-garde non-narrative essayistic films. But *Helsinki, Forever* is still a bit different; in addition to being a portrait of the city, it really is more a visual history that spans one hundred years. There are film clips from Finnish film history — everything from comedies to musicals— as well as images of strife and poverty, politics, and painting. As much as a cinematic document of the city, it is also about the artistic life of Helsinki; hence we get shots of architecture and hear contemporary Finnish pop songs.

The voice-overs are about urban economics and sociology, cultural and artistic history, historical fact, and modernity — in terms of urban and cinematic growth. It is a philosophical and aesthetic portrait ripe with startling images that convey a strong sense of Helsinki as place and presence. One of the more ingenious devices is the use of Finnish pop music to comment on (and often contrast) the history we see; some songs are about the city itself, highlighting the film's overall theme as a city symphony, and others about romance — again suggesting both the idealized/realistic nature of the city symphony type of avant-garde film that makes *Helsinki, Forever* a great blend of experimental technique and documentary approach. Helsinki "comes to life" as a vivacious, wistful, and clearly beautiful place, somber at times but also welcoming. The past and present collide, which makes *Helsinki, Forever* a bit different from the historical city symphony film (since most are of the moment); but its montage still captures the essence of the city, intimately and dreamily, a hallucinatory place of imagistic black/white contrast. Often sedate but never boring, *Helsinki, Forever* takes us on a poetic, elliptical, and metaphoric journey through a city using collage, essay, and pure cinematic display. Director von Bagh — ex-director of Finland's national cinema archive — knows the city, knows cinema, and acts as historian, using everything from home movies, newsreels, film archives, and voice-over to create, arguably, the most experimental and creative city symphony of recent memory.

*   *   *

The three types of avant-garde feature film I have briefly outlined here — and their corresponding examples — hopefully will direct readers to a more thorough investigation of each type. But certainly they all share characteristics beyond their representations as avant-garde films; these types all inherently prescribe to a tradition that has always been welcomed in the history of experimental cinema: essayistic film. Essay films do allow us to rethink preconceived notions about form and content through the ways filmmakers represent information in essayistic style. The essay film is a type of avant-garde film that arguably finds parallels among many other types of avant-garde films. That is, since many essay films are based on new forms of representation, theses and probing examination of issues, fictional and documentary, real and inauthentic — the list could go on — they engage us differently; because of these reasons, the essay film (and the theoretical-dialectic approach I have outlined) are very similar to avant-garde films in general. As Corrigan suggests,

> Situated between the categories of realism and formal expressivity and geared to the possibilities of "public expression," the essay film suggests an appropriation of certain avant-garde and documentary practices in a way very different from the early historical practices of both, just as it tends to invert and restructure the relations between the essayistic and narrative to subsume narrative within that public expression.[44]

Essay films stand as good examples of avant-garde films because they are very often a blend of formalist and realist aesthetics, combine historical practices while inventing new forms, and create *expressivity*— a fundamental characteristic of avant-garde films in general. Though these types are similar because of this, they are also, as I hope to have demonstrated, unique unto themselves. But to further understand the specifics of each avant-garde type, it is essential to discuss some at length — hence, the last section of this book, which analyzes several case studies in contemporary avant-garde feature filmmaking.

Some of the case studies are similar to those discussed in this section, but many create their own distinctness, forging works that are unlike anything else in film. Still, for the essay film, and specifically the theoretical-dialectic type, the women's experimental film, and finally the contemporary city symphony, major aspects of avant-garde history and culture become manifested in their styles and (often) thematic content. One of the reasons I have chosen the three is because they do share commonalities as different forms of essay discourse. For this reason, too, they will reflect how the films in the next section will demonstrate the variety — and overlap — among the varying types of contemporary avant-garde feature films. But the films that follow are representative of the historical avant-gardes while also creating new forms. There are other types of avant-garde films that warrant much discussion besides the essayistic form found in the three types outlined here, such as surrealist, collage-animation, or video installations/mixed media. Some of these will be addressed in the next part, and will reflect a number of the ideas presented earlier.

₰ Chapter 8 ₰

Case Studies

The following discussion of a selection of avant-garde films offers an array of films and filmmakers that are linked to the historical and canonical avant-gardes, but they are also decidedly original. Some of the films are well-known and have received a lot of critical appraisal; others may not have received as much but are still vital examples of the types of films outlined in this book. Much of the analyses are from my own judgment, but they are supplemented with some critical assessment, depending on the film, filmmaker, and the sources available. All of the films mentioned are also available for viewing. As previously discussed, not all of the films may be considered avant-garde by other critics or even the casual moviegoer or cineaste. I have chosen them because they reflect the kinds of films that typically operate outside the mainstream arena. The films are arranged chronologically.

The contemporary avant-garde feature film is diverse in construction and result — there are innumerable examples of films that relate to the criteria established earlier, which can be beneficial and practical yet also problematic. First, hoping to generate a cultural and aesthetic awareness, these films represent films that establish critical avenues of exploration: they reflect historical trends, but eschew standards. Second, they reflect personal vision, perhaps the strongest aspect of the avant-garde feature film one must consider as the ontological force for each film. Finally, even though I suggested different characteristics one may look for in identifying an avant-garde feature film, these films do not contain every piece of criterion, nor do they always possess more than one. Overall they provide spectators different kinds of films and film-going experiences that are not readily available from other contemporary films built upon economic or cultural concerns.

In essence, the films here are simply case studies: films that can be used as prime examples of contemporary avant-garde films. They all have idiosyncratic stylistic and formal choices and all clearly are more interested in producing a film that is an *aesthetic document*— that is, a work of art that is unusual, extraordinary, defiant, personal, and on the cutting edge, the forefront, the *vanguard* of cinema.

The Color of Pomegranates

Armenian director Sergei Paradjanov's films are extraordinary instances of visual narrative that rely heavily on the transformative practices of creation, poetic sensibility, and transformation. Relying more on symbolic or metaphoric imagery instead of straightforward dialogue — though epic indigenous stories inform his work — puts Paradjanov in rare company among filmmakers of the last forty years. By his own admission, he sought alternative methods of perception and reflection of life — and in so doing reflects certain avant-garde and modernist tendencies in his films. *The Color of Pomegranates* (1969) provokes the spectator into rethinking the form of film; watching the film creates a very direct sense of breaking from general filmmaking practices to something new. Using *tableaux vivant*, few intertitles, and emotive music, Paradjanov overwhelms the spectator with images rather than words, though the film is ostensibly a film about words, as it is a biography of the eighteenth-century poet Sayat Nova. The film is also an amalgam of themes — spiritual quest, inward journey, biographical musing, and love story. The intertextual nature of the film also makes it unusual and thoroughly modern, an avant-garde feature that eschews any kind of formula. Very broadly, Paradjanov's film draws attention to the modes of representation themselves. Paradjanov draws attention to *the way* representation organizes our often very different experiences of the world, thoughts, feelings, relationships and of everyday phenomena. For this reason, *The Color of Pomegranates* becomes less like a way *to* something else and more like something you have to take notice of *for* itself. Essentially, the creative, transformative, and adaptive process that Paradjanov undertakes (and successfully demonstrates) allows *images to narrate* his inimitable filmic world.

The Color of Pomegranates is a thoroughly avant-garde film, a film so rich in allegory, surreal imagery, and symbolism that it requires multiple viewings. Its simple-but-complex style and abstruse story marks it readily and easily as avant-garde. It is both theological and philosophical, literary (poetic) and lyrical, hypnotic and hallucinatory. The story revolves around the maturation of the young poet. We see him in childhood and as a young man, then in a monastery and finally at his death; and his growth as an artist is seen through the relationships he has with his family, his lover, and assorted other characters, from peasants to religious figures. The film's ornateness and indigenous references are grounded in Armenian folklore and history, so any viewing of the film is tempered by a willingness to accept its obscure subject matter and presentation. Also, the film is filtered through Paradjanov's imagination and Nova's poetry, making it both ambiguous and personal, trademarks of many (important) avant-garde films. But its true avant-gardism lies in its presentational and representational style; it is radical, idiosyncratic, and highly subjective. The film's matter of showing/telling is, according to Karla Oeler, akin to Joyce's narrative strategies in *Ulysses* by way of Eisenstein's interest in turning the "inner monologue" into a public form, a more collective and, I would add, associational representation of the particulars of private speech. She says, "*The Color of Pomegranates* realizes Eisenstein's Joyce-inspired dreams for the cinema, miming, simultaneously, the inner speech, the sensual thought, of both its central character and, through him, the spectator."[1] The emphasis on spectatorial recognition and presence suggests the active viewing necessary for (or necessitated by) avant-garde cinema. In one scene, for example, we see the young boy poet staring at a woman whose left breast is covered by a seashell. Symbolic? Metaphoric? Surreal? Yes, and all at once. And it also aligns our vision with the protagonists, even though the image is cryptic, poetic, and highly charged with significance. It is, perhaps, an example of the private thoughts made public.

Paradjanov's extraordinary film utilizes painterly images to construct its ambitious story recreated through tableaux, where the images themselves become pure poetry. It is one of the most stunning and astonishingly beautiful films ever made. But it is difficult because it not only addresses an unfamiliar subject in an experimental fashion, but it also is full of myths and rituals that are subjective interpretations of Paradjanov's understanding of Sayat Nova and of the ethnography of his culture and history. All of Paradjanov's films are difficult for these reasons, but their avant-gardism also makes them strangely compelling and attractive. Traditional mythology forms the basic visual and narrative style for the film, making it somewhat unapproachable. Andràs Kovacs describes Paradjanov's style as "ornamental," which he sees as a trend in late modernist cinema from the 1960s, the era of *The Color of Pomegranates*. He describes the ornamental style as "not mere decoration or spectacular effect. Ornamental films may have theater as a cultural referential background, but most typically, their source is somewhere else. The source of modern ornamental style is either in different national folklore or in a religious or mythological context."[2] This kind of cinematic language is different from traditional forms of filmmaking. Oeler calls this kind of filmmaking, specific to Soviet practice in the 1960s and 1970s, "Poetic" and "Archaic," wherein "films of this school often feature the folklore, costumes, decorative arts, and music of particular ethnic groups."[3] These kinds of descriptions might signify a documentary or at least an ethnographic film, and *The Color of Pomegranates* is, in a way, ethnographic; but it is far more experimental than a document of the traditions and folklore of a specific region. The film has close ties to the lyrical side of surrealism, particularly the poetic display of symbolic objects. Much of the film offers static long takes of characters positioned in places that make them grounded to a particular space and place, yet they seem utterly free, as unfettered as dream-objects whose significance is symbolic, metaphoric, or allegorical. According to James Steffen, "Paradjanov's scenarios tend to be impressionistic, with more of an emphasis on gesture and detail than plot and dialogue per se."[4]

He further adds, "*The Color of Pomegranates* is notoriously difficult to decipher.... [The] structure of the screenplay and its use of verbal repetitions underlines the influence of painting and poetry on the form of the film itself."[5] Indeed, the imagery of the film suggests that painting and poetry are as much of an influence on the visual style as the narration. Again, this might point to the film's ornamentalism. Though the film is, like many avant-garde films, concerned with a representation of reality, it is far more abstract. For instance, Paradjanov uses graphic blocking with objects and characters, and also frames most scenes as centrally-framed shots, like in theater; yet it appears more designed, where spatial harmony or tension is created through the alignment or juxtaposition of shapes, colors, light schemes, or persons. The film is full of definite and indefinite spaces, where the immobility of the camera captures the essence of the real and abstract, the literal and the symbolic. The poeticism derived from associational arrangement of shots also signifies a highly unorthodox approach to cinematic narrativity, marking *The Color of Pomegranates* as avant-garde. Kovacs suggests this characteristic is predominately at the core of ornamental films. He states:

> Ornamentalism can be a form of abstraction whenever a closed set of regular or irregular geometrical elements that are not meant to represent a part of surface reality becomes an essential part of the composition. However, ornamental elements in modern art are meant to convey some deeper meaning; they are meant to represent some kind of "inner reality" and express fantasy, emotions, or a psychological state of mind allegedly inexpressible by elements of surface reality.[6]

The Color of Pomegranates is steeped in rich colors and ornamental tableaux, making it essentially a "moving painting" (Paradjanov actual was a painter as well as a filmmaker); and as such, many of the scenes are like canvases where the eye is directed to specific areas of the frame/canvas, which heightens the senses as well as positioning the spectator in a unique way suitable for avant-garde film. There are numerous images referencing frames, for example, highlighting the dual nature of the moving canvas or illuminated painting. Empty frames surround people in more than one scene. In one, a small cherub hangs suspended from the ceiling with a golden frame, which swings side to side, in front of him. In another startling image, two boys dressed as angels walk through a graveyard carrying an empty frame. As they walk, the frame noticeably "captures" certain elements in the scene: vistas, stones, hills. Often, figures are framed through windows or doorways, or by building eaves. It is both abstract, in that it creates multiple frames through which to uncover the representable, and literal: frames direct our attention much like the frame of the film itself.

A description of a few other scenes will help clarify the power of the poetic that Paradjanov creates. In the opening shot a dagger lies next to a cut pomegranate that bleeds its red liquid onto a cloth that then forms into an abstract shape resembling Armenia. One of the most lyrical shots comes a few moments later when Sayat Nova, as a young boy, climbs onto the roof of the house with a book. He opens the book and then we cut to a larger shot of him lying down on the roof surrounded by many, many other books drying in the wind. Their pages flap in the breeze, creating a chorus of poetry. Many shots in the film are of figures centrally framed staring directly at the camera — at us, as it were. In one, the young poet stands erect with a tall ornamental staff in one hand held close to his body, while the other arm is outstretched at ninety degrees and has a chicken resting on top of his arm. In another, the poet's lover dumps a large vase of red wine over him as he kneels beside her, arms at his sides. Such weird or strange iconography fills the film, making many images dream-like.

There are many times when the actors look directly into the camera, essentially meeting our gaze. Having the actor look at the camera not only breaks the "third wall," it also suggests the way avant-garde films directly address us by "inviting us into" the world of the film, either through the direct confrontation on a conscious level or, more abstrusely, through the unconscious. Like in a painting, characters take on a life beyond the frame by exchanging glances with us. The breaking down of the diegesis is an avant-garde tactic, and it asks us to consider the method of presentation because it is self-reflexive and entirely anathema to mainstream film. This also signifies something both formal and cognitive; Paradjanov asks us to see the inner life of the poet *in* and *through* a particular perspective or view. Oeler sees this technique reflecting the frequent use of frames-as-windows, of "passing through and looking through." She suggests:

> One looks and is looked at. If the world is like an open window, it is this still, this threshold of consciousness and self-consciousness that arises from sensing oneself as not only seeing, but also seen. The film's human figures realize this duality on a formal level by gazing directly at the camera and, through the camera, at the spectator. If the film realizes in images the world of a man, then the images of *The Color of Pomegranates* are images of the poetic consciousness gazing back on itself. Paradjanov's film is a reflection on reflection. More specifically, it is a reflection on a self-consciousness that is at once individual and collective.[7]

To have the characters engage with the audience is both an ontological and phenomenological endeavor, one that deliberately experiments with narration, causality, point-of-view, and subjectivity. This technique, along with the complex symbolic figurations and costuming, the music, and the tableaux, creates a "collage of disparate elements" that potentially "overwhelms the viewer with its intensity and density."[8] Paradjanov uses repetition, rich symbolism and allegory to represent the inner life of the poet, creating an avant-garde film that bears little resemblance to traditional forms of narrative filmmaking. The film may even be described as fragmented, which helps create its hallucinatory tone. The film begins with a passage from Sayat Nova's writing, which is repeated several times: "I am the man whose life and soul are torture." Inevitably, this "torture" is seen through the fragmented images of his life and death, itself rendered poetically. The poet's aging, for instance, is shown more as a trompe l'oeil: When the child grows to a man, Paradjanov presents it as having the child step behind the older figure and disappear from our view in a single continuous shot. This technique also demonstrates Paradjanov's eschewing of more sophisticated techniques in order to establish the avant-gardism of the film. Much of the film is presented in such a way, where, instead of establishing narrative sequences, Paradjanov connects shots associatively so that "the poetic montage of tableaux emerges as a key cinematic stream-of-consciousness technique."[9]

Paradjanov also uses multiple actors to portray the same character, Sayat Nova, and also uses androgynous women to play men, another method of avant-garde representation and reconfiguring of character. There are also times when the young boy is in the same frame as the youthful troubadour and the old man version of himself. This condensation of time is another avant-garde strategy that also points to the larger suggestion of a shared collective consciousness of one's self and being, which is precisely what Paradjanov has set out to accomplish with his film — to render the inner life of the poet. The opening title of the films indicates this as much; it states, "The film does not attempt to tell the life story of a poet. Rather the filmmaker has tried to re-create the poet's inner world." Arguably, the film has ties to the "trance" film tradition in American avant-garde film, where Deren's *Meshes of the Afternoon* or Anger's *Fireworks* or Brakhage's *Anticipation of the Night* all signify the dream-like excursions through the filmmaker's psyche, rendered, of course, in poetic or surreal imagery. Similar to these films, the spectator is forced to interpret and construct meaning, which perhaps can find correlations to the duality, intermingling, or even dialectic of the conscious and the unconscious, "an experience of human consciousness [that] tends to collapse time and condense meaning, the same processes that define the syntagmatic distortion and syncretism of inner speech," giving *The Color of Pomegranates* an extraordinary level of cognitive involvement.[10] The film's detail is orchestrated in such a dense and symbolic manner that we construct schemas for comprehension during viewing, though the film also undermines complete comprehension by presenting tableaux instead of narrative, situations instead of actions. Like many avant-garde films, though, we can deduce an appreciation for the film's meanings even if they are multifaceted and highly personal or subjective to Paradjanov. As Oeler surmises, "We are presented with tableaux, complete in themselves, that often, through the eyes of the characters, look back at us. Through framing and through images that gaze back at their beholder, the film presents a highly mediated world, ultimately arriving at a representation of consciousness that frames, allegorizes, and symbolizes, using a long, collective tradition."[11]

The Color of Pomegranates is a difficult film simply because it challenges expectations. It involves us unlike traditional mainstream cinema. It is avant-garde because of its unique style, its method of presentation, and its unorthodox use of film form. Like many avant-garde films, it [resists] being reduced to a single, clearly stated idea; the sight threatens to explode, unable to support the plethora of meanings it attracts like a magnet. Paradjanov's dialectic of sound and image, his constant exploitation of asynchronized and post-synchronized sound, encourages the viewer to look beyond the immediate historical and biographical context of the film.... The viewer is invited to share in a game of associations.[12]

The formal techniques Paradjanov exploits in the film make it avant-garde and certainly unusual in terms of its relation to mainstream cinema. Its strange and beautiful imagery spill from the frames; they invite serious contemplation on their sublimity, like paintings in galleries or like the highest form of poetry. There are not too many films that do this sort of thing, but the avant-garde world of *The Color of Pomegranates* invites reflection for these reasons. We are, in many ways, engaged in the intertextuality of the film just as the film itself is engaged with intertextuality in creating its structure. Its blend of word, image, sound, and song is abstract and sensual. Despite its seeming simplicity — staged tableaux instead of frenetic movement typically associated with cinema — the film ultimately directs us to a heightened sense of perception, a meditation on consciousness that ultimately makes *The Color of Pomegranates* unlike any other film experience.

Eraserhead

David Lynch's first feature, *Eraserhead* (1977), has been written about extensively, so much of what I will address represents a small percentage of the criticism about the film. Mostly, I want to discuss its formal techniques, ones that immediately signify it as avant-garde. *Eraserhead* is, without a doubt, one of the most original, inspired and inspiring works of avant-garde cinema over the past forty years, and its reputation as a midnight movie and cult classic is warranted if only because of its boldness and originality. It is also an art-house avant-garde film, which positions it alongside the other films included in this section as case studies. Here are esteemed critics J. Hoberman and Jonathan Rosenbaum describing the film: "*Eraserhead*, the most original and audacious film ever to become a midnight blockbuster ... [is] an almost miraculous achievement: an avant-garde hit, an intellectual splatter film-cum-thirty-five millimeter nightmare sitcom of the urban soul."[13] There is no denying its power — to shock, amuse, aggravate, confuse, and prompt reflection. *Eraserhead* offers a unique combination of conflicting emotions and desires existing on separate planes, reality and fantasy, which ultimately makes it a very approachable avant-garde film; that is, its themes resonate with any viewer. The film juxtaposes the sacred and the profane, the transgressive and the transcendent, and carefully, even manically, builds tension and emotional meaning through the incomprehensible and irrational, and, perhaps most tellingly but not often recognized, its *surreal realism*, an idea I will elaborate on when discussing Jan Svankmajer and *Conspirators of Pleasure*. Put simply, surreal realism is the formal and stylistic aesthetic/practice that foregrounds the uncanny within an ostensibly real universe. *Eraserhead* does this magnificently.

Eraserhead is a very internal film, which means it is a projection completely of David Lynch — and particularly the sensorial *presence* of Lynch's imagery — that extends onto and through the screen to us. (In an interview about *Eraserhead*, Lynch said, "Certain things are just so beautiful to me and I don't know why. Certain things make so much sense, it's hard to explain. I *felt Eraserhead*, I didn't think it. It was a quiet process: going from inside me to the screen."[14]) It is also internal because it is about the irrationality that stems from the internalized fears and desires that become manifest through tangible, concrete things. And while this may be off-putting or hard to decipher (and *Eraserhead* does baffle), it does not mean the film exists solely in a dream-state; the film invokes dream states, but Henry (the protagonist) exists in a reality both known and unknown to us. While summarizing the film is difficult, it is not entirely impossible to offer a plot synopsis. The film begins with a surreal Prologue, where we see a man (Henry) disembodied and floating though twinkling stars in outer space. While the ambient hum-drone of the soundtrack increases, the camera moves directly toward a planet and then glides over the planet's rough surface before entering a room where a man, the Man in the Planet (as he is often called), sits by a dirty, smeared window. Then the camera focuses on the image of Henry, whose mouth opens and emits a sperm-like substance. The Man in the Planet then pulls some levers, and a sperm-substance flies offscreen. The Man then pulls other levers, and we see the sperm stuff splashing into a pool of water. The camera slowly moves into the puddle and into a bright light that consumes the frame in bright luminescence. Then, after the blinding white light, the film begins proper. The rest of the film follows Henry as he negotiates the trials of "normal" adulthood, a familiar Lynch motif: the subversion of classical Hollywood stories (here, romance, family films, melodrama, and horror) through abstract experimentalism and avant-garde style. Henry arrives home to a squalid apartment in a desolate-looking industrial wasteland. He goes to his girlfriend's house for dinner, where he is told she has had a baby. Mary and the baby soon move in with Henry, but she leaves, unable to take the constant crying of the baby. Henry fantasizes about a Lady in the Radiator, a short, ashen woman with huge cysts on her cheeks, who sings a beautiful song about being in heaven. Soon after, the baby falls ill. Henry has a surreal tryst with his attractive neighbor. He again fantasizes about the Lady in the Radiator and enters her dream-state realm where, in a nightmarish sequence, he loses his head, which is turned into pencil erasers. Back in "reality," Henry kills the baby, which causes a cataclysmic destruction of the universe — we see the Man in the Planet desperately trying to "save" things by pulling levers. Henry enters the radiator again, meets his Lady savior, and the film again flashes white before ending.

This brief summary does not do justice to the nuances of the story's dialogue (minimal) and characterizations, its humor, or its incredible mise-en-scène or cinematography, but hopefully it will provide (unfamiliar) readers/viewers with a basic outline. As Steven Jay Schneider says, "[No] mere summation of *Eraserhead*'s narrative, however 'accurate' it may be, can possibly succeed in conveying the tone of this picture, the feelings of unease, uncanniness, and out-and-out horror which result from watching it and which only increase in intensity upon repeated viewings."[15] The real power of *Eraserhead* is in its aesthetic approach to this subject matter. First, Lynch evokes a powerfully surreal world where the uncanny occurs in a hallucinatory, dream-like atmosphere of darkness and light. The brilliant black and white cinematography evokes a netherworld, a post-industrial landscape of fragmented spaces. The darkness of *Eraserhead*—and it is a darkness created through chiaroscuro lighting and many shades of grey — is one of its many strong points. Lynch mentions in an interview, "Darkness to me is a mystery. I don't know what's there and that's what draws me there. It's not necessarily evil, although that could exist there."[16] The expressionistic lighting and cinematography creates the absurd, disquieting sense of dread that stems from the claustrophobic room where Henry lives and the desolate world he seems to live in, which is never made clear. In discussing the setting, and its unique appeal to both himself and his audience, Lynch says:

> In my mind it was a world between a factory and a factory neighborhood. A little, unknown, twisted, almost silent lost spot where little details and little torments existed. And people were struggling in darkness. They're living in those fringelands, and they're the people I really love. Henry's definitely one of those people. They kind of get lost in time.[17]

This "place" is extremely unique to the world that *Eraserhead* generates through its careful construction of mise-en-scène. Not entirely a known, real location, but also not a complete fantasy land, it is a world where everyone seems strange, acts strange, says strange things, and produces strange actions/reactions from others. Again, the setting *appears* recognizable, but also alien; because of this, spectators have the potential to be ill-at-ease — just like the characters in the film. The deliberately slow pacing, the acute framing, the montages of bizarre images, the black and white quality of the film's presence, and the sense of something existing just outside or just within the reality of Henry's (nightmarish) world creates the surrealistic effects sustained throughout.

Henry occupies a world of greyness— where reality collides with surreality, or a place where the mysterious nature of the dream invades the real, creating discomfort and anguish. But, as we shall see, there is room for escape: "Greys are shot against greys, figures emerge out of grey and become translucent."[18] Not quite a dream — though some critics have suggested the film itself is Henry's dream —*Eraserhead* recalls the surrealist notion of making the dream palpable; that is, the tone of the film recounts the ambiguity or eeriness of dream logic. Lynch has also said the film is "a dream of dark and troubling things," which prompts the question: Whose dream is it? Henry's? Lynch's? Ours? Lynch is purposefully cryptic, I think. It is not clear, and that is part of the (surrealist) fun the film provides us. Critics Stephen Saban and Sarah Longacre suggest:

> The remarkable fact of the film is that, unlike other films that are dreams or have dream sequences, *Eraserhead* actually reproduces the dream state in all its nightmarish possibilities and impossibilities. The effect is not achieved by showing someone going to sleep and/or waking up (although there are dreams within the film). The film itself is the dream, the nightmare.[19]

While I do not necessarily agree the film is a nightmare (it *is* nightmarish), it does reproduce dream states — though, again *whose* remains unclear. Yes, Henry fantasizes about the Lady in the Radiator and effectively "escapes" there at the end of the film, which is not a nightmare at all but a surrender to and embracing of his fantasy. And there is a nightmarish sequence involving Henry losing his head. Both of these are meant to invoke or imitate the illogic or irrational that occurs in dreams, which is why one might conclude, "*Eraserhead* drifts like a troubled dream through relative degrees of lucidity."[20]

A second and equally important part of *Eraserhead*'s avant-garde aesthetic is its sound. Throughout the film there is a constant hum/buzz/drone/hiss amalgam of noises, ambient but loud and ever-present; it's another character, really, or certainly another presence in the film that is not just heard but *felt*. As mentioned, there is little dialogue, and it is spread out over the course of the film. But the use of sounds is amazingly done and only complements the unease the film's imagery suggests. We hear industrial noises, like steam and hissing, and prominent drones of buzz and hum. The sounds have been manipulated, distorted, and heightened, helping create the atmosphere of *Eraserhead* — dread, fear, anxiety, darkness. The sound is not used to create an emotional effect, like in typical Hollywood films. In addition to the ambient soundtrack, there are occasional Fats Waller organ tunes and, of course, the song sung by the Lady in the Radiator. None of the music proper is any indication of anything other than accompaniment for the weird things we see. Visually and audibly, *Eraserhead* is a tour de force of form; at times the sound changes with each edit, making us completely aware of its presence and significance to the industrial wasteland that marks the film as place. Both the sound track and image track create the unique atmosphere of *Eraserhead*, an avant-garde arena of juxtaposing and complementary elements that displace congruity with anxious excitement, something that noises do not usually do, especially in mainstream film. But for a major avant-garde film like *Eraserhead*, it is essential in understanding how the film operates and why it succeeds at fulfilling desire — ours and Henry's.

The film is structured in a way that allows us to see how the world operates. The Man in the Planet creates Henry's life and world, and then we see how Henry deals with his given circumstances. It is planned for him, and so when he discovers it is not a "good" life, he seeks change, a way out. A grotesque child or a tryst with his seductive neighbor does not help — they only complicate matters. Henry's recourse is to seek out his ideal life, which is with the Lady in the Radiator. That is his perfect dream; his perfect nightmare may be his total erasing of himself, which he feels is happening, hence his other dream of losing his head. This is why *Eraserhead* creates such feelings of uncanniness: The weird images disturb us but also force us to contemplate their bizarre and irrational meanings. But I should hasten to add that even though it seems we are given Henry's point of view, Lynch does not say. When asked about the point of view of the film, he says, "That's good. I wouldn't even know what to say about that. Maybe if I wrote, I'd do it in the first person, third person...I don't know. It is what it is."[21] Lynch's reply is typical for his discussion of *Eraserhead* (or any of his films) — that its meaning, including a particular perspective — is totally left for us to uncover, which is not always forthcoming. We have to work at it, using associative/constructive techniques in the hopes of making meaning, an important part of avant-garde film viewing. This is why Schneider can conclude,

> [It] should be kept in mind that the "associational" component here — because the activity in question gets placed within a pre-existing narrative context, viewers are encouraged to look for some connections — has always been a favored strategy of experimental and avant-garde filmmakers, and betrays Lynch's debt to these established traditions.[22]

Lynch's debt to the avant-garde tradition is reasonable, and it helps explain why the film is both familiar and horrifying at the same time. Its foreignness is akin to surrealism or expressionism — that is, it situates itself in a particular world that is grotesque and odd, unfamiliar and unknown ... but not completely without grounding. Henry's attempts at normalcy are thwarted, which is why he seeks the idealized life of his fantasy, something almost any viewer can relate to on a strictly personal level. Accordingly, K. George Godwin suggests:

> *Eraserhead*, while it dwells on shocking, even perverse images, seems in-turned, obsessively introspective. It provides an auditory and visual assault which isolates each viewer. The experience becomes intensely personal, unshared. Lynch achieves this by relentlessly applying alienating devices. Foremost among these is the setting of the film in a bleak world not recognizable as our own. The action which takes place there offers no narrative with an eternally meaningful coherence.... [The story] is couched in a collection of bizarre, seemingly meaningless images and inconclusive scenes which shatter the story's familiarity and make it frighteningly strange.[23]

Watching *Eraserhead* is a personal experience, but as a midnight/cult movie, it *does* have a shared, enthusiastic following, which does indeed create a communal viewing experience, however "alienating" the film may seem to be. So while not completely alienating — I think we can discover points of reference in the film — *Eraserhead* functions enigmatically, as something to be solved *and* enjoyed.

If the film deals with locating and embracing an idealized other, then Lynch has done a fantastic job of representing this fantasized dream life in the form of the Lady in the Radiator. Henry's life is full of turmoil; the baby — a hideous fetus-looking thing that is more animal than human — disrupts his attempts at happiness, which is why he turns his somber gaze to the radiator. To Todd McGowan, modeling his analysis after Lacan, this explains Henry's "lack" and his desire for fantasy: "[The] structure of *Eraserhead* separates into two disparate worlds of desire and fantasy — the social reality and the escape from that reality. Throughout most of the film, we see Henry existing in a desolate postindustrial landscape where he continually experiences nothing but dissatisfaction."[24] In some regards, then, the film shows how a person like Henry struggles to reconcile his rational world and his idealized world, which again is one way we can identify with him. Henry tries to accommodate his wife and child, but it does not happen because there will always be an insurmountable tension between thought/action and dream/fantasy that structures the film. In different ways, the entire film is about fear —fear of the present moment and the fear that circulates among people and creates unease, loathing, disgust, and dissatisfaction. And there is always a fear of the new and unexplained. Lynch touches on this in an interview:

> Henry is very sure that something is happening, but he doesn't understand it all. He watches things very, very carefully, because he's trying to figure them out. He might study the corner of that pie container, just because it is in his line of sight, and he might wonder why he sat where he did to have that be there like that. Everything is new. It might not be frightening to him, but it could be a key to something. Everything should be looked at. There could be clues in it.[25]

This might also help explain why Henry's curiosity, of wanting to know more, makes him attach such significance to the hissing radiator. In trying to figure things out in his reality, he keeps coming up short; turning to the fantasy provided through an escape from this reality feels reassuring. When Henry does enter the radiator — that is, his idealized world — he feels comfortable, something that does not quite occur in the world of the baby, the wife, her family, his neighbor, or the wasteland environment. It is why McGowan can conclude, after Henry enters the radiator and embraces the Lady,

> Henry finally escapes the dissatisfaction that has haunted him throughout the film. He discovers the enjoyment that derives from embracing one's private fantasy. Through the act of opting for his fantasy, Henry attains enjoyment but shatters his world and destroys his baby. Of course, this world is bleak industrialized wasteland, and his baby is inhuman. In this sense, Henry's act at the end of the film seems perfectly justified and even appropriate. However, even if the final turn toward fantasy is liberating, Lynch never allows us to forget that it necessitates destruction of the world.[26]

Clearly there is a general assumption here that Henry's world is divided, that there are spatial and temporal dimensions to the separation, and that he exists sometimes simultaneously in both. What is interesting is that the world does indeed fall apart when Henry elects to enter is idealized fantasy; The Man in the Planet loses control of his levers, sending sparks flying while he grimaces in pain (or defeat) as he loses control of Henry. It is quite a brilliant and startling ending, and its presentation only adds to *Eraserhead*'s mystery and surrealism. It is arguable if Henry *really* escapes, but that is beside the point (perhaps). He momentarily or temporarily leaves the plane of reality.

Lynch's film, "[the] most beautiful and brilliant film ever to become a midnight blockbuster," follows historical avant-garde tropes: ambiguity, the image-as-presence, the audio sound track as dominant feature, the combination of surrealistic and expressionistic tones and décor; it is a compelling blend of different-yet-similar characteristics that make *Eraserhead* as daunting as it is imaginative.[27] And while I have offered suggestions on how to read it, the film really is open to multiple interpretations, as it should be as an avant-garde film. Again, Lynch reiterates this when he maintains the film does mean something to him, but certainly should mean other things to different viewers:

> That's the way it ought to be. The whole film is undercurrents of sort of subconscious.... You know, and it kind of wiggles around in there, and it's how it strikes a person. It definitely means something to me, but I don't want to talk about that. It means other things to other people, and that's good.[28]

Elsewhere, when discussing secrets and the terrible desire or compulsion to know more, Lynch says, "There are some secrets that, when you learn them, something comes with that learning that is more than the loss of knowing. These kinds of secrets are different. And I believe in those. But talking about how certain things happened in a film, to me, takes a lot away from the film."[29] (This also refers to the exact thing used for the baby; Lynch has steadfastly refused to discuss what the baby is — animal, latex animatron — which, according to Hoberman and Rosenbaum, establishes "[the] taboo aspect of [whether the baby can be defined as a living creature, and] is, in fact, central to the film's impact."[30]) And finally, addressing ways in which to "enter" and experience the film, Lynch says, again cryptically, "In *Eraserhead*, there are a lot of openings and you go into areas and it's all.... There's sort of like rules you kind of go by to keep that feeling kind of open and I don't know, it's real important to it. It's more like a poem or a ... more abstract, even though it has a story. It's like an experience."[31] *Eraserhead* is definitely a prototypical avant-garde *experience*. Its audio-visual assault on the senses is unlike many other movies. And it is also funny — there is a dark humor circulating throughout, especially in the scene with Henry's girlfriend's family, but Lynch has succeeded in making a film that is an intellectual puzzle laced with surrealist humor and wit. *Eraserhead* "seems to capture the process of dream consciousness with remarkable precision," making it a film ready to be interpreted in many ways.[32] Its complete inversion of classical narrative strategies makes it an indelible avant-garde film, and allows for Lynch's "desire to 'speak directly' through the [film], combined with a faith in the audience's own eyes and ears, [producing its] strange, sensory power."[33] *Eraserhead* forces us into its strange and beautiful world, and once there we cannot remove ourselves—and that is a magical, thrilling thing.

The Falls

The Falls (1980) is one of director Peter Greenaway's most clever puzzles, a film about structure—though it is not necessarily structuralist—and organizational schemes, and a witty deconstruction of the documentary genre, government control, fictional re-creation, and ornithology. But this does not even begin to scratch the surface of everything that makes *The Falls* unique and avant-garde. A monumental effort (the film lasts over three hours), it is "a work of mind-boggling intrigue and wit" that addresses not just perception, but the means by which we receive information and the various manifestations comprehension takes.[34] Devised as a documentary about the victims of an unknown occurrence, the film strives for authenticity while undermining the precepts of the documentary film. Taken as a work of fiction, the film asserts its form over content, though content shapes form. Greenaway's inimitable style, which would mark him as a serious international director of experimental films, really begins with *The Falls*; the films he made prior to it helped establish its aesthetics, but with it, Greenaway has made something truly unlike anything else—something so different, unusual, and essentially *good* that the BFI awarded it the best British film in thirty years, which, I think, makes it also one of those rare films that remains completely outside the mainstream but received brief critical attention simply because of its complexity and not at all because it was embraced by anyone within the channels of film commerce.

The Falls structures itself with an abstract organizational system centered on lists, catalogues, scientific data, and the alphabet. Further, it offers numerous artistic allusions, linguistic strategies and puns, and encyclopedic information that is alternately discussed, contained, stretched, and theorized. In other words, Greenaway has made an epic film about the nature and use of images, words, and thoughts, presented as a documentary yet filtered completely through a fictional lens, so that we never are quite sure what is real, supposed to be real, truthful, authentic, or entirely false, though Greenaway would have us believe the entire premise—which is what ultimately occurs, despite the absurdity of its structure. *The Falls* certainly addresses the "longstanding prejudice regarding experimental films that if the pleasures offered are other than narrative (for instance, in visual style, montage, *homage*, tantalizing juxtapositions, and *ideas*), the films will be cold, distant, pretentious game-playing."[35] To some extent, this happens with *The Falls* because it is an intellectual film and asks the audience to work. It is full of repetitions, ellipses, references to itself and other things, and it constantly reminds us that its very appearance is essential to deciphering its subject matter.

The plot of *The Falls* is complicated but not impossible. The film documents ninety-two people who have been struck by a VUE — Violent Unknown Event — that affects their mental and physical being. A voice-over tells us that the ninety-two case studies will feature names of the victims drawn from a Directory, the Event Standard Dictionary, and who are connected through their names, all commencing with the letters "FALL." The catalogue's subtitle, "An Investigation Into Biography," informs us of the way the film will approach its subjects while also stressing the official report itself as structured, catalogued, and numerical. For instance, as the ninety-two names scroll over the opening shot, we are told they are "taken from the latest edition of the Directory, published every three years by the committee investigating the Violent Unknown Event — the VUE for short." But the film is still more intricate than this simple premise. As Bart Testa describes it,

> *The Falls* has as its main narrative conceits two overlapping fictions. The first is the "VUE Directory" and the "VUE Commission" that maintains it. The second is the Violent Unknown Event itself. The VUE Commission has made a three-and-half-hour compilation documentary from its Directory that Greenaway's *The Falls* calls "The Falls." This isomorphy is offered as a deadpan assertion, and it is crucial to the film's vastly extended irony, which involves a fictional-yet-systematic denial of Greenaway's authorship, of his own expressivity. It is also an affirmation that the film's own fictional system is the gargantuan task of a collective, institutional author, the compilers of a vast anthropological archive.[36]

This structure makes the film not just knotty in its presentation, but particularly and distinctly avant-garde, because it is built around the premise of accumulation and dissemination of learning, watching, and reacting. The VUE itself is obscure and mysterious, and the government's Directory and attempt at justification is equally puzzling. All of the characters profiled or documented in the film have undergone transformations; the narration describes them all in detached, straightforward, monotone. "The VUE Directory Commission itself gains its authority and its aura of objectivity by maintaining a certain bland innocuousness characteristic of bureaucracies, a willed anonymity that means safety."[37] Some of the transformations are irrational: one changes sex, one changes skin color, others have become immortal. But all of the victims suddenly have a vast knowledge of birds, and there is some indication that the physical transformations that most go through resemble birds (indeed, the film is full of references to birds, the name of birds, and images of birds). What does it all mean? There is no explanation given, making it all the more intriguing. The scatological information the film yields provides a basis for the VUE Directory: The event in question happened one night and affected 92 million people, all of whom speak one of ninety-two new languages. The minute details of each of the ninety-two victims chronicled in *The Falls* makes it both funny and maddening; the build-up of such abundant detail overwhelms the spectator. Each segment (of the ninety-two) is brief, and the film starts over with the next person. Greenaway is "concerned with organizing diverse forms, still, documentary, live action, interview, reportage, within an incoherent text."[38] *The Falls* is a document about documentation, and Greenaway both provides a framework for examining his document and a way to undermine it through its status as a game of jokes and linguistic fascination, and through its sheer fascination with the way discourse alters perception. As David Pascoe suggests, "For Greenaway, what is real is precisely that physical truth which cannot be represented."[39] Likewise, Amy Lawrence concludes, "In *The Falls*, Greenaway parodies every technique which traditional documentary seeks to substantiate its ties to reality. Of course, by the end every aspect of the film has been revealed to be a complete fiction."[40] The dialectic Greenaway creates makes the film's experimental style all the more impressive. Its combination of structuralism — its structural film techniques— and mock documentary foregrounds its formal construction over any kind of narrative coherency, causal logic, or plot development. In essence, it "could be said that [Greenaway] deconstructs structuralist practices the way he deconstructs documentary practices. Fundamentally, Greenaway trusts no system and is suspicious of any structure's potential to become hegemonic, even when a particular system is deployed with a counter-hegemonic intent."[41] *The Falls*, then, is an avant-garde film that is intellectually stimulating because of its content, its style, and its formal (de)construction.

We are told at the beginning of the film that "the ninety-two people represented in this film all have the names that begin with the letters F — A — double L." Hence, we get people named Fallanway, Falla, Fallstoward, Fallfree, Fallwaste, and so on. Lawrence points out that "as the incongruities pile up, basic identification of each subject becomes less and less certain. Names get changed and explanations for how and why point to conspiracy, fraud, and the heavy hand of the commission itself."[42] In some cases, the featured victim reverts to previous names (though they still begin with "FALL"). Sometimes photographs of victims are replaced by actual real-life people, blurring further the lines between documentary and fiction. In an interview, Greenaway admits, "*The Falls* poses this problem: it consists of fictional material presented in a documentary manner. According to the English school of filmmakers, documentary reality *is* reality. But we know that the pursuit of reality is a waste of time."[43] Greenaway is in some ways asking the spectator to acknowledge the falsity offered through his "documentary" film, that a certain reality can never be attained, which is at the core of *The Falls*. According to Testa, Greenaway "imaginatively underscores the fact that fiction and nonfiction films share systematic properties: shaping materials that always imply that they existed before finding their place in a construct," a foundation predicated on the ability to build and destroy simultaneously.[44] This is why the viewer constantly has to work while watching the film; "self-reflexively, Greenaway solicits from the viewer our recognition of how arbitrary rational systems and the procedures of data-formation are joined by the institutional will to order."[45] But the nature of representation is called into question: how does one document and explain the unexplainable (VUE)? Do words tell the truth as much as images do? Do neither? The fact that ninety-two separate languages were formed as a result of the VUE is significant to Greenaway's agenda. "Ninety-two languages and ninety-two subjects suggests a connection between identity and language to the extent that each human being's use of language is so distinctive, it becomes an idiolect."[46] Greenaway's use of language and different linguistic devices, both spoken and recorded, is encyclopedic. It is why Lawrence concludes, "[The] material contained within each segment and the style in which it is presented are largely unpredictable. Living lives beset by incongruity, explainable solely by non sequitirs, redundancies, odd emphases, and the errant detail, the subjects of *The Falls* exist in a conceptual landscape out of Borges via Lewis Carroll."[47] The point made in *The Falls* is that the more that language is used, the less decisive it becomes. It can *tell* us facts, but the facts are untenable. In a manner befitting of documentary filmmaking, which Greenaway mocks, language is often used to "tell the truth" about the subject or object documented. Accordingly,

> Documentary cinema offered Greenaway his most attractive ready-made form because of its word-to-image relation. In most conventional nonfiction expository films, the formal system is arrayed so that language provides cultural, discursive, and interpretive anchoring for the image. This image-language relation is Greenaway's preferred found-format in ... *The Falls*. As a formal and lexical system, the use of this found-format's language strengthens the "textualizing" tendency of his films and has collateral effects on his style of shooting and editing.[48]

What the movie demonstrates is how Greenaway simultaneously takes the referent away from the sign, hence creating a gap between image/word and meaning/intent. Avant-garde films often ask us to question the representation of things (and reality), and they often offer particular ways to view reality through new visions. Lawrence likens this method to "conspiracy," wherein conspiracy equates to a way of reading the text(s) Greenaway puts onscreen, both verbally and visually (and, of course, audibly too). She says:

> Conspiracies (planning and carrying out frauds and hoaxes) become models for how spectators make sense of fact *and* fiction. In watching a film, we reconstruct characters, events, and their authors by imaginatively fusing the evidence presented into a coherent unified whole. The perception of character, event, and author is dependent on faith; characters, whether "real," based on fact, or entirely fictitious, are the product of *our* imaginations. As Greenaway reveals, the process is thus open to illusion and sleight-of-hand. Documentary in particular becomes a magic act that Greenaway is at pains to undo. Like the canniest of magicians, first Greenaway performs his trick, shows you how it was done, then he does it again.[49]

In essence, what Greenaway does with *The Falls* is create a new form of storytelling that breaks down generic tropes, builds new ones, destroys them, and then repeats the process. It is no easy task to assemble all of the material Greenaway has with the film; its all-encompassing strategy forces itself upon us, both in terms of its accumulation and through its formal strategies that utilize structuralism and documentary. *The Falls* willfully subsumes the notion of art (the film *The Falls*) and artifact (the documentary "The Falls") as true testaments to perception, each instead offering alternative ways to perceive *at the same time*. It is truly remarkable, and completely avant-garde.

Greenaway has long been a maverick director, and *The Falls* was the first of many adventurous works that touched upon various themes but always carried the distinct mark of personal vision and style. He has continually made works for exhibition in museums, which stem from his excessive cinematic style: His films are so conceptually dense that film cannot contain the limitless and visceral nature of his cinematic exercises. Trained as a painter, Greenaway sees the richness of the history of visual art, best captured in painting, as the driving force behind his avant-garde cinema:

> I wanted to make a cinema of ideas, not plots, and to try to use the same aesthetics as painting which had always paid great attention to formal devices of structure, composition and framing, and most important, insisted on attention to metaphor. Since film is not painting — and not simply because one moves and the other doesn't — I wanted to explore their connections and differences— stretching the formal interests to questions of editing, pacing, studying the formal properties of time intervals, repetitions, variations on a theme, and so on.[50]

This sentiment adequately summarizes the goal of *The Falls*. The film does not have a narrative in any traditional sense and instead relies upon the formal queries or investigations regarding time, space, repetition, variation, metaphor, and pacing. Like many of Greenaway's films, it quotes and references architecture, landscape, painting, scientific theory, myth, and tradition. Because he is interested in metaphor, the mise-en-scène is elaborate, dense, multifaceted; attention is given more to how a scene is framed and shot than it is to montage, forcing viewers to get accustomed to the pacing (often slow) and to the style, where process itself becomes the locus for meaning, as opposed to simple plots. *The Falls* could arguably be the best example of this kind of filmmaking. The Directory's archive consists of a structure that also structures the film. In summing the objectives of the film, and particularly the methods Greenaway uses in this double form of structuring, Testa asserts that Greenaway's inversion of narrative affects the material in the film and the way we see it. It is a valid point. He suggests:

> *The Falls* inverts the process by which narrative arises. Modern stories arise out of elements in an arrangement that we habitually term representation: the tabulation of the narrative archive that consists of semantic items, stock oppositions, icons, and actants. It is Greenaway's recurring gesture to return these to that originating precondition of representation: by thwarting narrative dynamism, he returns the narrative elements to the archive, to the table-like grid structure. This inversion, achieved through the entropy of diegetic complication at which Greenaway excels, always remains his favorite strategy and the means by which he always is a structural filmmaker. Nonetheless, Greenaway archives, for the first and last time, the hypertrophic and programmatic realization of this strategy in *The Falls*.[51]

The self-reflexivity found in *The Falls* (and indeed in much of his filmic output) takes the form of radical free play of meaning that typically does not lead to narrative closure. Greenaway straddles art cinema's illogic and ambiguity, avant-gardism's experimentalism and subjectivity, and modernism's inherent questioning of realistic representation. All of these tropes or characteristics can be found in *The Falls*; it conflates the author and the text like no other Greenaway work because it manages to use documentary as a fiction, and fiction as a documentary. The film ironically tries to present a method of containing chaos and catastrophe (the VUE) while it simultaneously becomes increasingly chaotic itself. There is a constant apprehension or anxiety in *The Falls* because the film tries to make chaos calm. It is also why, ironically, "The logic of the format (orderly, sequential) is precariously balanced against the progressively more incredible tale contained within it. The more information we receive, the harder it is to believe what we hear."[52] The film is always using different types of structuring mechanisms to obtain order, from lists to grids to maps, and they all lay claim to establishing a specific means by which to control the uncontrollable. He uses an array of documentary styles, including interview, voice-over, and still images, to create the documentation. Pascoe suggests, "Particular discourses, such as maps, catalogues and recorded data, may be understood as tools for creating order from chaos, providing particular opportunities for making connections whenever this is socially and politically appropriate."[53] Hence, the government's zealous role in making "The Falls," which rests precariously on systems of organization based on bureaucratic obsession and piecemeal assumptions. Greenaway's own work in editing documentary films for the British government during the 1960s obviously influenced the way he criticizes and lampoons their rigorous attention to detail, though the detail itself is also the structuring device for his film. As Lawrence notes,

> For the former editor and director of informational films, the explanatory power of organized data (mathematical, visual, linguistic, scientific, and artistic) becomes progressively less tenable the more it is insisted upon. All of Greenaway's feature films are obsessed with the way principles of organization (alphabetical, numerical, statistical) have a tendency to become ends in themselves.[54]

The Falls is a remarkable "documentary" about the way we receive information. Its avant-garde status rests upon its labyrinthine structure, its audacious story, and its method of representation, which, as mentioned, is a unique combination of fact and fiction that takes perception into new territory. It uses language as a tool for investigation and representation — in the form of voice-over and in the detailed cataloguing — as opposed to a straight image representation. It therefore puts forms of cinematic (and actual) discourse in doubt, as it complicates an entire way of rendering images as opaque instead of entirely referential. It is a film about trying to capture the splintering forms of the world through image and word, where fiction trumps reality, and where art measures truth over artifact. Or, more precisely, it asks us to question how film form, as presented in documentary or fictive ways, is authentic; "literal-minded application to the factual and the material in his discourse is one of the strongest characteristics of Greenaway's work."[55] Because of this, one must approach *The Falls* with the understanding that it asks us to be open-minded toward its unbelievably large cache of formal devices, allusions, and theoretical musings—as many good avant-garde films do.

Tetsuo: The Iron Man

One of the most original and influential films to emerge from Japan over the last twenty-five years, the highly surreal and avant-garde *Tetsuo: The Iron Man* (1989) is a mind-blowing and ear-shattering excursion into a visual "metal machine music." It has many characteristics of uninhibited amateurism — but in a good sense — and a strong and acute visual sense, not to mention a stylized cinematography reminiscent of silent cinema (light/shadow play, expressionism, pantomime acting). But to be sure, the film is difficult to watch and hard to decipher; its narrative takes a backseat to the audio-visual style director Shinya Tsukamoto creates through graphic black and white photography, expressionistic close-ups, and intensely provocative imagery both sexual and mechanical in its straightforwardness. *Tetsuo* is about the merging of metal and flesh, and its graphic representation of this blending or commingling leaves one exhausted (and perhaps confused) by the end. Make no mistake about it, though, the film is a no-holds-barred tour de force of stop-motion animation, live action, unforgettable imagery and avant-garde aestheticism that makes it dark and foreboding, prescient and thought-provoking.

The plot of *Tetsuo: The Iron Man* is convoluted and bizarre: A salaryman and his girlfriend hit a man crossing the street with their car. They take the body to a forest, where they discover he is not quite dead. The woman, now aroused, initiates sex with her boyfriend against a tree as the dying man watches. It turns out the man they hit with the car is a "metal fetishist" who had just inserted a metal rod into his calf before running into the street and being struck by the car. In a kind of beyond-the-grave revenge scenario, the metal fetishist causes a woman on the subway to mutate and attack the salaryman, who, as a result, begins to change himself into a metal-man. His transformation reveals some of the more graphic and astonishing sequences in the film. At one point his penis turns into a giant drill, which, when used by his again-aroused girlfriend, quickly leads to her demise. The salaryman eventually becomes more and more metal, which leads to a final showdown with the original metal fetishist, who is still alive. During their combative sequences, ingeniously shot in stop-motion photography and animation, they merge to become one giant metal-human who vows "to conquer the world."

This brief synopsis does not do the film justice; there are larger themes that emerge from the ideas Tsukamoto puts forth. However, knowing the plot is actually not that essential in appreciating exactly what Tsukamoto has done with his film. It is the style and the form that make *Tetsuo* a real avant-garde film.

Japanese film expert Tom Mes has described *Tetsuo* as a watershed film in both Tsukamoto's career and in broader terms relating to Japan's film climate during the late 1980s. Arguing that Japanese filmmaking was not as prestigious during this time as it once was, Mes suggests the international acclaim and recognition, not to mention the outright awe, toward *Tetsuo* created a new generation of fans, fan culture, and energy in Japanese cinema. Mes's argument makes perfect sense when considering the inventiveness and outright lunacy of *Tetsuo*. Mes says:

> What *Tetsuo* did was to create a following, in particular overseas. With his film, Tsukamoto found and perhaps created an entirely new audience for Japanese films. These were not the cinèphiles that had grown up with Akira Kurosawa, Yasujiro Ozu and Kenji Mizoguchi and who discussed the work of the New Wave in the pages of *Sight and Sound, Film Comment* or *Cahiers du Cinema*. This was a new generation of fans, who regarded *Tetsuo: The Iron Man* not as a rupture with an established image of Japanese cinema, but as a film that fitted snugly into a pantheon of genre works that included Ridley Scott's *Blade Runner*, James Cameron's *The Terminator*, David Lynch's *Eraserhead* and the work of David Cronenberg, Sam Raimi and Clive Barker.[56]

Such intertextual references suggest a strong affinity with cult cinema, both in type of films and directors Mes links to the film, but also in the development of a particular kind of audience. As a result, *Tetsuo* has been accepted as one of the most groundbreaking films made during the "cyberpunk" era, a notion that suggests a subgenre of science fiction writing (and film) that examines or situates the body-as-performance, loss of self, and the search for identity and meaning in a future urban environment that has become over-reliant and dependent upon, or dominated by, technology. In this manner, *Tetsuo* is, arguably, a film about the encroachment of technology on the body and the inevitable merging of the two. Mes also points out that Tsukamoto was not familiar with the term "cyberpunk" when making *Tetsuo*. However, it certainly appears that the significance placed on machinery might be echoing cyberpunk literature, where, traditionally, the body becomes a site of investigation into its role in an increasingly machine-like atmosphere. But *Tetsuo* has much more to say about the ways metal/flesh creates moments of anxiety and eroticism. Despite its graphic nature, the film explicitly deals with the way man-as-machine not only has the power and potential to destroy, but also to multiply and carry forth, mainly through melding machinery-as-flesh. This point is made clear by Tsukamoto himself:

> The combination of metal and flesh came in part from the wish to express eroticism. I found it very difficult to do that in a direct way and I felt I needed a metaphor

to express that aspect, which became the invasion and erosion of the body by metal. I tried to make an erotic film by way of science fiction, to express eroticism through iron.[57]

The film shares with other science fiction (and horror) films the idea of technology run amok, but here it is shown in a manner totally original because the metal fetishist in the film *wants* to insert metal into his body, *wants* to merge with the salaryman, and *wants* to build himself stronger and faster by accumulating other people and metal objects in his quest for domination. We see this quite clearly at the end of the film when the fetishist and the salaryman have become a gargantuan pile of twisted and fused metal, standing tall in a heap reaching the eaves of roofs and towering over cars in the street. Different faces protrude from the metal body, suggesting they have begun making people into metal/flesh entities that make up part of their own large body. It is truly nightmarish, grotesque, and rather darkly humorous. The entire imagery is also avant-garde, and its collage-like stop-motion animation calls to mind Jan Svankmajer, while its noisy soundtrack and expressionistic lighting recall David Lynch's *Eraserhead*.

Mutation is a traditional theme in monster movies, and one may be so inclined to call *Tetsuo* an avant-garde monster film. *Tetsuo* is firstly an audiovisual assault on the senses, an overwhelming cacophony of heightened sounds, industrial music — literally sounding like metal on metal — and eye-popping cinematography. Its surrealism and expressionism also make it avant-garde. The film is experimental in many ways because of these unusual stylistic and formal choices. For instance, the actors move jerkily, almost in pantomime or in modern dance; there is very little dialogue, making it atypical for a feature film; and the kinetic, frenetic pace of the cinematography, editing, and visual presentation establish a film difficult to watch, yet pleasing for its aesthetic accomplishments. It is both an indication of Tsukamoto's style and a highly charged and enigmatic take on modern society, where industrialism, consumerism, and materialism become one. As Mes states:

> *Tetsuo: The Iron Man* marks a point of maturity for Shinya Tsukamoto as a filmmaker. The personal style that evolved from the do-it-yourself approach truly becomes a signature style, a fusion of stop-motion animation, varying film speeds, handheld camera movement, sound effects, music and rhythm, all combined in the editing. This maturity is witnessed by the fact that the film's style succeeds in telling the story almost entirely by itself; *Tetsuo* communicates with the viewer through its style. Style has gained a narrative function, meaning that form equals content.[58]

This description also suggests just how avant-garde the film is; because it relies on its visual strategies to communicate with us, it eschews almost all types of classical narrative or formal construction. *Tetsuo* is a hyper-active, hyper-real take on surrealistic and apocalyptic cinema, where the bombardment of images, cut sharply, jaggedly, and rapidly, force us to be highly attuned to its idiosyncratic schemata. The coalescing of metal and flesh is actually quite stunning, even when it is totally bizarre, such as when the fetishist inserts the metal bar into his skin or when the salaryman's face sprouts coils, metal bars, and metal springs (the giant rotating and whirring metal penis notwithstanding). While Tsukamoto may be interested in how machinery or technology can overpower us to the point of *becoming* us, the film really is more a shock-horror avant-garde art film — perhaps the only one of its kind.

Tetsuo has an amazing power to entrance the spectator. Besides its visual acuity, it is incredibly loud. The constant pounding of the industrial music, the heightened sound effects, which include a thunderous scraping when the girlfriend sticks a fork into her mouth, do as much to dazzle as disorient, given the convoluted story, which, admittedly, is not told to us in any manner befitting traditional narrative cinema. The story must be deciphered only after the viewing (or after several) because Tsukamoto gives no indication what is happening onscreen. Not much is explained, in other words, so it is left up to the audience to fill in the gaps or essentially create the story, which is something quite common for avant-garde films. Along with *Tetsuo*'s strong visual sense, the noise and lack of clear narrative are a couple of the reasons Mes considers the film to be much like a silent film, admitting "this might sound like an odd way to describe a film as noisy as this one." He says:

> *Tetsuo* contains very little dialogue and what dialogue there is adds nothing to what is already conveyed through the form. There are indicators to be found in the film itself that suggest that the similarity to silent film wasn't certainly coincidental. Firstly there is the use of black and white film, a choice initially based on the film's theme of fusion with metal (the color of the film mirroring the color of metal), but a suitable one for a contemporary silent film. Additionally, image compositions, lighting patterns, performances and make-up are all strongly expressionistic in nature: high contrast light, over-accentuating face paint, exaggerated body movements.[59]

I would suggest that all of these descriptions or descriptive categories for silent film really illustrate why the film is avant-garde. Its experimentalism can be found in the lighting, the performances, the costumes/make-up or, really, the entire cluttered mise-en-scène, and its expressionistic and, as I have mentioned, its surrealistic imagery.

Tetsuo: The Iron Man can also be aptly described as an experimental cult film. It has a loyal following — much like Tsukamoto does as a filmmaker — but it has never entered the mainstream nor has it moved beyond art houses, midnight showings or, most importantly, ever left its greatest popularity base: DVD. Like many cult films, its subject matter is off-putting, risky, offensive, and somewhat gory. But it also shares with some cult films the lasting quality of its influence. As already mentioned, the visual style — indeed the *visionary* style — the film presents allows for a deeper appreciation for the type of cinema Tsukamoto participates in, where his films, and *Tetsuo* in particular, makes "the audience for his films relatively restricted, probably due in no small part to a style and subject matter that are too intense and overwhelming to appeal to mass audiences, either at home or abroad."[60] Tsukamoto is also avant-garde in attitude as much as he is in style. Again, this kind of defiance of mainstream cinema and the production machines that guide Hollywood or national cinemas (like Japan's) marks him as a true iconoclast and auteur, a lone filmmaker following his own rules and methods, much like the canonical avant-garde filmmakers in the United States. It is important to remember that the way a film gets made can also sometimes make it avant-garde. As Mes suggests,

> [Tsukamoto] is the sole creator of his work. Evidently he works with a cast and crew, but he is one filmmaker who can truly be called independent, one who writes his own screenplays, raises his own money and produces, designs, shoots, edits and frequently also stars in his own films. Directors sometimes complain that they never got to make the films they care about most. Shinya Tsukamoto, however, makes only the films he cares about most. Very seldom accepting offers to work with an outside producer, he is literally uncompromising when it comes to cinema.[61]

Tetsuo: The Iron Man is an uncompromising film. Its kinetic pacing, visceral gore, surreal representations of man/machine and metal/flesh, and sophisticated themes about tormented individuals revolting against and/or conspiring with metal machines is extraordinary. A "monster" movie unlike any other, *Tetsuo* was the first of its kind that spawned many imitators, but none that are as wildly innovative, avant-garde, or breathtaking as it is. Its cinematography is brilliant and its propulsive soundtrack cloyingly perfect, while its hectic, confused, and exciting editing create a chaotic and often claustrophobic experience that is as visceral as it is imaginative. It is certainly an acquired taste, but once viewed it likely will cause one to want to see it again, simply because of its originality and experientialism.

Begotten

Perhaps there is no better way to describe watching E. Elias Merhige's *Begotten* (1989) than painful: Its content exudes pain, and our witnessing of it does as well. One of the most visceral films ever made, *Begotten* is an experimental tour de force that is as baffling as it is mesmerizing. A surreal, metaphysical, horrific, wordless, and sometimes beautiful avant-garde film, *Begotten* offers a (non) story — and I suggest "offers" rather than "tells" — about primitive myths, divine birth, and punishment, a cryptic passion play about the Earth's birth and torture, told quite literally (with blood and gore) but meant to evoke a more metaphoric, symbolic realm of experience and understanding. Ultimately, "*Begotten* hovers between traditions, creating an ambiguous experience that challenges viewers' sense of decency, their ability to understand, and their patience — while simultaneously providing both narrative fascination and sensual engagement with the film's remarkable chiaroscuro."[62]

The film begins with a grisly and grotesque scene where a character called

"God Killing Himself" disembowels himself with a razor, arms flailing, blood splattering, and entrails dropping. From this emerges a second character, "Mother Earth," who, having been inseminated from/through the God's entrails, eventually gives birth (in another horrific display) to the third enigmatically named character, "Son of Earth — Flesh on Bone." Mother Earth and Son of Earth — Flesh on Bone then go on a kind of pilgrimage, traversing a barren landscape where they suffer intense pain from some type of nomadic tribe. Eventually they die, and from their grave a new cycle of life begins: At first we see flowers wither and die, then, more pointedly, flowers sprout and grow, shot ingeniously through time-lapse photography. None of these characters' names are revealed until the final credits, which suggests *Begotten* is a film to be deciphered while watching (active viewing), with little interference, and then considered anew after getting the names. In other words, watching it once, we never truly know who these people are or what exactly is going on, even though one can deduce. But once we know the names, a narrative of primitive myth, rebirth, and cyclical behavior emerges. Merhige also shoots the entire film on a grainy, dirty, sometimes pixilated black and white stock; he also rephotographed each minute of the film, creating an otherworldly (and highly surreal) image throughout. This hallucinatory effect adds to *Begotten's* mystery — a film that appears as hazy as its contents, where form matches its content.

Slow, methodic, mystifying, and highly formal, *Begotten* is not a film that will win many viewers with its gore, elusive narrative, and strange and disturbing imagery. There is no dialogue to help us, and the sound track is full of ambient cries and moans, human breathing, and other indecipherable noises (animal cries, scratches, etc.). Existing "somewhere underneath conventional cinema," *Begotten's* main attributes come from its visual inventiveness— immediate, off-putting, yet mesmerizing if one is willing to accept its oddness.[63] The film looks like it is a document of another era, an ancient ritual/remnant from centuries ago, "found" and projected as some sort of rune, testament, or relic. The film's surrealism stems from the idea of its hazy, unrecognizable quality, a record of an event (a documentary), and a fictional recreation of the same event, that casts shadows on its authenticity or "realism." This is done quite on purpose. In discussing the film's hypnotic power of suggestion and its "oldness," Merhige says:

> The idea of time working on the surface of the medium itself was important to me. I wanted to create a sense that the film was going through its own trial, its own sufferings. The idea of ruins, of things falling apart — not because of the overt violence of one body against another, but through the subtle violence of time — has always fascinated me. I wanted *Begotten* to look, not as if it were from the twenties, not even as if it were from the nineteenth century, but as if it were from the time of Christ, as if it were a cinematic Dead Sea Scroll that had been buried in the sands, a remnant of a culture with customs and rites that no longer apply to this culture, yet are somewhere underneath it, under the surface of what we call "reality."[64]

Indeed, what Merhige has done is create a film that *looks real* and has stood the test of time, an object discovered. The fact that the film defies (ostensible) logic or any sense of "reality" (indeed, it affects a "hyper-real" just as much as a surreal world) makes it all the more intriguing. *Begotten* is an experiment in representation; its strange and horrific images are grotesque to be sure, but it forces us to engage in its unrelenting — and stunning — vision of creation and death. As Merhige himself says of this difficult process, "There's a very peculiar and fascinating psychological process going on, of simultaneous release and repression. On the one hand [viewers] *see* it, but on the other hand, they don't want to see it. These polarities are at odds with each other."[65] *Begotten*'s bizarre abstraction is so intense that it does provoke discomfort and attraction *simultaneously*— a strange mix of the lyricism found in poetic trance films, the repugnancy of gore, and the ambiguity of incomprehensible symbols or metaphors. It is a film, too, that ultimately is personal for spectators because we are forced to create meanings for ourselves.

Begotten's experimental structure, which is on formal, stylistic, and thematic levels, produces an active viewing experience — something, as mentioned, that is essential to avant-garde films. In addition to the many ways one might understand the film, Merhige also utilizes canted camera angles, extremely slow pacing, and chiaroscuro to reveal the elemental landscape of *Begotten*, a landscape equally created through viewer imagination and stylized filmmaking. As Merhige suggests,

> *Begotten* is a chrysalis made of archetypal materials, gestures, and forces that defy the "moral" and rational structure of meaning. The film is a launching pad for the mind, a "watering hole" where the imagination drinks to intoxication. The drama of *Begotten* is in the anthropomorphic rendering of forces that nobody can touch or see, but are there right at the edge of every moment — in the film, they're right at the edge of your perceptions. The twentieth century mind has become estranged from the very foundation of creation. *Begotten* is not new; it finds its home in histories and ages when the Imagination was not fantasy, but in fact the substance of God. The historical narrative ... is the voice of the collective Imagination. This is precisely how *Begotten* works: it activates a bridge that runs between universals and individuals. In other words, *your* narrative is part of the same process that produced *Begotten*.[66]

Begotten is a very organic film, and, judging from Merhige's remarks, it is a film that also is associated with the mental properties of perception and conception. It creates as it tests our patience and disorients our normal film expectations. Eccentric, weird, surreal — however you label it, *Begotten* is an impassioned argument for total involvement. The images are so unique and extraordinary that there is no other means of understanding it unless you disengage from your own reality and enter its allegorical (biblical?), otherworldly presence. Seeing "God" eviscerate Himself or the torture and death of "Mother Earth" and "Son of Earth" takes deliberate and considerate effort and fortitude — just like the creation of the film itself.

Begotten certainly can be considered a surrealist film, since its imagery is mostly unexplainable, unrecognizable, associative without clear referents, and possibly related to the unconscious. But Merhige seems to be interested in heightened reality — a surrealist engagement with the real — so that "the photographic image acquires the unique value of a 'precious article of exchange' only in as much as it transcends the mere reproduction of reality, in order to become the faithful yet indeterminate, and therefore disquieting, reminiscence of an irretrievable object of desire."[67] The power of *Begotten* stems from its "disquieting" attractiveness — its ability, that is, to present the unrecognizable "object of desire" in ways befitting the avant-garde sensibility of paradox. *Begotten* also defies traditional codes of conventional filmmaking, undermining means of comprehension through representational strategies that are incongruous or illusionary. *Begotten* is not a readily approachable work; its graininess, ambient soundtrack, and intensity make it an eccentric curiosity that is puzzling to discover and behold. Both engaging and disengaging, the film plays like either an exercise in self-indulgent artistry (I would say it does not) or an ambitious experiment in the power of cinema to transform us. Playing like a dream with symbolic/allegorical characters that undergo extreme trauma, the film is a highly subjective experience. In his review of the film, Richard Corliss said *Begotten* is a test "for the adventurous eye," adding,

> It's as if a druidical cult had re-enacted, for real, three Bible stories of creation, the Nativity and Jesus's torture and death on Golgotha — and some demented genius were there to film it. No names, no dialogue, no compromises, no exit. No apologies either, for *Begotten* is a spectacular one-of-a-kind (you wouldn't want there to be two), filmed in speckled chiaroscuro so that each image is a seductive mystery.[68]

This "mystery" is its appeal. Watching it is both a physical and mental undertaking, which is good. Its violence is surreal and disturbing, a phantastic, phantasmagoric, primordial ritual of strange beauty. God's unflinching death, Mother Earth's birthing, and Son of Earth's burning, beating, and burial are grotesque and difficult to watch, but the shadowy black and white imagery, which is sometimes unrecognizable, creates an unusually sympathetic portrait; if indeed we are to mourn the death and destruction of God/Mother/Son, then we can because of the immense mistreatment and suffering. And when flowers wilt and then bloom, we *are* offered salvation.

Begotten is an exercise in avant-garde filmmaking that tempts, teases, and *hurts* the spectator. Its unconventional narrative strategy — no dialogue, strange noises — and its formal eclecticism (rephotography) makes it immediately difficult, but not completely foreign, if one can make it through and give it a chance. As a contemporary avant-garde feature, *Begotten* is unparalleled in its ingenuity and craftsmanship, a real testament to the power of experimental filmmaking.

Archangel

Perhaps no other contemporary filmmaker is more adept at creating strange and beautiful worlds than Guy Maddin, where Expressionism meets Surrealism, melodrama walks steadily with silent-film conceits, and experimentalism couples nicely with amateurism. Guy Maddin's film world, simply put, is so artistically and aesthetically personal and idiosyncratic that it deserves special attention as its own weird genre. A truly visionary and iconoclastic director, Maddin subjects us to places so peculiar and stories so uncanny and inadvertently complex that they require particular attention in terms of their overall status as avant-garde films. In other words, Maddin's unique approach to cinema is unparalleled; no one working in film today is as far-out, far-flung, or voraciously adventurous as Maddin. *Archangel* (1990) is merely one of his brilliant features that demonstrate his unnatural leanings in film aesthetics, which are entirely avant-garde.

Maddin's films are certainly acquired tastes, given his affinity for silent cinema, part-talkies, surrealism (though he often disavows allegiances to it), expressionism, mannerist styles of acting, "primitive" sets, hallucinatory stories in strange places, melodrama, detailed mise-en-scène, exquisite cinematography, and (of late) rapid montage editing. All of these elements work together to create films "lost in time." They seem displaced from any specific temporal or spatial orientation, even when they have "actual" settings, like *Archangel* in the town of Archangel, or *Careful*'s mountain haven. One critic even suggests, "[Maddin's films] look out of time in that they seem to prophesy a future that has already gone by. He is the laureate of Futurepast."[69] But each film is carefully constructed, nuanced, and very funny. Even while we are admiring the films for their astonishing eclecticism, we inevitably find ourselves laughing at the absurdity stemming from the story, the language, the playfulness, the props, or the acting, though none of this humor is meant to be critical of his work. In essence, "His sense of humor is witty, self-deprecating, and unconsciously wicked. So are his films: their self-consciousness is a strength, their weirdness comforting ... he has already shown the workings of an alchemy that transforms the strange, the curious, and even the disgusting into a world of beautiful bewilderment."[70] Maddin's films are full of different stylistic and formal innovations; he changes perspectives by alternately using close-ups and long shots, and creates melodrama and focus through iris shots (an admittedly anachronistic technique but highly suitable to Maddin's inimitable universe) and occasional tinting or toning of the film strip (again, a technique used primarily in silent films, but certainly part of the history of avant-garde film as well). He is an intuitive filmmaker, where image often trumps narrative for dramatic effect (hence his films are typically described as "part-talkies," using intertitles, sound effects, and little dialogue, which is the case with *Archangel* in particular). Described as a "throwback" filmmaker, which is part of his charming insouciance, Maddin "proves that it's still possible, even in today's bland and hypertrophied movie climate ... to make feature films that couldn't have been made or even imagined by anybody else."[71] More than anything, Maddin revels in the gorgeousness of the anachronistic absurd, the deadpan inappropriateness of illogical, incongruous, or even silly things, and the demented enchantment discovered within the (sur)realities that configure his plots and unconventional characters. In short, though not an avant-gardist who looks to his avant-garde forebears, his works immediately can be recognized for its avant-garde sensibilities, charms, wickedness, and technique — but he is definitely in a class of his own.

Archangel tells the story of dashing one-legged Lt. Boles, a Canadian soldier wandering through and into the town of Archangel, an outpost in Russian Siberia. Set during the Bolshevik Revolution, the film sets in motion an absurd premise of criss-crossing loves, lovers, and people who need love. The central motif for the film is amnesia, a trope Maddin uses in other films, but perhaps here it reaches its apogee. Almost everyone in Archangel seems to suffer from some kind of memory disorder. Boles is in love with Iris, but she is dead; and when he meets the Soviet Veronkha, he believes it is his dearly departed Iris. The opening of the film is a touching and hilarious monument to love. Called "The Dirge of Lt. John Boles," it has Boles clutching the ashes of his departed Iris in a small urn. Boles looks wistfully over the side of the boat when the captain informs everyone on board (en route to Archangel) that he must confiscate all of their liquor. Boles's urn is indistinguishable from the bottles, so the captain takes it and throws it overboard. And so Iris vanishes (again), and Boles is left to reminisce, mistake others for Iris, and try to carry on. Boles is again heartbroken; "This brief scene — a mélange of emotional loss, confident error, and dutiful acceptance — is like a microcosm of the film."[72] When he meets Veronkha, she unfortunately is married to the Belgian pilot Philbin, who keeps forgetting he is married to her. Veronkha, meanwhile, mistakes Boles as Philbin and so keeps falling deeper in love with him. A second woman, Danchuk, also falls in love with Boles because she is so dissatisfied and disgusted with her own husband, Jannings. In this weird triangle of love/lust/loss, Boles follows a literal map with a giant "X" that marks the spot for discovering romance, where he hopes his occluded memory will help him realize which woman — Iris, Veronkha, or Danchuk — he will end up with forever. Though the plot sounds fairly straightforward, its execution is lost amid the flow of images, the lack of dialogue, the absence of exposition, and the various moments where warfare is foregrounded and used metaphorically.

Archangel is quintessential Maddin: strange and somnambulistic, it is fixated on behaviors that come from forgetting. Called a "post-traumatic fever dream," *Archangel* also is a spherically structured narrative roundelay that keeps repeating (or retreating) back on itself, as Boles's amnesia anchors Maddin's odd tale of the Bolshevik uprising, the rituals of war, and the fleetingness of love.[73] The whole film is reminiscent of those strange movies made just after the advent of sound cinema, when "part-talkies" arose and straddled the innocence of silent film with the supposed modernity of talking figures. The film "clarifies Maddin's cinematic allegiances, making it clear that his principal points of reference were the lost codes of late silent/early-sound cinema."[74] The films from this era were experimental, especially the Soviet films that *Archangel* somewhat echoes, but also the highly melodramatic films that involved stories that showcased emotive, mannerist acting. *Archangel* is similar to these films also because of Maddin's flair for re-creating texts that resemble, pay homage to, mimic, and even parody their sensibilities, when the "trepidatious transition between silent films and 'talkies' [employed] sound subjectively. Characters' voices hover before their lips, aiding in the creation of a world of unreality, perfectly suited to a story populated with amnesiacs."[75] Maddin has always used a trademark blend of silent-film attributes (irises, intertitles, sound effects) bordering on nostalgia, and amplified it through an awareness of further film history: melodrama, experimentalism, and expressionism. As Maddin said in interview about his predilection for silent-film tropes and stylistic similarities,

> At the time [of *Archangel*] I liked to justify it to people at film festivals and so on with the simple logic that silent movie vocabulary has been discarded, and it's free to be picked up off the busy roadside of the filmic industry. I was a scavenger picking up these lost vocabulary units and was free to use them in any way possible.... I felt like I had a palette full of options at all times: I had intertitles, mime, dialogue, voice-over, and I was going to use them all.[76]

Indeed, *Archangel* uses these characteristics of silent film language and makes them unique to the world Maddin creates in and through them. He has said elsewhere, "*Archangel* utilizes Soviet editing techniques and minimal camera movement — both Eisenstein influenced. But I don't copy anything intentionally, it's subconscious plagiarism. The silent era used a whole roster of similar phrases repeated in each film."[77] This is important to remember, because even though one might align *Archangel* with silent film, it is a contemporary film and bears hallmarks of a postmodernist sensibility about the way images can be deployed for varying purposes; in other words, Maddin does not copy anything — he calls our attention to a lost era of filmmaking while making it entirely his own.

Archangel utilizes primitivism in the best sense of the term: The sets are minimal, the special effects crudely effective, and the innocence of the characters and their behaviors (and the actors' ability to capture this innocence) is completely engaging. The battlefields and the recreated battles are so staged (and there is even a section of the film, called "Illumination," that uses *tableau vivant* to recreate dark and humorous famous battle scenes) that it may be easy to laugh at the seeming amateurism. But it is not; Maddin is able to generate so much through such a small(ish) environment. Fake snow, fake airplanes, fake carriages— none of it is too distracting if you believe in the method Maddin uses to establish the world of Archangel, the town, and its environs, and the entirety of the film *Archangel* itself. William Beard, in his indispensable book on Maddin, describes *Archangel* as the best example of "the peculiar chemical process of the Maddin cinema — the emergence from a most unlikely and even uncompromising collection of indigestibly disparate components of a strange, absurd, poetically moving, and finally emotionally compelling aesthetic object."[78] Admittedly, the film can be as alienating as it is engrossing, but it reveals itself through its multi-layered plot (confusing at times, but nevertheless original and absorbingly silly), its careful attention to detail (rendered through mise-en-scène and its silent-film associations), and its outright experimental nature. Its ability to float in a region between two eras of filmmaking, and its uncanny use of different styles, really suggests it will remain in a state of hallucinatory somnambulism, where sound teeters off into silence, and silence prefigures any and all forms of communication. It is also perhaps why Caelum Vatnsdal can rightly conclude, "[*Archangel's*] themes of amnesia and confusion rise up off the screen like opiate to infect the audience; viewers seem to have as much trouble identifying the characters as the characters do with each other."[79] Conceivably, the amnesia motif helps assure the film's status as being too paradoxically *advanced* — despite its primitivism — to be remembered beyond its cult boundaries. Maddin himself acknowledged the film as having a "high walkout quotient."

Loss, jealousy, and amnesia are all disquieting conditions or mental states that ultimately create a rather elegiac tone for *Archangel* (as they do in other Maddin films). In addition to being the main theme of the film, amnesia is also the cultural metaphor used in representing a moment in history (the Bolshevik uprising), as well as the film's links to a bygone era of filmmaking that has created a type of cultural amnesia for too many spectators brought up on mainstream cinema. For Maddin, "Amnesia explains how people can forget their responsibilities to family, loved ones, and friends. This dominant narrative motif appears in many guises throughout his work ... reaching its apotheosis in *Archangel*."[80] Forgetfulness is a constant state for the characters in the film, and Maddin seems to suggest that this constancy also structures people's lives in general; disavowing the past through amnesia allows one to erase bad memories, pain, suffering, lost loves, or the trivialities of everyday life that affect the psyche. As Dana Cooley remarks,

> Maddin's *Archangel* ... is an allegory for memory, loss, and grieving as processes that haunt human existence. The characters in this film are constantly forgetting or are on the verge of forgetting their loved ones. They misrecognize and mistake, perhaps even willfully at times, in order to align the past with present wishes.... Given the precarious and perennially new world of Maddin's films, his characters occupy what seems to be a perpetual state of amazement. Dazed, meandering over the flickering screens that Maddin creates in homage to his filmic roots, the characters are constantly so startled by scenes, so shocked by revelations, that they can't quite seem to figure out why their experiences would be so jarring, nor recall what has brought them to their present state. They cannot remember but they are constantly bewil-

dered, or on the threshold of amazement and uncertainty, perhaps precisely *because* they cannot recall and so must as every moment meet the world unknowingly, so without the reassurance of foreknowledge and familiarity.[81]

As this long explanation suggests, the characters in *Archangel* exist in a realm akin to a half-etherized state where memories are created through present moments instead of the past, which ultimately creates the precarious relationships among the characters. It is why Boles sees Iris in Veronkha, why the soldiers continue to fight, and why Philbin, most tellingly and amusingly, forgets he is married *on his very wedding night*, and so tries to seduce the hotel desk operator after he goes downstairs for only a brief moment after leaving his wife upstairs. The lack of any solid foundation or familiarity with faces makes everything ritualistic—from romance to war. Boles can only recall his lost love's name ("Iris!" appears repeatedly in intertitles and on the lips of Boles) and his sense of patriotic duty. "In other words, in the absence of any sense of history, personal or otherwise, Boles finds refuge in the comforts of ritual itself. For him, playing soldier, fighting enemies, and making war is necessary precisely because it needs no explanation to be meaningful."[82] All of the characters in *Archangel* are somehow afflicted with a sense of loss, making them (and the film) opaque, plagued by obsessions ranging from duty to apoplexy brought on by amnesia and mustard gas, itself a narrative motif that helps explain *some* of the characters' behavior. In an interview, Maddin expands on this:

> [Mustard gas] serves a dual purpose. *Archangel* is about fogginess and forgetfulness. Mustard gas was a neat visual equivalent for the cloud of confusion the players find themselves in. I made it up for fairytale purposes to give the movie a folklore feel, hence the Iris, apple, and eye symbolism. Filigreeing on simplicity with careless boldness is the basic freedom a storyteller has. It's also an excuse for the story being more unfocused than I had initially hoped.[83]

Maddin admits the film's "fogginess" stretches beyond the visual motif and into its somewhat unintelligible narrative, though I would suggest this is what gives the film some of its charm, and certainly contributes to its avant-garde standing. The film offers a radical sense of discombobulation—both in its style and its themes. But beyond its shadowy state of forgetfulness, *Archangel* is really about love and the loss of love, a common theme in many mainstream films, but given a drastic, experimental makeover here. Stephen Snyder suggests, "The convoluted psychology of the characters could be described as the condition of wanting to be loved without risking one's life or self-image to receive such love. Openness is not a possible choice...for it seems to open the door to identity loss. Amnesia can be a way of saving one's sense of identity as well as losing it."[84] Either way, the film's evocation of a lost era and a lost place exemplifies Maddin's filmmaking style and thematic preoccupation with surreal melodrama, archaic allusions, and strange characters.

Archangel contains scenes that are weird and often grotesque (the most infamous being the strangulation-of-another-by-one's-own-intestines; it is monstrous *and* funny). Maddin has crafted a fairy-tale world where mystery dominates the action and brief instances of dialogue. Thoroughly avant-garde in its technique and approach to filmic representation, the film reminds one of the power *to create*—its world is so convincingly established that you really do feel the languidness, the forgetfulness, the outright bizarre and outlandish character behavior and mannerisms as if it were so. To understand Maddin is to understand his passions, motivations, eccentricities, and his unapologetically intense and personal cinema. William Beard's description of Maddin's first feature, *Tales from the Gimli Hospital* (1988), is equally fit for *Archangel* (though I will caution that Beard is not making the analogy). He says:

> Everything in the film that tends toward abstraction falls immediately into this category: the soundtrack crackle, the images sometimes smeared and fogged almost to indecipherability, the pacing sometimes slowed to the point of emptiness, the aggressive blankness or disconnection of soundtrack events, the bewildering juxtapositions of styles and tones and imitative modes, the manifold disruptions of any straightforward reading of events or meanings—these may all comfortably be described as "avant-garde."[85]

Each Maddin film uses some of these methods, and each offers a unique simplicity that couches the avant-garde characteristics in formal innovations, enough to deem Maddin's films elegantly mesmerizing works of art. *Archangel* is the type of film that forges new directional forms of intensity and processes that are anti-commercial and stubbornly personal, subjective, and eccentric, where silent cinema aesthetics, "surreal tapestries of precisely pitched tableaux blending absurdist satire, warped horror, eccentric gore, and wrenching melodramas" (not to mention perverted humor and dark material), make this film (and Maddin's others) so incredibly unique that it defies categorization, except to say only that it is *out there*.[86] But Maddin is no mere fabulist or conjurer; he is a dedicated craftsman, artist, and surveyor of film culture and history. *Archangel* is both a historical epic and a melodramatic love story, and it is also about the simple glory of its images: the Illumination scene, the battles, the Love Prologue. Maddin constantly reminds us of the past through the film's visionary look and its main theme of amnesia; oblivion, or the slip into oblivion, is a reminder about the preciousness of the present, even though it is untenable at best. The oddness (and oldness) of his films is what makes them appealing. The sparse dialogue, the title cards, the use of sounds and music, the exaggerated gestures and facial expressions—all inhabit *Archangel* to such an extent that despite whatever one's criticism of it, it must be admired for its sheer audacity and limitless creativity in replicating a bygone era. But he is doing more than simply repeating the tropes of silent film. He uses them in such a way as to uncover a new method of filmmaking that invites us to journey with him through the past's relics that connote many things and offer many suggestions to extend practice to theory, and theory to practice. In other words, the sense of muted and muffled memory haunts and permeates Maddin's films.

Maddin has said, "I'm a gently quiet director who seeks viewer investment. I'm working towards beauty, placidity, and exquisite strangeness."[87] *Archangel*, like so many other avant-garde films, typifies this sentiment. Maddin's ability to maintain viewer investment is key to appreciating his films; if you are not invested, they will prove too elusive, foreign, different, or just plain weird to handle. But if one is to see how he carefully uses parody, homage, pastiche, exaggeration, simplicity, and other techniques and styles, then his world comes alive and knocks us unlike anything else in contemporary cinema. I will again revert to Beard and his summation of a key scene in *Archangel*, where a whipping occurs primarily because it is the accepted ritual, as it relates to Maddin's oeuvre:

> This, then, is one of the principal functions of the past, or fantasy-past, in Maddin's imaginative world: to find, or to suggest, a place which is full of unacceptable ethical and ideological limitations but which is capable of a solidity and coherence that may even only be there because it is imagined to be there in this act of fantasy-creation. The simultaneity or fusing of these opposite qualities (fantasy-historical-world meaning, real-world ethical knowledge and skepticism) is one iteration of the project going on throughout Maddin's cinema: the project to hold incompatible paradigms somehow together.[88]

In essence, Maddin's films bring together so many disparate chords to create a polyphonous whole that to describe them as avant-garde is not even enough to merit their formidable dreaminess and talent. *Archangel* is a film that is only one of Maddin's unmatched and incomparable masterpieces.

Bullets for Breakfast

Holly Fisher's collage film *Bullets for Breakfast* (1992) is both a deconstruction of the Western genre and a filmic essay about representations of women. It uses John Ford's *My Darling Clementine* as the backdrop — or template — for Westerns in general, and intersperses footage of photographs and other images of women, particularly art postcards of Renaissance paintings, all of which have women as the object of the artistic gaze, though the images themselves are innocuous simply because they are generally accepted well-known, or well-worn, pictures of Renaissance paintings. Fisher seems to be interested in the way multiple lines of narrative inquiry create incongruent, contrasting conclusions about representation. Counterpointing Ford's landscapes and masculinity with, respectively, shots of landscapes in Maine and underscoring the women as objects of beauty through Renaissance painting, and positioning women at work (the film also offers sequences of women working in a fish-smoking house) *Bullets for Breakfast* is the kind of collage film that ultimately suggests how found footage combines with new images in a densely textured and interrelated tapestry.

In addition to the various images, Fisher uses different forms of audio narration. The pulp–Western writer Ryerson Johnson reads selections from his autobiography, and feminist poet Nancy Nielson recites her poetry. Both instigate a dialectical play of forms of representation: While being first-person accounts of life experience, they are used to help distinguish and distort the images in ways that create tension, ambiguity, and humor. Overall, *Bullets for Breakfast* is a film that foregrounds its hybrid structure — part documentary, part collage film, and part narrative — to expose the ways stereotypes are formed and perpetuated through myths (John Ford's landscapes), ideals (Renaissance art), or memory (fiction, poetry, autobiography). Its strange eclecticism makes its "message" unrestricted, in that we get a sense of how images and words combine to form lines of inquiry or even lines of ideology; but there are no definite means by which to subsume one to the other — they always intermingle and outlast one another in perpetual interplay. Part of the aesthetic of collage filmmaking is to disrupt causal narrative, to present different forms of narrativity. A collagist quite literally takes various forms, which can be various forms of media, or visual and audio rhetoric, and combines them in ways antithetical to expectation, since we have to work to uncover how they are used.

Bullets for Breakfast is really a film about the women depicted through imagistic representation, whether in Western films or painting, or other forms of verbal discourse, like autobiography, pulp novel, or poetry. It is experimental in its form, and Fisher aims to break linearity apart in order to show how women have been illustrated through the seeming cacophony of collaged images, voices, sounds, and texts. The juxtaposition of the readings, for example, highlight the ways biography counters history and fictional re-creations of historical circumstance, making the personal "visible." Fisher has described the film as "a Western filtered through a post-feminist sensibility," and that her film "shows ... that history is relative to who is writing and when."[89] History, as portrayed through narrative film, can sometimes be discursive or didactic, which I think is part of Fisher's critique of a film like *My Darling Clementine*, which is both romanticized and moralizing. By contrast, *Bullets for Breakfast* is a Western that makes one reconsider the tropes of the Western and how they have been used in popular culture, or how they are interrelated with other forms of representation that can be misconstrued as forming a linear, "real" history. Watching the clash of images—when superimpositions intrude on *Clementine*, or when the fish-house workers toil—creates the irony and jarring sensibility Fisher wants.

Collage films are based on the notion that a complete (re)assembly of different elements will creates new meanings of expression, representation, and aesthetic sensibilities that may owe something to the parts or may stand alone (or both). In this way, the film functions from a critical perspective. With *Bullets for Breakfast*, Fisher is analyzing the perceived accepted roles of women, especially in how the masculine identity is constructed (in the Western), and therefore situates the woman as "other" or opposite to the man. Also, the film deconstructs the Western using *My Darling Clementine* as the template. In creating the assemblage that resulted in the finished film (the sounds/texts/images), Fisher said:

> To lay in the sound effects of bullets was amazing, to just feel the power of those tiny pieces on the soundtrack. Bang! You realize, ah, so that's how you get power. I'm hoping, in the language and structure I'm trying to evolve, to find another way to make a powerful statement — not through loud noises and dramatic plot structure and cliffhangers.[90]

The key point made here, that Fisher is interested in the *evolving* of language and structure, reminds us of the film's experimental nature. Hoping for progress, change — evolution — is something many (if not all) avant-garde filmmakers try to achieve. To develop a new form of cinematic language, which collage films do, and also to resurrect structure by divorcing it from plot or "cliffhangers," is a particular way to enhance the meaning through theme and form. For example, by including a selection of art postcards, the film announces a clear dichotomy between our understanding of the iconography of the Western and a more nuanced understanding of the way images of women have helped shape memory, meaning, and ideological representation. As Fisher says, "I knew by single framing these cards in location I could explore questions of representation and perspective in a nonverbal way."[91]

Bullets for Breakfast is often quick; the editing and music/sound effects work in tandem to present the stories of the images. The film is a dissection of the particular codes that direct meaning. It also is an examination of genres — Westerns, melodrama, documentary, collage — that often dictate emotional response. Here, though, Fisher breaks them down as well, suggesting that meaning is not predicated on what we ought to know, but on what we do know. *Bullets for Breakfast* is an example of collage filmmaking that ultimately presents us with a new way of reconsidering sexual difference. In using disparate elements, Fisher asks us to view images (to read texts) anew. Collage films generally offer a wide array of images and sounds, and places them in carefully edited positions for informational purposes. In this sense, *Bullets for Broadway* provides a very distinct way of (re)interpreting reality inasmuch as it gives us a new way of understanding differences between men and women that are based on recycled images or photos or texts.

Lyrical Nitrate *and* Decasia

Both *Lyrical Nitrate* (1991) and *Decasia* (2002) are types of avant-garde films that are (or can be) alternatively called found footage, collage films, compilation films, or abstract-montage experimentations; however, most often they are a combination of all of these aesthetic and/or formal techniques. As early as the 1920s, and in some cases before then, experimental filmmakers began formal and theoretical investigations of film's capacity to render ephemeral and phenomenological moments of time in fractured, collagist, and abstract ways—meaning they explored how fragments of film are expressive, enigmatic bits of ontological spaces forged through celluloid. Quite literally, found footage films assemble fragments of (primarily) early silent films into avant-garde features that follow conceptual frameworks that re-imagine the original bits of film in new ways that distinguish them — and the completed found footage film — as something at once familiar and exotic, continuous and ruinous, and disembodied yet interrelated. In some regards, the found footage film (and I will refer to both *Lyrical Nitrate* and *Decasia* as such) are aesthetic, philosophical, and even metaphysical inquires into the past and how it shapes, conflates, or disintegrates memory, time, and/or fragments of things captured, preserved, and finally lost. They are archives of previous moments of creation. Cinema, and particularly the cinematic form of found footage films, "is a trace of historical time rendered *visible*: it invents a new relationship to time and contingency. This "time," in our common encounter with films, can become even more *visible* if gaps and accidents fragment and stain the film," as is the case with both *Lyrical Nitrate* and *Decasia*.[92]

Rediscovering the very materiality of decayed film and the fragments of early cinema forms the basis for much found footage films. Using an assortment of film clips in a particular manner creates entirely new meanings and associations for the spectator, so much so that the question arises over the very authenticity of meanings of the originals that serve as the sources: Anything and everything becomes connotative. According to Andre Habib:

> *Found Footage* is an open category of avant-garde or experimental cinema that presents, according to Catherine Russell, all the aspects of an "aesthetic of ruins," often animated by nostalgia, or by apocalyptic themes, which resonate through their style, based on fragmentation, elliptic narration, temporal collisions and visual disorientation.... Found footage ... appears as a form of cultural recycling, often informed by a social critique, by discourse concerned with the end of history, and subverting the material through ironic and violent montage.[93]

Several ideas here emerge that are (mostly) characteristic of fond footage films. Experimental filmmakers interested in rediscovering the past-on-film have often exploited older films for the poetic possibilities created through fragmentation, ellipses, recycling, spatial-temporal dislocations (or collisions), and perceptual confusion based on the composite form of found footage film. The avant-garde montage that gives rise to the found footage film valorizes "lost" and "discovered" cinema. The concept of an "aesthetic of ruins" seems apt for describing the found footage film, especially the experimental nature (or dialectic) of using something "dead" to create a "resuscitation." Again, Habib sees this idea of the ruinous, which I take to mean the literal destruction and eventual disappearance of an artifact, as a fundamental aspect of the found footage film:

As with ruins, the film object had to be taken out of its regular function, so that it could *appear as a cultural artifact....* When an object loses its physical integrity, its shape and coordinates that permit it to actualize or accomplish a certain number of actions or tasks, we say this thing is in ruins. But it is by falling into ruin that it appears as *image*, since its usage has ceased to replace it.[94]

The found footage film, then, is arguably an attempt to re-capture the essence of something ruined through its image, here preserved on celluloid (and, in particular, nitrate, which itself disintegrates over time), and re-presented in fractured, fragmentary form. One may also refer to the "ruin" of any film narrative since the found footage film assembles various images from disparate sources to create the final film; yet narratives *do* emerge as the compilations assert a form of associative montage that serves as a new narrative based on the tension that arises from the non-linearity of the found footage and its juxtaposition or collision in the finished film that establishes original, innovative means of storytelling.

The formal experimentation that is part of the assembly of found footage films is a decidedly avant-garde one, in that it eschews any type of classical filmmaking. There is no essential construction of mise-en-scène, no "original" cinematography, and no script that outlines a narrative. These types of avant-garde films use rephotography and optical printing to re-imagine and reuse "footage that was originally shot for another purpose, whether portions of the finished film, or footage that was never used in a film."[95] Found footage films offer a radical disassociation of content and form that becomes reconstructed, reconfigured, and creates a "dialectic between memory and oblivion, preservation and destruction."[96] *Lyrical Nitrate* and *Decasia* both use images that stand alone and work in tandem to create something gloriously new, evoking a melancholic nostalgia for the images lost in space and time, while also thrilling us with their remarkable aesthetic technique. Jonathan Rosenbaum suggests watching such films (particularly *Lyrical Nitrate*) is "closely related to the voyeuristic appeal of pornography, specifically the old-fashioned stag reels."[97] He clarifies this by adding, "The experience of watching these fragments is, like the fragments themselves, fleeting and therefore tantalizing, suggestive and therefore provocative — and so far off the beaten track of what's supposed to be viewer friendly in our culture."[98] Indeed, the fragmentary nature of the found footage film is part of its charm, since it allows for multiple kinds of viewing and cognitive experiences. Further,

[These] films untie the knots of narrative continuity to focus on gestures, facial expressions, visual tricks, producing a poetic montage of "distant fragments," revisiting the damaged remnants of a damaged history or the ghastly beauty of decomposed celluloid. They document a gaze in time, offer a look at a history of looking — the multifaceted visual culture of a certain age.... These montages all produce the impression that a world is disappearing *before our very eyes*, and that the *display* of this disappearance has something to do with the very nature of cinema.[99]

Since many found footage films are composed of silent films, they are examinations of nitrate film (hence the title of Delpeut's film). Nitrate was used in cinema until the 1950s; it was a highly organic, perishable, flammable material that was out of necessity and safety replaced by an acetate stock ("safety film"). It decays by itself (hence Morrison's title of *Decasia: The State of Decay*). The idea of a simultaneous acknowledgement of the older image as an existing monument and its corresponding disappearance provides the viewer with a confrontation with the past, articulated through assemblage yet expressed fully in the present as an experiment in filmmaking technique. This is one reason why found footage films are unique and can arguable suggest the fundamental ways perception van be articulated more fully through avant-garde cinema.

Lyrical Nitrate

In many ways, *Lyrical Nitrate* is an abstract homage to a lost era, a lost art — silent cinema. Using a wide variety of assorted clips — newsreels, documentaries, travelogues, fiction films — from different sources, director Peter Delpeut has crafted an ingenious experimental feature whose shifting color tones and tints, and close-ups of faces and ephemeral objects, make it beautifully hypnotic, the ghosts of the past hovering slightly within our minds as they penetrate our deeper consciousness. None of the films that Delpeut uses are identified until the final credits, so we are dealing with a film unmoored, a film seemingly uncomplicated or undemanding in its presentation of the images, yet ultimately complex in its hybridity. *Lyrical Nitrate* is indeed a highly lyrical film, as the title indicates, where "its lyricism stems from the material properties of the film material: the different coloring processes, often of astonishing brightness, are not only preserved; they are often accentuated by biochemical degradation."[100] Delpeut also slows down the speed in some places, creating an eerie, uncanny effect, as most silent films were shown at higher speeds. This affective manipulation of the rate at which the images are projected allows us to see the beauty that nitrate stock emits, as well as the beauty of the enigmatic images. Images are lost in time without referents — they infer alternate spaces of reality, which gives the film its poetic force. Delpeut abandons the stories behind each clip, instead giving fragments that float by, carrying their own private stories. The film does have a loose structure; it is divided into six categories, indicated by intertitles: "Looking," "Mise-en-Scène," "The Body," "Passion," "Dying," and "Forgetting." This arrangement only suggests a connection among the images through subject matter, a pattern of association. Most of the clips are run at different speeds, including freezing them. Some are sepia or blue, some have musical accompaniment (from the likes of Bizet and Puccini), and a handful have sound effects. A certain surrealism emerges in their foreignness; strange pictures of women walking through a garden, a crucifixion scene, giggling children, men crossing the street and eyeing the camera, railroad cars, and even a glimpse of a movie theater audience all suggest a netherworld presence. The strange collage of documentary and fiction yields a fascinating ambiguity. We see images of boats on water, cityscapes and country idylls, melodramatic scenes and comedic ones, people at work and play; it is the ephemeral nature of these "lost" fragments of people and objects and scenes that creates for us a wonder that is both anthropological (even archaeological) and historical, as it is avant-garde and experimental. "The fragment has become a mode of knowledge and of poetic expression, carrying its own history."[101] The film ultimately becomes a celebration of the past and a cautionary tale, an allegory of cinematic history that relates memory as abstract, searching for something tangible.

Lyrical Nitrate is an amalgam of genres simply because it has many images extracted from their original narratives, and it plays with how one constructs meaning through narrative or the lack of a coherent one. In this regard, the film

> borrows heavily from *found footage*'s aesthetic of ruins, while refusing its more ironic, theoretical or visually radical aspects. From the compilation films, it retains a *documentary* dimension, as trace or testimony of past visual practices, while keeping those films relatively anonymous [, a negotiation of] space between avant-garde practice and archival exploration.[102]

It is visually stunning because it is a compilation of *nitrate* film, and also because Delpeut is doing something completely innovative himself cinematographically, especially with the deep focus, the slowing of speeds and the tinting, though I would suggest there is a theoretical basis for understanding how these images work on a cognitive level, especially in terms of their associative or attached meanings. Delpeut seems to be addressing a fundamental aspect of moviegoing — and one I have stressed is essential to the understanding and enjoyment of avant-garde film — perception. The film may seem "deliciously prurient" because of its very otherness, its exclusive nature of outsider status deeming it experimental, "old-ish," and anathema to the giant Hollywood productions that tend to forget the silent era altogether.[103] The discontinuity of the film's structure and narrative make it difficult for audiences used to classical modes of filmmaking, but it is the type of movie that fascinates because it takes the opposite extreme: an avant-garde collage film that not just stands in opposition, but declares its beauty and wonder in every frame, whether it is an image from a melodrama, a biblical film, children at play, adventure film, scientific examination, or exterior shots of trains, landscapes, and street scenes.

Lyrical Nitrate is a self-reflexive film about deterioration — decay, ruination — that asks us to consider how film is used on an ontological level. Many of the images in the film are already at the point of decomposition, so it is decidedly harder to make them out; yet that is precisely what makes them compelling. Perhaps the ending signifies the self-reflexive tendency of nitrate the best. It is a scene from a movie about Adam and Eve in the Garden of Eden; a figure representing Father Time stands nearby, spinning a globe. Its image is haunting, mesmerizing, stunning: it appears to be in color, but it is too hard to tell because the film has deteriorated so much that the surface is full of bleeding colors, from white to red to green to yellow — all because the nitrate is "dying." This ending to the film is poignant: Adam and Eve partaking of the forbidden fruit and immediately burned — but in this case literally, in front of our very eyes, as the film deteriorates. This effect produces some of the more ambiguous and strong reactions to the film as a whole. As Rosenbaum suggests, "Delpeut places the most extreme examples of deterioration at the very end of his compilation, and the emotions they arouse are rather complex because the effects of deterioration are in some cases as beautiful and mysterious as the images that are being devoured."[104] The disappearance of the film image — Adam and Eve — and the disappearance of the filmstrip itself creates the elegiac, melancholic tone that lasts through much of the film. To Habib, this final scene encapsulates Delpeut's endeavor to simultaneously create a film about ruin as it ruins itself. He says:

> The elegiac tone of the film culminates in a final blaze, which seems to consume all the film fragments seen up to this point, as if this blaze represented their inevitable destiny. During the last minutes of the film, the celluloid strip becomes unstrung, destroyed by mold, to the point where the imprinted scene appears shredded by rapid flashes of colored blots and filaments, bright flares, sumptuous ochre stains.... Here we find the most striking alliance between the medium and its "content" — the destroyed celluloid performatively exemplifies the scene, by ruining it. Amidst the flickering serpentines of dismantled celluloid, we see Adam and Eve sharing the forbidden fruit, on the verge of being plunged into a temporality that is no longer exempt from corruption or contingency ... and this is precisely what the film exposes.[105]

It is here where *Lyrical Nitrate* exposes the lyrical nitrate itself as something to behold and something as rich in texture and meaning and nuance as any image that has come before it. Its transient existence shows its beauty in color tints, lights, and surfaces. Ultimately the film gives the impression of rediscovery-through-destruction, an uncovering of the "auratic" and autonomous status of nitrate at the very moment of its disappearance. The discrepancies, discontinuities, and the fragmentation work paradoxically *to create* continuities among the images (and their pattern placement), as well as suggest a stronger link between the undiscovered/lost past and the immediate present. In exquisite detail, *Lyrical Nitrate* posits that cinema exists as a fragmented yet lyrical art able to capture, retain, and destroy. It is in this idea/l that the film more profoundly, perhaps, is about how "the detail ruins, from the inside, the unity of the work: detailing, in truth, is ruining. The detail forces the part to manifest itself, disjointed from that unity. It is this *stripping* — this powerful extraction of the part from its totality — that is at work in [*Lyrical Nitrate*]."[106]

DECASIA

Decasia is much like *Lyrical Nitrate* in its construction and execution: Filmmaker Bill Morrison uses archival and found footage to construct an ode to decaying film. In some regards it is more experimental, though the themes are similar. Morrison uses decaying film stock as his raw material, focusing on a more ideological aspect of decay and how it is inevitably similar to humanity's mortality. It is a film about creation and destruction, where decomposition of film serves as a metaphor for existence. In an artist's statement that accompanied retrospectives of his films, Morrison makes this point clear. He wrote, "Like our own bodies, this celluloid is a fragile and ephemeral medium that can deteriorate in countless ways." The nitrate film used to create *Decasia* takes on an expressive means, and its inherent qualities—like those of *Lyrical Nitrate*—render it an artifact itself. The film uses a variety of images—travelogues, newsreels, fiction films, wildlife documentaries—to create an experiment in the style of collage films and found footage films, where the randomness of images both stand alone and work together to create the story. The film is made up of assorted black and white images of silent cinema, evoking a tone caused by the very way the nitrate film is displayed — with holes, cracks, scratches, blotches, and light refractions that make the fragments unconditionally obscure and surrealistically beautiful and bizarre. To add to its strangeness, "Each frame of *Decasia* was stretch-printed two or three times, slowing down the image and enabling the eye to capture the passing of the film strip and the stains, marks, and holes that have attacked it, making this struggle between image and matter a fascinating experimental laboratory."[107] Morrison is attempting a more involved look at how the past mingles with the present in the form of presence and absence. Again we are forced to reckon with images divorced from their places and times, so that each fragment becomes its own means of communicating with us about the nature of decay, where "each image seems to be suspended between the creation or the origin of the world and its fascinating and irretrievable destruction."[108]

Found-footage films are ones that are avant-garde examples of media archaeology. The filmmakers who make these kinds of pictures, like Delpeut and Morrison, excavate the past in order to rescue and reuse what has been buried by time and advanced technology. *Decasia* can be considered avant-garde for this very reason; its method highlights the ways in which matter transforms and is transformative. *Decasia*, like *Lyrical Nitrate*, is innovative and offers many rewards to the viewer eager to uncover the past and to experience the present, *as conceived or constructed by the past*, in startling ways.

Blue

Derek Jarman's *Blue* (1993) is one of the few feature films to not have a single image projected onto the screen. The entire film consists of a fully saturated blue color filling the screen space, accompanied only by the sounds of voices, including Jarman's own, reading verse, poetry, and other fragmentary narration, and sound effects and music. Blue is a conceptually challenging film, one that asks the viewer to construct all the visual aspects of the narrative (and there is one) while not being able to see anything other than a deep field of blue. Jarman was losing his sight as a result of AIDS-related HIV, so the film stands as a metaphor for the significance of inner sight and therefore *forces* the viewer to see the same way. It is a powerful testament to Jarman's will and audacity, and it exemplifies the avant-garde tendencies of Jarman and also of radical explorations into the ontology of the film medium itself, as is the case with many avant-garde films.

Blue is fascinating simply because of its concept: There is only a blue screen to look at. And while that might sound like something less enjoyable than watching an actual series of images play out a visual narrative, Jarman has still crafted a very intriguing, interesting, and enthralling film. The film is a philosophical inquiry into the idea of representation and what images, or especially the lack thereof, suggest through their absence. In other words, *Blue* asks us to construct a narrative based solely on the things we hear — which is a lot — and on the shape-shifting blueness that permeates the screen and bleeds into our consciousness. Watching the screen, you *do* see it move — or at least that is the idea, that a seemingly still image takes on form despite its formlessness. Jarman wants us to see the world differently through perceiving the way cinema can operate differently. Watching a blue screen enables us to visualize almost anything, and the sound track serves as a guide to doing so. The various elements on the sound track take precedence over the visuals, something very different in cinema, which is one reason we may consider it avant-garde. The sound track consists of four separate voices (the actors Nigel Terry, John Quentin, Tilda Swinton, and Jarman himself) who read different things, mostly from an autobiographical journal, bits of poetry, and a story of a young boy named Blue. The different voices also often reflect on the color blue and Jarman's treatment for his blindness. Adding to this dense layer of voices are sound effects (everything from bird calls to bells) and a minimalist score from Simon Fisher-Turner. This amalgam of different voices, sounds, and music ostensibly becomes the visual field of narration for *Blue*: We *see* what we hear.

Blue started as a biographical film portrait of the artist Yves Klein. Jarman had long been an admirer of Klein, mainly because he saw a similarity in their approaches to both painting and artistic creation in general. Klein is best known for IKB — International Klein Blue, a deep ultramarine blue that he used for his monochrome paintings and various installation projects. According to Jarman biographer Tony Peake, it was the color itself — blue — that struck Jarman as something that could serve as a metaphor for his struggle with blindness and, by extension, his battle with HIV. Peake says about the origins of *Blue*, first called *International Blue*, then *Bliss*, "*International Blue* is a clear indication of how, as he rode the emotional rollercoaster of HIV, Jarman was desperately seeking an oasis of peace within himself; somewhere without the pandemonium of image..."[109] Further, Peake clarifies Jarman's connection with Klein as "spiritual" in nature, since both artists were so fully invested with creating works that were inextricably linked to their own concerns about aesthetics and ideology (though Jarman would trumpet the cause of gays more loudly, fervently, and politically than Klein). He adds, "Klein believed in the power of [IKB] to vivify and sensitize not only the viewer, but the object it covered, especially when that object or canvas was without the trammels of form and line."[110] So in a very similar vein, Jarman wanted to expose the film medium by placing a color on the screen, by projecting something solid, unchanging, formless and lineless, into a particular space. Tim Ellis also notes the instigation for *Blue* in the aesthetic deconstructions of Klein. In discussing the relation between Klein's gallery work and Jarman's final vision for *Blue*, he suggests:

> One of Klein's ongoing preoccupations concerned the transformative potential of aesthetic space, evidenced most famously in a work called *The Void*. This was an empty room, painted white, in which was manifested a "sensuous pictorial state," a spatialization of his monochrome paintings, which would "act upon the sensuous vehicles or bodies of the gallery visitors." Entering the space, writes Klein, "one is literally impregnated by the pictorial sensibility, refined and stabilized beforehand by the painter in the given space." This challenge to the boundaries of the artwork and to the relation between artwork and viewer is a precursor to the radical reimagining of cinema that takes place with *Blue*.[111]

Clearly inspired by Klein's method, Jarman takes the idea further by making the monochromatic texture of the color blue a limitless opening into the mind's eye — an ever-expanding radicalization of perception as constructed through something that firstly does not move, and secondly is essentially imageless. For this reason, too, Ellis can claim, "Jarman's innovations go beyond the matter of what is represented to address the matter of representation itself. He was a lifelong experimenter with aesthetic forms, often reclaiming conservative genres for radical purposes."[112] Jarman's radical purpose in deconstructing cinema with *Blue* is completely avant-garde, and the film's ambitious simplicity makes it a wonder.

Interestingly enough, *Blue* pulsates with energy; the blue seems to diffuse, meld, contrast, and shape-shift the more one looks at it. It is not simply a trick of the eye, a *trompe l'oeil*–like blending of the real and the imaginary, where we become so entranced that the mind hallucinated movement. The screen literally throbs with blueness. Such concentration yields a specifically new way of thinking about how images create experiences for spectators. Peter Wollen described *Blue* as "an evocation of pure vision," which, ironically, is exactly what Jarman-as-blind-man wants us to see.[113] The screen disappears from view because there is no set "framing" for the color, opening an entirely new field of vision. Similar to works by Brakhage, *Blue* undertakes the task of reinventing the way we perceive things— our surroundings, ourselves, others; it reminds us that seeing is inherently sensorial and also constructive. And for Jarman it is also instructional, since much of the film (its soundtrack) is concerned with his illness and approaching death. Becoming blind, for Jarman, had allowed for a way of seeing (blue) and a way of vision (metaphoric, political); his virus rendered him blind, so he "sees" blue, while he also is ultimately concerned with the larger politics of vision that encourages others to see the world differently. *Blue* thus supposes that spectators will have a personal investment in its story, which is, essentially, a lamentation or elegy for Jarman and his ordeal.

Jarman's experimental aesthetic for destroying our notions about cinematic representation, and the resulting re-constructing of it through his film, ultimately points to a larger agenda: gay activism. According to Peake,

> Slowly but surely, Jarman was inching the film away from Klein and the immaterial towards something more social and more personal. Intersecting with the idea of a voyage through history, and of tracing a London life from cradle to grave before floating into the blue, was Jarman's newfound passion, queer politics, which took the film in a new direction.[114]

Inasmuch as *Blue* is about opening up new fields of vision, it is a harrowing (and sometimes brutal and funny) account of Blue (the character), and about Jarman's torment and treatment. Because there are no images onscreen, we have little choice but to become absorbed into what we hear; the film makes us *listen* to film just as much as it radicalizes our ways of seeing. In this manner, *Blue* is also a theoretical film about how cinema is a means of constructing new methods of hearing — if there is nothing to look at except one color, then we *have* to pay attention to what we hear. As Ellis surmises, "[The] intimacy of the voices in our ears encourages an identification with the experiences described, at the site of that experience. With no images on the screen, we are given no way to distance or hold ourselves away from the narrative."[115] For example, when the film begins, the pronoun used is "you," not "I," though it eventually becomes a first-person film told through multiple voices. The opening lines are enigmatic and thematically all-encompassing:

> You say to the boy open your eyes
> When he opens his eyes and sees the light
> You make him cry out, saying
> O Blue come forth
> O Blue arise
> O Blue ascend
> O Blue come in

The themes are both personal (losing his sight and coping with the breakdown of his body) and metaphysical (an "ascension"), and Jarman realizes these concepts through a field of blue and an elaborate multipart sound track consisting of poetry and storytelling and music, "a perfect way of addressing his own concerns while taking his audience on an elegiac journey towards immateriality" in both senses of the term.[116] So in many ways *Blue* is about the ethics of representation and about the way representation alters one's personal and communal perception. While his eyes have failed, Jarman challenges the spectator to see anew through blue and through sound, which conjures images through words and music. It is a remarkable testament to his imageless film that Jarman can make us feel a particular way; "the gently ironic voices do not encourage the usual pity or sympathy for the sufferer, but rather encourage us to feel the horror of being in the situation, a 'normal' person caught in a nightmarish scenario."[117] If this happens, then Jarman has succeeded in establishing a mode of thought about life and toward art in general. While the film is sure to distance many through its unusual aesthetic stance, it just might be able to wrangle people into its world through the narrative of Jarman's (and Blue's) life.

The lack of image and the full force of sound create an interest aesthetic and philosophic idea concerning sound. Watching films is an audio-visual experience, but because *Blue* rids itself of a series of images (the typical way of filmmaking), we have less control over the way the sounds infiltrate our cognitive means of interpreting film. That is, sounds are used to direct us rather than images, so they help orient us in cinematic space. Because there are no stabilizing images for the sounds, the effect is disarming, yet it compels a new way of recognizing the image. "The film attempts to imagine a seeing that is more like a hearing: a vision that connects us to the world, rather than separating us from it."[118] The sounds force us to create a visual counterpart in our heads. In this radical reversal of image construction, Jarman has created an avant-garde film that seduces us into its world through the essence of its blueness and also through its competing and complimentary sounds. The formal experimentation in *Blue* is a way of allowing the spectator to create control in assumed chaos, where no image exists and sounds penetrate continuously.

Film for Jarman — a trained painter and set designer — allows for a creative freedom to explore experimentalism. All of his features are avant-garde, but *Blue*, his final film, focuses on how the spaces of cinema can be torn apart through the disintegration of mise-en-scène and editing. Many of Jarman's films are mash-ups. *The Tempest, The Last of England, Edward II, Wittgenstein* all combine radical content, new media practices, and forms of cultural appropriation, and all experiment with form, style, and cinematic space. And by extension, they all examine different ways of seeing the familiar and unfamiliar. *Blue* is in many ways a culmination of the artistic and ideological concerns that engaged Jarman through much of his career, as Ellis notes:

> *Blue* further develops a number of investigations that preoccupied Jarman throughout his artistic career. The first is the relation between the spectatorial space, the screen and the space of the film, an investigation undertaken in order to remake that relation. Here the productive void of blue becomes the logical extension of the notion of the cinema as heterotopia, as the screen disappears as boundary in favor of pure color-space. Related to this is the investigation within his films of painting, and the studio as ontological laboratory, a place to experiment with being-in-space.[119]

Not many films that fall into the mainstream are concerned with the ontology of the image, the aesthetics of space, or the metaphysics of spectatorship quite like Jarman is with *Blue*. Jarman wants to reeducate via Klein's idea of the void — the limitlessness of space that opens up through formal experimentation and the exploration of "pure color-space." *Blue* forces us to reconsider how cinema communicates, while fostering empathy about the tragedy of the AIDS epidemic. Some may regard the film as didactic, but its manner of storytelling — through multiple voices that are sometimes angry, sometimes funny — does not hammer the point; it simply tells us the facts and recites ideas poetically. Listening to the words allows us to recognize the ephemeral nature of life and the immateriality of the image. The film allows Jarman to recount his own disease — seeing blue as a result of medical treatments — and creates for us the experience of seeing with and through this particular vision. The color blue itself becomes symbolic, metaphoric, transcendent — the voices often discuss sky, water, sadness, the infinite, making the film self-reflexive as well as experimental. To reiterate, *Blue* is an avant-garde work of art that fully envelopes the audience in its artistic creation. In essence, "We are offered a boundless void of possibility and potentiality, although the proffered transformation is not without its pain. But here, as elsewhere with Jarman's work, privation can potentially lead to a fuller apprehension of being. The restriction of sight in *Blue* opens up a boundlessness of vision."[120] Or, put another way, the pure blue screen suggests "a mystical connection with the infinite. While it leads us away from manipulative images and stimuli, it opens what a mystic — like Klein or Jarman — might call the inner eye to visionary experience: Not blindness, but literally in-sight, that might allow us a direct connection to ourselves, to deep understanding, to ultimate release, to limitlessness."[121] It is tempting to conclude that *Blue* is too radical to solicit this kind of response, but if one gives it the chance, the rewards are indeed extraordinary. Because of its avant-garde nature as an imageless, sound-focused film that paradoxically opens up the realm of seeing to unprecedented and unfettered limits, *Blue* takes the abstract (and the world of abstract expressionism) and makes it tangible. Perhaps Jarman's words can speak best for themselves:

> In the pandemonium of image
> I present you with the universal Blue
> Blue an open door to soul
> An infinite possibility
> Becoming tangible

Conspirators of Pleasure

Jan Svankmajer is one of the most admired avant-gardists in cinema, a filmmaker who encompasses many different means of creating inimitable film worlds: alchemist, surrealist, collagist, and animator. His unique aesthetic approach and imaginative vision are particularly well-suited for films that deal with unconscious desires, as does his unparalleled excursion into surrealist daydream, fantasy, and reality, *Conspirators of Pleasure* (1996), a film that combines live action with stop-motion animation (a trademark of most of his films), to create a truly bizarre yet fascinating peek into the lives of others, who, it turns out, are much like the rest of us, even if we don't care to admit it. Svankmajer has the strange power to make us feel the realness of his characters and their situations, even when using animation and surrealism to substitute the phenomenal world with the un-real, or at least with the unconscious. *Conspirators of Pleasure* "is the first of Svankmajer's features to be set principally in the 'real world' and the first to deal explicitly with the relations (or rather non-relations) between men and women," making it new for him (as most of his short films use a lot of animation and puppetry), yet still maintaining the hallucinatory or surrealistic tone of his films (because he still uses some animation and puppetry).[122] Or, as Frantisek Dryje states,

> *Conspirators of Pleasure* is completely different, at least in terms of form. A shift in emphasis is immediately apparent: acted sequences predominate and animation serves only to supplement or complete them. At the same time, the basic building blocks of Svankmajer's personal style — his use of close-ups, rapid editing — are preserved. As with the majority of Svankmajer's previous films, there is an absence of verbal dialogue: an expressive form that poses a certain risk in the case of a feature film.[123]

Conspirators of Pleasure is a remarkable avant-garde film that asks us to "conspire" with Svankmajer and the characters in order to believe both their behaviors and to admit culpability. *Conspirators of Pleasure* is about the strange sexual fantasies that people have — what they do behind closed doors — but they are entirely real yearnings. The film contains black humor and sarcasm about the human condition, and about how we are all interconnected through our fantasies — we are all "conspirators" of pleasurable things. I like to think of Svankmajer's films as instances of "surreal realism" — films that are grounded in reality yet present that reality in uncanny ways.

Svankmajer is a highly distinctive filmmaker who rejects classical filmmaking and embraces surrealism, particularly the Czech influences of his own country, avant-garde tropes and techniques, and finally the ambitious projects associated with animated art cinema, only because many of his films exist only in the periphery of mainstream distribution and exhibition. Like other avant-garde artists, Svankmajer challenges traditional means of representation by presenting surrealistic scenes that signify something beyond the realm of the ordinary, even when the events are couched in reality. According to Peter Hames, Svankmajer "conspires" in the surrealist notion of co-mingling the real/unreal and the conscious/unconscious. He says:

> Svankmajer accepts the position of Bretonian Surrealism as an investigative quest. His objective is to examine the apparent confrontation of two worlds, not to assert

the dominance of one over the other, but to explore a continuity, an interpenetration. His interest in magic and alchemy is a logical extension of this quest: the cognitive power of the senses, the importance of dream thinking, the transformation of the separate into the linked, the transmutation of the senses, a rejection of the superficially rational and utilitarian.[124]

Conspirators of Pleasure followed two other feature films, *Alice* (1988), an adaptation of the Lewis Carroll novel, and *Faust* (1994), an adaptation of Goethe. Svankmajer had already spent over two decades making short films that were primarily animated, specifically stop-motion animation, and occasionally mixed live action — actors — with animated objects, like he does in *Conspirators of Pleasure*. Svankmajer is also one to acknowledge his inspirations; at the end of the film, the credits list as "technical consultants" Luis Buñuel, Max Ernst, the Marquis de Sade, Sigmund Freud, Leopold von Sacher-Masoch, and Bohuslav Brouk. By having such an eclectic list of "consultants" (co-conspirators?), Svankmajer openly announces his ties to surrealism, psychoanalysis, and transgressive behavior. In the majority of his works, by focusing on live action and animated objects — the mixture of reality and the unreal — Svankmajer expresses the fantasies and desires and fears that motivate human behavior, which, I think, is the reason why we can relate to his films — and this one in particular — because they express commonalities but through an avant-garde agenda. Surrealism aims to change the way people consider living — indeed, the very way they perceive their surroundings. Surrealism conspires in revolution, and it also provides moments of the un-real or hyper-real. In an interview discussing the film, Svankmajer said, "Their conspiracy is aimed against this civilization, as they do not respect the reality principle. Desire is their driving force. In that sense, *Conspirators of Pleasure* is indeed a surrealist film; Surrealists have always invoked the 'omnipotence of desire.'"[125] *Conspirators of Pleasure* is an explicit examination of the surrealist idea of desire, but the film transcends any sort of bland recognition because all of the conspirators are both sad and funny, and because their actions are entirely absurd. One conspirator rolls a bread loaf into tiny balls and snorts them through long tubes, giving herself an extreme form of pleasure; two others engage in a sadomasochistic ritual of courtship; another builds erotic hand-made implements in his woodshed to garner self-pleasure; another builds a masturbation machine. In discussing the relevance of humor and the strange things his characters often enact, Svankmajer says, "Yes, of course, there is a bit of sadism and a certain 'enjoyment' of it, in other words the principle of pleasure is also involved here, but it is also black humour [sic] with subversive metaphors and metamorphoses."[126] What makes the film avant-garde thematically is the "subversive metaphors" that underlie character behavior. What is remarkable (and also avant-garde) about the film is that there is no spoken dialogue; the characters act and interact through furtive glances, sheepish looks, or pleasurable grins. The only things we hear are hyper-real sound effects that give credence to the idea of how fantasy coexists with reality, a surrealist idea that lends the film its black humor as well as reiterating its theme. According to Hames,

> The lack of communication between the film's protagonists suggests not only that desire and sexual love can never be satisfied by the other but that it is consistently returned to the self as auto-eroticism: the sadistic treatment of puppets, the sniffing of balls of bread, rolling brushes and nails over the skin, having one's toe sucked, constructing a surrogate masturbator. In all instances, desire is deflected from real people to things and ends in fetishistic and solitary activity.[127]

The film is ingenious in showing how the desires that people have individually are also somehow collectively interrelated, even when the desire results in "solitary activity."

Svankmajer finds the marvelous in the banal, a key ingredient to surrealism's insistence on irrationality as a guiding force in our daily lives. The mundane activities of each individual conspirator's daily routine are subverted because we see their "true" selves through their pleasure-seeking personae. The film is completely expressive: devoid of dialogue, we become transfixed by the images, sounds, and behaviors of the conspirators. Svankmajer's films are highly inventive and ambitious in form and style, combining live-action, puppets and marionettes, collage, object-, drawn-, and clay- animation, and montage, which makes them avant-garde. Animation has the potential to "free" objects from their moorings, and in *Conspirators of Pleasure*, "They fulfill a secondary 'realization of the imaginative,' achieving a final and meaningful purpose."[128] When they "come to life" in the film, they operate within the logic of dreams—anything seems possible. So when rolling pins move by themselves, bread balls scurry through a bowl, or effigies come to life and interact with real people, we see — and feel and hear — the surreal, illogical humor. Surrealism, and, arguably, avant-garde filmmaking itself, is about freedom, or at least the capacity for momentary freedom that comes through release — through pleasure or creativity. The conspirators of pleasure of the film

> move around us— inconspicuous, ordinary and tedious, but above all, they live (and let us state in awareness of all its banality) within ourselves; because the desire of every human being for freedom, for free action without any external motivation, is as intensive as the forces of cultural tradition are repressive, oppressive and domesticating. We should not be confused by the pathetic appearance of these rebels— they are hardly more pathetic than our own privacy or the norms and conventions of public hypocrisy, as the film also shows.[129]

Subverting our own desires through the faces of others, Svankmajer is able to induce humor through discomfort. The actions of the characters are so bizarre and strange but *normal*; even though he uses Surrealism, and is therefore very much an avant-garde filmmaker, the film is universal because it appeals to and is reflective of general notions of identity, culture, and freedom that inform any individual's sense of self. Svankmajer's film balances the dreamlike absurdity and danger in the true spirit of Surrealism. The display of the uncanny is an anxious, psychological place and space prone to unusual or eerie situations and circumstances, which are, ultimately, couched in the reality of everyday life. Herein resides the avant-gardism of *Conspirators of Pleasure*. Surrealism is a catalyst for exploration and for uncovering meanings in the nuances of everyday activities. Svankmajer's film makes the unconscious seem palpable; the animated objects and interaction between humans and marionettes-as-effigies represent the constant conflict of the real and the fictional.

Conspirators of Pleasure is uncompromising in its presentation of "the permanence of desire and, in these manifestations, the obsessive and secretive behavior through which it is expressed."[130] The plot, as indicated already, revolves around the clandestine sexual desires of six separate individuals. Two neighbors engage in a ritualistic and masochistic game of lust and desire, where they create effigies of one another that ultimately leads to violence; a mousy mail carrier rolls tiny bread balls in a large bowl and then sniffs them through long tubes for personal gratification; a man who sells pornographic magazines constructs a masturbation machine that he uses when watching a television anchor deliver the nightly news, while she surreptitiously has her toes sucked by fish in a bowl under her desk; and finally, a policeman, who is the husband of the TV woman, builds instruments out of women's boas and scarves, nails, rolling pins, lids, and other assorted things, which he rolls over himself in order to obtain pleasure and fulfill his desires. All of these strange behaviors may be described as transgressive, but the characters do them in order to obtain a form of self-pleasure, so they are not essentially harmful or dangerous (except maybe the violent ritual performed by the neighbors and their effigies). They do their acts to achieve freedom, a point Svankmajer has stressed, since it combines traits of surrealist release, Freudian unconscious desires, and masochistic behavior:

> [*Conspirators of Pleasure*] is, however, about freedom. As we know, Freud's pleasure principle, to which all the characters in the film are subjected, is generally considered to be a synonym for freedom. The film might be described as Sadeian though, not so much because the relationship of the two protagonists (Lovbalova, Pivunka) is sado-masochistic, but rather because all the characters fulfill their desire, hot for "absolute freedom," disregarding the reality principle, disregarding personal effort, obstacles, suffering. Freedom, in Sade's view, always takes this absolute form.[131]

The film then uses avant-garde techniques to demonstrate these themes or ideas, which are articulated through Svankmajer's blending of surrealism and realism, animation and live action. The characters in *Conspirators of Pleasure* are all somehow trapped by their circumstances and so are compelled to follow their instincts in order to escape, which means crossing sociological or cultural boundaries. The need to transgress stems, perhaps, from their need to question "the relationship between the core of social life and the periphery, the center and the margins, identity and difference, the normal and the deviant, and the possible rules that could conceivably bind us into a collectivity."[132] But "rules" are created to instill normalcy, and normalcy often begets transgression, a paradoxical and cyclical pattern that inevitably suggests that when people commit transgressive acts, and especially those in these two films, they do so because they are enacting "normal" behavior. Transgressions are also highly subjective and often metaphorical events. When the characters in *Conspirators of Pleasure*, for example, engage in perverse sensual activity, we feel as if we are spying on them and their personal pleasures. Transgressions are indeed "part of the social process, [but they] are also part of the individual psyche."[133] But I would suggest that inasmuch as we pry into the lives of these characters, we identify with them because they manifest the desires we all share.

The animation Svankmajer uses brings to life the puppet-effigies and the objects used by the conspirators in the film, making the effect startling and clever. As Hames notes:

> Added to Svankmajer's actors and puppets, which are not only interchangeable but frequently enjoy the same status within the narrative, are his objects. As he has noted many times, he does not regard objects as dead artifacts. While he collects them for their associations and the feelings they evoke, he also suggests, more mysteriously, that they have an interior life, and the possibility of links with our unconscious impulses.[134]

Animation becomes an essential tool for capturing the power of the imagination so that in his films one sees how objects have personalities of their own. This process of animating the inanimate is painstaking—since he primarily uses stop-motion animation—yet serves a very clear purpose: Animation makes the imaginary real, a key idea of Surrealism. Animation also is a locus for resistance to traditional forms of narrative storytelling because, quite literally, anything may "come alive" and interact with the live characters. In addition, "The animation of actual objects could be understood within the notion of a realist mode and self-generating two-dimensional work with a more semiotic one."[135] Svankmajer's animation emphasizes how it can change the parameters of the everyday, destabilize our accepted ideas of reality, and challenge the conventional understanding of our existence. Indeed, animated films generally examine areas of visual communication disregarded in conventional cinema, which is why Surrealism flourishes in his work. As Svankmajer puts it, "I use real animation for mystification, for disturbing the utilitarian habits of the audience, to unsettle them, or for subversive purposes."[136] Objects provide an emotive message, and most people do not realize this, yet Svankmajer shows how plausible this idea is by focusing on the tactile dimension of everyday things. He shows how objects that are usually trapped in the ordinariness of life take on new meanings as metaphors for sentiment, thoughts, and dreams. As Dryje says, describing *Conspirators of Pleasure*, and indeed most of Svankmajer's films, "Another new element in the symbolic and symptomatic language of Jan Svankmajer is the direct presentation of his long-term interest in tactilism and tactile art as an independent imaginative phenomenon."[137] In this sense, *Conspirators of Pleasure* focuses on how objects become both physically and emotionally playful, rebellious, terrifying, and humorous: They bring to full life the unconscious, the nonsensical, the nightmarish, and the uncanny — the stuff of pure Surrealism, where real things play significant roles in shaping both dreams and reality.

Svankmajer has been called an alchemist throughout his career, and with good reason. The alchemist mixes a range of ingredients together to form a unique assemblage of various items or one final product, which then has a transformative and enchanting power. Alchemical transformations arise through a deconstruction process that eventually yields a hybrid product. The alchemist finds unity among disparate parts; he discovers universality among discontinuities. In *Conspirators of Pleasure* he brings together collage, animation, found objects, and live action to show how they become connected to one another after mixing them. Alchemy brings hidden qualities and characteristics of objects to the forefront, which Svankmajer then highlights as having subtle or overt associations among people. In general, "alchemy is about trying to connect things that you cannot connect, that are un-connectable," which is why his films come across as alternatively humorous and grotesque.[138] In this same vein, Svankmajer is also inherently concerned with magic and the irrational; it is not often we see bread balls come alive, or puppets suddenly have sight when eyeballs roll into their sockets, or tin cans, feathers, and rolling pins move on their own and interact with other objects or with actual people.

A collage is considered a random collection or hodgepodge, but essentially it is the combination of things that are used to produce something new and whole. Svankmajer's work is sometimes described as being like a collage simply because he uses different elements that not only fill the mise-en-scene, but also the entire film. It may be best to describe the films as "kinetic collage," since he is creating moving images. Svankmajer's method of representation is so uncanny that is strikes us as being alien, yet the way the objects interact and act just as real people jar us into recognizing something totally original in his collage-like approach. Accordingly,

> Svankmajer's cinema of incongruities is designed, through collage and juxtaposition, both to categorize and control the worlds created and imagined but also to suggest the contradictory and provisional nature of the process.... In aiming for the surreal, Svankmajer can also be argued to be seeking a world of nondifferentiation. Alchemy, he says, "is about trying to connect things that you cannot connect, that are unconnectable."[139]

The strangeness resulting from incongruities, juxtaposition, and surrealist imagery fuels the alchemical process of transformation and alignment, where things become equal with people. The images in *Conspirators of Pleasure* are edited in such a way to create a sophisticated form of lyrical montage. Montage is a very important component of Svankmajer's style. His use of montage, which harkens to both Soviet aesthetics and Surrealism, emphasizes the artificiality and confrontation that occur both thematically and stylistically in his films. A collage is in some ways a static way of representing montage; the practice of collage (and montage) can bring together suggestive fragments as well as instigate psychic or emotional disruptions. For Dryje, Svankmajer's style also complements the idea of object-animation and surrealist desire, particularly effective in *Conspirators of Pleasure*: "[The protagonists'] energetic charge is kept alive by Svankmajer's surrealist technique, a 'transfer of perception' in which the most banal objects acquire the highest, magical meanings, in which sources of creativity are uncovered through the release of the much glorified and vilified pleasure principle."[140] Svankmajer uses the collage technique because he combines live action, marionettes, objects, and other incongruent elements. This merging of elements creates a "total montage" that emphasizes the tactile dimension of textures and objects.[141] The rapid editing technique that is montage accentuates the already unusual or disturbing visuals that Svankmajer wants us to focus on, which includes the juxtaposition of extreme close-ups with wider shots or the movement of objects. In fact, the disarming use of close-ups, combined with the exaggerated use of sound, is a large part of Svankmajer's signature style. The unexpected use of the close-ups in combination with other actions is disarming, macabre, and an example of "brute reality" because they visually assault the senses. In *Conspirators of Pleasure*, for example, we are shown extreme close-ups of the actors' faces, the objects, and the puppets. The camera zooms in frequently to heighten their connections—their conspiracies—and it directly forces us to view them in new ways, a trademark of avant-garde films.

Svankmajer is completely unorthodox in his approach to filmmaking, which makes his work avant-garde. His style immediately sets him apart from the mainstream, and, like with many avant-garde filmmakers, it is recognizable to those who appreciate his work. Svankmajer's films are certainly subversive and avant-garde, but given his aesthetic approach, they have to be. But there is also a sense of revelation after viewing; the films, and especially *Conspirators of Pleasure*, move us in different ways, through humor and sheer wonder at his ingenuity. Perhaps the film connects with us because they do intertwine the real and the fantastic, blurring the lines between dreams and waking life. Or it could be based upon Svankmajer's dedication to the remarkable "realization of the real" as it has been mediated through surrealist approaches. Hames sees Svankmajer as being anathema to mainstream film, stating:

> Compared with conventional cinema, Svankmajer's work is subversive in almost all of its categories: narration, representation, characterization, editing. Most of his recent films have moved away from music in favor of the sounds of objects and substances.... His photography rejects lyricism and any attempt to present his puppets as exotic. If they appear mysterious, the effect is immediately undercut. Their disruptive power must reside in their credibility as real objects. Disturbances replace catharsis. Black humor and horror replace realism. The focal point of identity—man or woman—is questioned.[142]

Conspirators of Pleasure is disturbing and has moments of black humor, but I would suggest it does offer catharsis because we identify with the characters' behavior, their seeking of pleasure. And the puppets *do* become credible, as do the objects. Svankmajer's greatest achievement comes from applying surrealist ideas to film, whether from awakening dormant objects or the interaction of marionettes and people. *Conspirators of Pleasure* "surprises in its imaginative nature and in its supremely poetic metamorphoses of perception (or vision) of space, time and the world in general."[143] This estimation sums up the film as avant-garde, and, indeed, Svankmajer's approach to cinema as avant-garde. His vision is at once witty and irreverent and often macabre, but always distinctive and individualist. It is the focus on *surreal realism* that allows us to understand the seemingly incomprehensible moments in his films. Svankmajer's film is original in so many ways; it is rhythmical and highly expressive, while simultaneously bizarrely beautiful, violent, and always thought-provoking.

Blood Tea and Red String

Christiane Cegavske's *Blood Tea and Red String* (2006) is a startling adult fairy tale made in stop-motion animation. Much like the darker works of Jan Svankmajer or the Quay Brothers, this film is a marvel of ingenuity, clever characters, and obscure narration. It is disturbing, humorous, and often brilliant in its execution. Many feature-length animated films are released regularly, but often there are some that defy categorization, ones that are indeed avant-garde, like *Blood Tea and Red String*, and so announce themselves as something different because of the aesthetic approach undertaken by the director. *Blood Tea and Red String* is like a moving sculpture: The herky-jerky stop-motion animation is both "amateurish" (not in any negative sense, but instead one full of enthusiasm and careful detail) and sophisticated, and the moodiness of the creatures that make up the film — from mice to assorted beings consisting of different parts — also make the film an exercise in experimental filmmaking. The very fact that it took director Cegavske thirteen years to make the film suggests an ongoing love affair with the process of creation itself as the starting point for obsessive detail, and, perhaps, a method that is compulsive yet appropriate for the painstaking stop-motion animation process.

The film is about a group of mice and their battle with the Creatures Who Dwell Under the Oak over a doll that the mice commissioned the Creatures to make. Told completely without dialogue — the creatures squeak, grunt, or squawk throughout — the film pits abnormal vs. abnormal, grotesque animals who have as much in common with fairy-tale monsters as Disney does with Looney Tunes. In other words, the frightening menagerie of critters who serve as protagonists and antagonists of the film are at times horrifying, deformed, bizarre, monstrous, and wondrously strange — which is to say they are unlike any cartoon at all because they are (or appear) real. Stop-motion animation renders things life-like, and the way Cegavske has worked makes them all menacing and completely original.

The Creatures have made a grim life-size doll with a large egg sewn into its belly, which they have hung from their tree in a crucifixion-like pose. In the middle of the night, the Mice come and take her away, scurrying off in a coach drawn by a turtle. The Creatures follow, encountering dark obscure woods, a cellophane water fountain (rendered beautifully), and a monster spider, all under a lustrous moon. The Mice are all dressed in haughty Victorian garb and have deep, blood-red eyes. The Creatures are a mix of things—ears of a bat, a giant bird beak like a crow's, the fur of a rabbit—making them macabre and darkly foreboding, yet charming as well in their clumsiness and desire for the doll. The Mice take the doll back to their lair, a dark home surrounded by death's-head sunflowers (flowers with skulls in their center), where they play cards and drink blood tea, becoming intoxicated in their revelry-like celebration. There is a giant human skull with a protruding raven's eye that watches over their shenanigans. The Creatures eventually find themselves journeying to save their doll, which "births" a bluebird from the egg in its belly. This plot summary, however, does not do justice to all of the other exquisite details found in the film, from a frog-like sorcerer to a lush garden within a maze, or the way each creature has its own unique personality (intriguing, since there is no dialogue—or voice-over—but simply squawks and squeaks).

Dark, mysterious, hypnotic, and astonishingly assured, *Blood Tea and Red String* is a fairy tale that is marvelous to see and stimulating enough to decipher. There could be some larger issues at work here—tyrannical bourgeois power run amok, the worshiping of idols—but overall, the film simply plays for itself and asks us to imagine this world where the weird roams freely. The main reason the film is avant-garde (besides its execution of stop-motion animation) is that Cegavske has created a really inimitable style. The camera moves, examines the miniatures in close-up, and creates juxtapositions through editing that draw our attention to various places in the mise-en-scène. There is also an ambient avant-garde folk soundtrack, at times plucking or peaceful, which adds a certain amount of mood to the strangeness of the created world. The film is hallucinatory and dream-like; its surrealism (and poeticism) comes from the depiction of an otherworld that is tactile, immersive, and modern. What *Blood Tea and Red String* is, is a truly original piece of experimental art, a film that is enigmatic and imaginative. As a work of animation, it signifies a completely different form of narrative construction. According to Paul Wells, "Animation has inherent spectacle in the freedom of its graphic vocabulary, but it is a spectacle that has been naturalized into its vocabulary in a way that enables the form to infiltrate generic conventions almost unnoticed."[144] A film like *Blood Tea and Red String*, then, positions itself within a broader interetextual network that consists of psychoanalytic desires of the unconscious, which gives rise to its surrealism; it participates in "spectacle," which connotes a demonstrative manifestation of the form itself, particularly useful for examining stop-motion animation where form is always foregrounded; and it alludes to fairy tales, a genre that is ripe for deconstruction (as it always has been). The graphic and plastic style of *Blood Tea and Red String* heralds it as an innovative type of avant-garde exercise, where direct experimentalism creates the narrative and the method of presentation.

Not a film meant for the masses, and essentially a film made for the director herself, *Blood Tea and Red String* is one of those obscure features that finds devoted audiences at festivals or midnight screenings. It is not a stop-motion-animated film that will ever turn up on television during the holiday season. Its avant-garde aesthetic creates the components of the film where narrative is usually subordinated to the visual elements. Cegavske's unyielding and unerring imagination, which brings to life seemingly "dead" objects, is alternately serious and playful, straightforward and symbolic. There is tension and anxiety that occurs in *Blood Tea and Red String* as a result of its ambitious and weird process, instigating the same in viewers as well. The surreal imagery can be seen as an allegory about the destabilization of order and rationality. Animation becomes an essential tool for capturing the power of the imagination so that the creatures in the film "come alive," possessing personalities of their own. This process of animating the inanimate is painstaking — since she uses stop-motion animation — yet serves a very clear purpose: Animation makes the imaginary real, a key idea of Surrealism. The film also participates in the uncanny, a realm of the mysterious, the unconscious, and the grotesque, but altogether inviting — that is, this unusual world is rendered so imaginatively that we believe it.

Many reviews of *Blood Tea and Red String* refer to it as a "fairy tale." Certainly the film could be interpreted as one, as it has fantastical creatures who battle over a makeshift god, and who engage in struggles for control, identity, and community. Fairy tales "offer archetypal stories available for re-use and recycling by different ages and cultures," and their significance may be found in "their stories and characters [that] seem to transgress established social, cultural, geographical, and temporal boundaries."[145] A dark film like *Blood Tea and Red String* also taps into myths about the monstrous that fills nightmares. (I should make clear, though, that the film is also playful, humorous, and spirited — not entirely sinister.) But the film is also its own creation, meaning it does not echo any well-known fairy tale but simply alludes to them. It ultimately is highly enigmatic, open to interpretation, and thought-provoking. Still, its avant-garde status rests on its camerawork and its intricate mise-en-scène, where mice, trees, stars, frogs, chariots, flowers, and handmade creatures come to life in staggeringly imaginative ways. The doll that is constructed is at once ugly and beautiful, a rag-tag amalgam of porcelain face and wild hair. The "red string" in question holds it aloft from the tree, where it also at one point seems to protrude from the doll's hands in a stigmata-like image. There is a certain intense level of poetic sensibility at work here, and Cegavske keeps our attention because of the paradoxically unnaturalness-yet-realness of the animation. Without using dialogue (an experimental tactic for a feature film, much like that used in *Conspirators of Pleasure*), *Blood Tea and Red String* is very much a film to immerse oneself in. It washes over the viewer through its colors (reds, golds, greens), sounds (music, animal noises), and images. It is reminiscent of Eastern European animated films, perhaps the greatest tradition of experimental stop-motion (and other forms of) animation. Truly a mesmerizing film, it requires a diligence on the part of the spectator to believe its world, to experience it sensorially, and to applaud the director's ambition and avant-garde sensibility.

Glass Lips— *aka "Blood of a Poet"*

Lech Majewski is a Polish-born, Lodz film school–educated, American-residing film and conceptual artist (not to mention author) who, with *Glass Lips* (2007), has created one of the more enigmatic avant-garde feature films of recent memory. The production was originally devised as a series of thirty-three video/art/photographic pieces called "Blood of a Poet" (as a direct nod to Cocteau's film of the same name), where visitors— as it was shown in museums— were instructed to walk from room to room to see the video installation as both separate and interrelated parts that form a whole work. The installation itself is a complex form of experimental video art; the film makes the videos come alive in new ways, particularly through colors, mise-en-scène, tableaux-style positioning and framing, and clever manipulation of time/space. In short, *Glass Lips* is an ingenious and haunting film that undermines traditional narrative logic to suggest the inner workings of the mind, a theme that resonates with any viewer of avant-garde film.

Majewski is not very well known in the United States, despite having retrospectives of his work shown at different museums. Critic Michael Atkinson describes Majewski as "a tireless and passionate Euro artiste of a kind that often gets relegated to the 'underground' or 'experimental' categories in [the United States], but who also employs old-fashioned surrealism..." which designates him as an artist existing in the margins.[146] Another critic says Majewski's "haunting aesthetic is formed of much deeper stuff, processed through a lively mind and idiosyncratic imagination, chastened and tempered by history, and captured on screen with the rigor and perfectionism of an artist who might also carve castles out of toothpicks."[147]

While the "Blood of a Poet" installation piece is undoubtedly an important avant-garde work in itself, I will focus these brief comments on the film version of it. But *Glass Lips* is, of course, tied to the "Blood of a Poet" installation, so its significance cannot be overlooked, especially since it articulates Majewski's vision and method similar to that of the film. "Blood of a Poet" is video art, and

> what distinguished Majewski from others who use video art is that he creates his works through purely filmic means. DiVinities, as the artist himself calls his works (a combination of words: divine with the digital technology DVD) are characterized by a painterly composition of takes, a refined game of shadow and light and subtle color used for conveying an often brutal and dramatic plot.... DiVinities are shown on a loop on many monitors in their natural habitat, the gallery. Either simultaneously displayed on walls as if moving frescoes, or frozen in monochromatic photograms and colorful light-boxes, they can be put together in countless combinations. This is a break from linear narration, and so each screening can be different.[148]

This method obviously is compulsive, original, and experimental, and it distinguishes the film version, *Glass Lips*, as a remarkably inventive use of film to visualize the video project. *Glass Lips* is one of the more beautifully photographed yet confounding avant-garde films that attempts to tell a story without any dialogue, relying solely on the expressiveness of the actors and the scenes themselves. The film's plot, a very loose one because its narrative is more associative than anything, details the story of a young poet who is beset by many insurmountable problems that mainly stem form a hellish (childhood) home life. The film depicts the artist's struggle to find himself amidst the indifference of the home and the world, where nature and nurture provide very little comfort and instead a lot of heartache, grief, pain, and suffering — all things some may consider to be essential for the creation of "great" art. *Glass Lips* is ostensibly set in an insane asylum or psychiatric ward, where the poet resides and reflects upon his traumatic experiences. Many of his remembrances overlap, mingle, or interfere with actuality, so memory becomes cloudy, like unconscious thoughts and desires, where reality and the imagination blend to create absurdly surreal situations. The poet's father was violent toward the youth, and his mother was apparently passive and also subject to his, the father's, authority. Left with little recourse to create a stable, nurturing, sane environment, the protagonist-poet spends his life in the asylum, where he is harassed and punished for seemingly deviant thoughts and behavior. There are many intertextual references throughout the film, some of which inspire Majewski's aesthetic, from Francis Bacon to Bruno Schulz to Roger van der Weyden. But the real power of the film lay in its visualizations/remembrances of the poet's past, which, as mentioned, often appear as present situations and possibly even future events. *Glass Lips* portrays the horrifying ways that childhood trauma affects the condition(ing) of the adult, and also examines the ways the effects of shock and suffering lead one to have severe bouts of isolation, grief, and madness. For these reasons alone, the film actually is an excellent case study of paternal abuse and motherly compliance, regardless of its avant-garde status.

The haunting tableaux vivants that make *Glass Lips* so disarming are rendered in mannerisms befitting stage or still life painting because they are so mesmerizing and hallucinatory. The hypnotic feel the film generates is due in large part to the fact that there is no dialogue so that all we have to measure coherence are the strange images Majewski has concocted to show the inner workings of a man's unconditionally abnormal consciousness and/or subconscious. It is quite an idiosyncratic method to tell such an important story; by having no dialogue, or overt linear chronology, *Glass Lips* is structured more like the (un)conscious mind at work: free association, image overload, and dramatic tableaux. Majewski, though, is a true artist compelled to translate to screen the ideas existant in the video installation of "Blood of a Poet," and also establish the visionary images and ideas that make the film so evocative. In addition to writing the film, Majewski also directed and photographed it, and even wrote the music — a true "auteurist" approach that leaves no doubt about its status or authenticity as avant-garde imagination and creativity, since he serves the primary roles of the film's creation, much like other canonical avant-garde filmmakers. Describing Majewski on the set of a separate film (though the description is apt), documentary filmmaker Dagmara Drzazga says, "When Lech Majewski appears on the film set, time starts to flow at a different rate — it thickens to form a new reality, the world of his vision and his film. From now on nothing else exists. He is the absolute master, the emperor of this microworld."[149] Majewski clearly has an alternative approach to making a film; the result is unconventional, abstract, and bizarrely staged, but it is still enthralling, and for these very reasons. There are many baroque images, religious images (and metaphors and possible symbols), surreal tableaux, and ambient noises. At times it feels fractured — like the poet's mind — because it is constructed of many separate pieces that either recount the past or acknowledge the present without transitions that indicate a particular narrative coherency. Some of the images are admittedly hard to decipher, or at least they can be interpreted in many different ways, which is always a good thing for spectators because they are forced to construct meaning or make connections among the ostensibly disparate images. This is also an important part of watching an avant-garde film. For example, in one tableau there is a group of people holding a figure of Christ before a giant cross; in another there are sheer cloths wrapped around faces; and in another there are nude figures standing in the woods surrounded by clothed people. What these symbolic images tell us varies, even though they all have something to say about the poet's trauma and nightmarish past/present.

Glass Lips extends the ontological condition of the "Blood of a Poet" series by presenting it as a hallucinatory realm where time-space is dislocated and discorporated. Many strange and compelling "scenes" fill the film. A woman stands before a mirror and tub and pours milk over her breasts. The poet stands alone in a snowy wood before a tree, almost in a Sebastian-like pose. A woman dressed in formal wear boxes a punching bag while standing center stage in a grand opera house. The poet becomes emerged in water, a "re-birth" of his former self. As a boy, the young poet is forced by his father to drink his soup on all fours like a dog ... and later the father does the same thing, but this time eating dog food. There are many different odd images throughout the film, and while they may seem contrived (which I would say they are not, given the subject matter), they exert a power over the dialogue-less film; the power of the film is in the striking visuals and the way they have been constructed like "visual moving" paintings. The life of the poet is one of trauma, from his childhood to the present, and Majewski's manner of presenting this experience is avant-garde. In reviewing/describing the plot of the film and Majewski's themes and methods, Magdalena Lebecka says:

> The plot centers around [sic] the intimate biography of a poet who has been placed in a psychiatric hospital. The film has a strange and dreamlike texture; it depicts the poet's painful experiences of clashes with hostile surroundings, the mythologizing of these experiences, traumatic memories from his childhood, erotic fantasies, expectations concerning the future filled with fear and the sense of disabling loneliness. This is an extremely subjective perspective — a complex model of the psyche on which a vivisection is carried out, uncovering — layer after layer — deeper levels of meaning.[150]

What the film succeeds in doing, then, is visualizing the inner world of the poet, something that shows its ties to Cocteau's *Blood of a Poet*; but in this instance, with *Glass Lips*, the visualization is more intense, experimental, and multifaceted because the psyche-writ-large is always a personal area for exploration, and Majewski has accomplished something remarkable and remarkably avant-garde with his film of the consciousness-on-display that is *Glass Lips*.

Glass Lips "exerts a chilly fascination from minute to minute" because it is so unorthodox in its presentational style, even when mimicking representational strategies of painters.[151] Its surrealism stems from the unexplainable images of manifested fears and thoughts, and without the benefit of dialogue or voice-over to situate it or the narrative. Majewski mainly holds the camera very still, only occasionally panning slowly or using an abrupt edit. The style is also a condition that lends the film its surrealism; the irrationality of the mind that is openly on display in the film — as its subject matter — is directly related to the libidinal form of filmmaking Majewski practices. The film's thirty-three "scenes" all are enigmatic, profane, and even metaphysical, delving into religious iconography, the unconscious-made-conscious (or concrete), and often unsettling and frightening images. But they hold a transformative power, which I think is partly what Majewski is up to with *Glass Lips*; it is a film that tries very hard to make us recognize its theme through its style, mostly succeeding, as the images remain with us long after the viewing. The complex nature of the film's style and themes make it avant-garde. In one review of the film, the critic writes:

> The pungent layers of narrative that make up *Glass Lips* may cross and collide — and occasionally confuse — but the intelligence behind them is clear.... This haunting look at the nature of nurture uses the childhood memories of a traumatized young poet to explore themes and visuals ranging from the biblical to the baroque.... *Glass*

Lips contrasts natural sound — a gurgling stream, a wailing infant — with unnatural behavior, and meticulously controlled images with emotional anarchy. After a while the film's expressiveness becomes so hypnotic that it's difficult not to make your own connections: the discovery that the gaping mouth of a blow-up doll resembles nothing so much as a silent scream says as much about me as it does about Mr. Majewski.[152]

This review accurately gives the portentous sense one gets when watching *Glass Lips*— that, in fact, we are participating in the surreal ourselves. This experimentation is an acquired taste. But *Glass Lips* succeeds in making us at least notice the ways in which memory and reality, hallucination and recollection, present and past, can all collide or conflate, creating instances that are disarming and revelatory. Majewski tells his story without words, a re-imagining of film narration, as well as a way to represent the inner vision of the protagonist through rich tableaux and enigmatic images. Painter Rafal Olbinski aptly sums up the experience of watching *Glass Lips* as both creatively inspiring and provocative:

> Majewski's films are poetic, surreal. They use shots full of metaphors, this forces you to think and stimulates the imagination. After watching his last film ("Blood of a Poet"/"Glass Lips") I dreamed about new paintings. This type of inspiration appears in contact with truly great Art — when you go to the Louvre, or the Metropolitan Museum, or when you watch Lech's work.[153]

Such inspiration, I think, is due in part to the truly experimental nature of the film. *Glass Lips* is a bold visual poem, a stream-of-consciousness associative montage, an avant-garde rumination of creativity — material highly personal yet resonant for many.

Conclusion

Film spectatorship indicates that the vast majority of films consumed in the United States are those that often reinforce dominant ideology, participate in classical paradigms, including genre, and are seemingly innocuous even when they are "daring." The avant-garde feature film, by contrast, offers a more nuanced form of spectatorship that is built upon historical tradition, cultural assumption and appreciation, and, to some extent, an "established" audience of art-house lovers or museum-going, university-sponsored private/public screenings. But avant-garde films will always remain challenging — difficult, demanding, and intensely personal, even if there is a community of like-minded viewers together watching, interrogating, and interacting with the film. The contemporary feature films that I have described in this book, particularly in Parts III, are more accessible to most audiences, which may prove a relatively "easy" (if not always smooth) avenue of exploration into avant-garde film. The one thing required of the spectator for the avant-garde feature film is participation. And, as Stan Brakhage argued, avant-garde films and their viewing processes are *liberating*. If we expand on this term and take it quite literally — what it denotes — then watching an avant-garde film is invigorating but beneficial, freeing and emancipatory. It liberates from the confines of typical classical form and style; it liberates from social and cultural constraints, which includes ideological constraint; and it liberates the mind, as the films themselves require and demand and encourage active spectatorship.

The ways I have delineated the contemporary avant-garde feature film hopefully suggest that it is not a hermetic genre or type, but a category/genre/type wherein the films (and filmmaking) have historical ties while always forging ahead. The films discussed here are by no means representative of any or all types of avant-garde feature films; indeed, they are a small percentage, but they do, hopefully, allow us to recognize them as such — even when they may be called other generic names or types (like art-house film, independent film, foreign film, and so on). This approach, which is socio-cultural more than theoretical, allows us to see the intertextual nature of avant-garde feature films, and that they do indeed intersect with other cinema and other forms of cultural representation. So, while I will readily admit that some of the films I discuss in the part of this book may not align with many critics' definitions or peoples' assumptions of avant-garde cinema, I offer them as a way of re-thinking the boundaries that genre often creates, so that we may re-examine longer avant-garde films and perhaps situate them into a newer type that can create a genre (like, for example, City Symphony, Collage Film, Women's Experimental Film, or Surrealist Film).

Abstract works of art, which can include avant-garde feature films, minister themselves to others in unique ways. The current avant-garde both embraces technology and loathes technology; video formats and computer manipulation can create abstract forms of representation, but so can the film strip itself, however obsolete some may deem it. Avant-garde films speak forcefully and directly as "uncorrupted expressions of resistance and transformation."[1] *Participating* in the *liberating* force of the avant-garde feature film allows for a better understanding and appreciation of motion pictures as a whole.

The longevity of the avant-garde is another important issue that I hope to have made clear in this book. One of the greatest attributes that avant-garde cinema maintains is a formidable achievement that has never subsided; unlike more standard genres, like the Gangster Film, Film Noir, or the Musical, that have waned over the past century, the avant-garde film has *always* remained in practice (and popularity) with devoted filmmakers and audiences. Running *ahead of* (or underneath) the mainstream, avant-garde cinema remains as prolific as any traditional genre. In essence, it has always remained a viable alternative to dominant aesthetic and ideological assumptions about the nature and purpose of art in cultural production and consumption. But it also remains contrary — even reactionary — to accepted notions of representation. Hence, the *use* of avant-garde cinema as a critical tool remains far behind the barometer established by Hollywood. But if the savvy filmgoer chooses to heighten his or her awareness of what the cinema can do and what it can accomplish, then he or she will actively seek the avant-garde, for it is there where true vision and originality lies.

The films I have discussed in this text are not difficult except by choice; otherwise, they need repeated viewings for their sheer artistry, their anti-establishment techniques, and their personal visions that are uncompromising and categorically *different*. And accepting and embracing difference is crucial in establishing a particular *taste* or knowledge that acknowledges the "other" as potent and relevant. Avant-garde feature films are pure aesthetic moments of artistic vision; their creation and subsequent consumption relies upon distinction, diversity, and particular positioning in cultural channels. These films will almost always provide a means to counter (a *counter-cinema*) expectations, and therefore will open up many new opportunities for critical discourse, participatory viewing, and pure intellectual and emotional enlightenment. Feature films *should* engage us in such a manner, and the avant-garde features I have mentioned will, hopefully, *lead the way* to a better critical and evaluative form of spectatorship.

Some Avant-Garde
Feature Films

The following is a brief list of films that are avant-garde features. It is not an exhaustive list by any means, and there are several purposeful omissions. For instance, I have not included all Warhol films or Godard films. Nor have I included all Maddin or Svankmajer films, both of whose entire feature film output would certainly be considered avant-garde. Instead, I have tried to compile a range of films from various countries that span the various types of avant-garde feature films outlined in the book, and in the cases of Warhol, Godard, Maddin, and Svankmajer, just those films mentioned in the book as well. I have also attempted to focus primarily on contemporary features. These directors, and others, are included in a separate appendix. One should bear in mind that this is only a small sampling of avant-garde feature films; anyone interested in compiling a longer — and diverse — list certainly may do so. By no means should this list be considered a definitive compilation of avant-garde feature films; it is a sampling.

Films are in chronological order.

Films are listed as: title (date), director. All films are listed by their original titles as released in the United States — some in English, original language, and translation.

1900–1920s

Haxan: Witchcraft Through the Ages (1922), Benjamin Christensen
The Adventures of Prince Achmed (1926), Lotte Reiniger
Napoleon (1927), Abel Gance
Berlin: Symphony of a Metropolis (1927), Walter Ruttmann
Man with a Movie Camera (1927), Dziga Vertov
A Page of Madness (1927), Teinosuke Kinugasa
The Passion of Joan of Arc (1928), Carl-Theodor Dreyer

1930s

Borderline (1930), Kenneth MacPherson
Blood of a Poet (1930), Jean Cocteau

L'Age d'Or (1930), Luis Buñuel
People on Sunday (1930), Robert Siodmak, Edgar G. Ulmer and Fred Zinnemann

1940s

Beauty and the Beast (1946), Jean Cocteau
Distant Journey (1949), Alfred Radok

1950s

Venom and Eternity (1951), Jean Isidore Isou
Closed Vision (1954), Marc'O
8 × 8: A Chess Sonata in 8 Movements (1957), Hans Richter
Heaven and Earth Magic (1957–1962), Harry Smith
Star Spangled to Death (1957–1961; 2003–2004), Ken Jacobs
A Midsummer Night's Dream (1959), Jiří Trnka

1960s

The Flower Thief (1960), Ron Rice
Testament of Orpheus (1960), Jean Cocteau
Mother Joan of the Angels (1961), Jerzy Kawalerowicz
L'Année dernière à Marienbad (1961), Alain Resnais
Dog Star Man (1961–1964), Stan Brakhage
The Woman in the Dunes (1962), Hiroshi Teshigahara
Queen of Sheba Meets the Atom Man (1963), Ron Rice
I Am Cuba (1964), Mikhail Kalatozov
Songs (1964–1969, 1979–1987), Stan Brakhage
The Saragossa Manuscript (1965), Wojciech Has
Who Are You, Polly Maggoo? (1966), William Klein
Daisies (1966), Věra Chytilová
Finnegan's Wake (1967), Mary Ellen Bute
Portrait of Jason (1967), Shirley Clarke
Scenes from Under Childhood (1967–1970), Stan Brakhage
Love Affair, or the Case of the Missing Switchboard Operator (1967), Dušan Maka-
    vejev
Fando y Lis (1967), Alejandro Jodorowsky
Deux fois (1968), Jackie Raynal
Innocence Unprotected (1968), Dušan Makavejev
Symbiopsychotaxiplasm (1968), William Greaves
Teorema (1968), Pier Paolo Pasolini
The Color of Pomegranates (1968), Sergei Paradjanov
L'Amour Fou (1969), Jacques Rivette
<---> (*Back and Forth*) (1969), Michael Snow
Walden: Diaries, Notes, Sketches (1969), Jonas Mekas
Dillinger Is Dead (1969), Marco Ferreri
Eros + Massacre (1969), Yoshishige Yoshida
Invasión (1969), Hugo Santiago
Mr. Freedom (1969), William Klein
Le Gai Savoir (1969), Jean-Luc Godard
Tom, Tom, The Piper's Son (1969), Ken Jacobs
Reason Over Passion (1969), Joyce Wieland

1970s

Fruit of Paradise (1970), Vera Chytilova
Vampir-Cuadecuc (1970), Pere Portabella
The Hart of London (1970), Jack Chambers
El Topo (1970), Alejandro Jodorowsky
Zorns Lemma (1970), Hollis Frampton
Fata Morgana (1971), Werner Herzog
Out 1 (1971), Jacques Rivette
W.R.: Mysteries of the Organism (1971), Dušan Makavejev
The Discreet Charm of the Bourgeoisie (1972), Luis Buñuel
Umbracle (1972), Pere Portabella
The Holy Mountain (1973), Alejandro Jodorowsky
Themroc (1973), Claude Faraldo
Up to and Including Her Limits (1973–1976), Carolee Schneemann
The Hourglass Sanitorium (1973), Wojciech Has
Je Tu Il Elle (1974), Chantal Akerman
Vase de Noces (1974), Thierry Zéno
The Phantom of Liberty (1974), Luis Buñuel
Immoral Tales (1974), Walerian Borowczyk
Mahler (1974), Ken Russell
Jeanne Dielman, 23 quai du Commerce, 1080 Bruxelles (1975), Chantal Akerman
The Mirror (1975), Andrei Tarkovsky
Black Moon (1975), Louis Malle
We Can't Go Home Again (1976), Nicholas Ray
Hitler, a Film from Germany (1977), Hans-Jürgen Syberberg
House (1977), Nobuhiko Obayashi
That Obscure Object of Desire (1977), Luis Buñuel
Eraserhead (1977), David Lynch
A Grin Without a Cat (1977), Chris Marker
Madame X — An Absolute Ruler (1977), Ulrike Ottinger
Cinématon (1978–2011), Gérard Courant

1980s

The Age of the Earth (1980), Glauber Rocha
Journeys from Berlin/1971 (1980), Yvonne Rainer
The Falls (1980), Peter Greenaway
Arrebato (1980), Iván Zulueta
Mon oncle d'Amérique (1980), Alain Resnais
Arabic Numeral Series (1981–1982), Stan Brakhage
Is This What You Were Born For? (1981–1989), Abigail Child
Chronopolis (1982), Piotr Kamler
On Top of the Whale (1982), Raúl Ruiz
Powaqqatsi (1982), Godfrey Reggio
City of Pirates (1983), Raúl Ruiz
Born in Flames (1983), Lizzie Borden
The Ties That Bind (1984), Su Friedrich
The Angelic Conversation (1985), Derek Jarman
Angel's Egg (1985), Tokuma Shoten
The Pied Piper of Hamelin (1985), Jiří Barta
Manoel's Destinies (1985), Raúl Ruiz

Nidhiyude Katha (1986), Vijayakrishnan
The Cure for Insomnia (1987), John Henry Timmis IV
Tetsuo: The Iron Man (1989), Shinya Tsukamoto
Surname Viet Given Name Nam (1989), Trinh T. Minh-ha

1990s

Archangel (1990), Guy Maddin
Begotten (1991), E. Elias Merhige
Europa (1991), Lars von Trier
Lyrical Nitrate (1991), Peter Delpeut
Prospero's Books (1991), Peter Greenaway
Talking Head (1992), Mamoru Oshii
Bullets for Breakfast (1992), Holly Fisher
24 Hour Psycho (1993), Douglas Gordon
Wax or the Discovery of Television Among the Bees (1993), David Blair
Libera me (1993), Alain Cavalier
Blue (1993), Derek Jarman
Satantango (1994), Bela Tarr
Cremaster Cycle (1994–2002), Matthew Barney
Lumière and Company (1995), various
Codex Atanicus (1995–1999), Carlos Atanes
Conspirators of Pleasure (1996), Jan Svankmajer
Flat Is Beautiful (1998), Sadie Benning
The Idiots (1998), Lars von Trier

2000s

De Udstillede (2000), Jesper Jargil
Timecode (2000), Mike Figgis
Subconscious Cruelty (2000), Karim Hussain
Mysterious Object at Noon (2000), Apichatpong Weerasethakul
Reconstruction (2001), Irene Lusztig
Claire (2001), Milford Thomas
Naqoyqatsi (2002), Godfrey Reggio
Blissfully Yours (2002), Apichatpong Weerasethakul
*Corpus Callosum (2002), Michael Snow
Decasia (2002), Bill Morrison
Rabbits (2002), David Lynch
Certain Women (2003), Peggy Ahwesh with Bobby Abate
Woodenhead (2003), Florian Habicht
Dogville (2003), Lars von Trier
Bodysong (2003), Simon Pummell
Alila (2003), Amos Gitai
Georges Bataille's Story of the Eye (2004), Andrew Repasky McElhinney
Daniel — Der Zauberer (2004), Ulli Lommel
Tropical Malady (2004), Apichatpong Weerasethakul
Funky Forest: The First Contact (2005), Katsuhito Ishii, Hajimine Ishimine and
      Shunichiro Miki
The Joy of Life (2005), Jenni Olson
Manderlay (2005), Lars von Trier
Blood Tea and Red String (2006), Christiane Cegavske

Matrjoschka (2006), Karin Hoerler
The Book of the Dead (2006), Kihachiro Kawamoto
Inland Empire (2006), David Lynch
We Are the Strange (2007), M dot Strange
Dustclouds (2007), Filip Jan Rymsza
Glass Lips (2007), Lech Majewski
Helsinki, Forever (2008), Peter von Bagh
The Philosopher's Stone (2008), Raymond Salvatore Harmon
Canary (2008), Alejandro Adams
The Lollipop Generation (2008), G.B. Jones
Saturn Returns (2009), Lior Shamriz
Trash Humpers (2009), Harmony Korine
Maximum Shame (2010), Carlos Atanes

❧ Appendix B ❧

Directors of Avant-Garde Feature Films

The following is a brief list of directors whose feature film work is almost always consistently avant-garde and experimental. Like the list of films, it is not an exhaustive list, but serves as an introduction to only some whose work does not fit into any particular category or genre — other than avant-garde. And, I will stress, I have tried to list only those directors whose *features* may be considered avant-garde, so many names have been omitted simply because the majority of their work is in short film production. Again, one should bear in mind this is only a *very small* sampling of directors.

The list is alphabetical.

Fernando Arrabal
Craig Baldwin
Stan Brakhage
Luis Buñuel
Vera Chytilova
Jean Cocteau
Hollis Frampton
Su Friedrich
Abel Gance
Jean-Luc Godard
Peter Greenaway
Wojciech Has
Katsuhito Ishii
Ken Jacobs
Derek Jarman
Alejandro Jodorowsky
Jerzy Kawalerowicz
Kihachiro Kawamoto
William Klein
Guy Maddin

Dusan Makavejev
Chris Marker
Jonas Mekas
Shunichiro Miki
Trinh T. Minh-ha
Ulrike Ottinger
Sergei Paradjanov
Brothers Quay
Yvonne Rainer
Alain Resnais
Raúl Ruiz
Ken Russell
Carolee Schneeman
Michael Snow
Jan Svankmajer
Hans-Jürgen Syberberg
Bela Tarr
Shinya Tsukamoto
Andy Warhol
Apichatpong Weerasethakul

Chapter Notes

Introduction

1. See, for example, P. Adams Sitney's *Visionary Film: The American Film Avant-Garde, 1943–2000* (2002); Wheeler Winston Dixon and Gwendolyn Audrey Foster's *Experimental Cinema: The Film Reader* (2002); or Michael O'Pray's *Avant-Garde Film: Forms, Themes and Passions* (2003).

2. A good example may be Hitchcock's *Spellbound* (1945), whose dream sequence was created by Salvador Dalì. A more recent example would be Darren Aronofsky's *Requiem for a Dream* (2000), which uses fish-eye lenses to over–dramatize and distort scenes.

3. See MacDonald, *Adventures of Perception*, pp. 15–16 for a very brief listing of various types of avant-garde movements.

4. See, for example P. Adams Sitney, who, when referring to avant-garde films of the 1970s through 1990s, writes, "A brief push for feature–length, narrative films failed, yet again, to open an avenue toward wider commercial acceptance…" p. 410.

5. For instance, anyone from Marcel Duchamp to Picasso to Andy Warhol has been discussed as such.

6. Stravinsky's *The Rite of Spring* caused a riot when it premiered in 1913. John Cage's compositions are routinely described as avant-garde, and he is considered a major influence on minimalist music.

7. Merce Cunningham, Alvin Ailey, or Martha Graham have all been applauded for their innovative choreography.

8. Michael O'Pray, *Avant-Garde Film: Themes, Forms and Passions* (London: Wallflower Press, 2003), 49.

9. Robert Stam, *Film Theory: An Introduction* (Malden, MA: Blackwell Publishers, 2000), 55.

10. Murray Smith, "Modernism and the Avant-Gardes," in *The Oxford Guide to Film Studies*, eds. John Hill and Pamela Church Gibson (London: Oxford University Press, 1998), 397.

11. Timothy Corrigan and Patricia White, *The Film Experience* (Boston: Bedford/St. Martin's, 2009), 312–325.

Chapter 1

1. Jeffrey Skoller, *Shadows, Specters, Shards: Making History in Avant-Garde Film* (Minneapolis: University of Minnesota Press, 2005), xxiv.

2. Andras Balint Kovacs, *Screening Modernism: European Art Cinema, 1950–1980* (Chicago: University of Chicago Press), 32.

3. David Bordwell, *On the History of Film Style* (Cambridge: Harvard University Press), 4.

4. Bill Nichols, *Engaging Cinema: An Introduction to Film Studies* (New York: Norton, 2010), 83–84.

5. Robert Ray, *How a Film Theory got Lost and Other Mysteries in Cultural Studies* (Bloomington: Indiana University Press, 2001), 75.

6. Skoller, xxiii.

7. Ray, 76.

8. Skoller, xiv.

9. Nichols, 116.

10. Ibid., 77.

11. Scott MacDonald, *Avant-Garde Film: Motion Studies* (Cambridge: Cambridge University Press, 1993), 2.

12. Nichols, 86.

13. Ibid., 85.

14. MacDonald, 2.

15. Dudley Andrew, *Concepts in Film Theory* (London: Oxford University Press, 1984), 66.

16. Nichols, 89.

17. Skoller, xxiv.

18. MacDonald, 1.

19. Ray, 76.

20. Nichols, 89.

21. James Peterson, *Dreams of Chaos, Visions of Order: Understanding the American Avant-Garde Cinema* (Detroit: Wayne State University Press, 1994), 21.

22. Skoller, xxxii.

23. Tom Gunning, "The Cinema of Attraction: Early Film, Its Spectator, and the Avant-Garde," in *Film and Theory: An Anthology*, eds. Robert Stam and Toby Miller (Malden, MA: Blackwell Publishers, 2000), 229.

24. Paul Arthur, *A Line of Sight: American Avant-Garde Film Since 1965* (Minneapolis: University of Minnesota Press, 2005), xvi.

25. See Sitney's *Visionary Film* (2000) primarily for discussions of these types, but also his *Eyes Upside Down* (2008) for expansion on other types.

26. See Horak's *Lovers of Cinema* (1995) for brief outlines of types of avant-garde films.

27. Timothy Corrigan and Patricia White, *The Film Experience* (Boston: Bedford/St. Martin's, 2009), 334.

28. Jacques Derrida, "The Law of Genre," in *Acts of Literature*, Ed. Derek Attridge (London: Routledge, 1992), 230.

29. Nichols, 90–91.

30. Steve Neale, *Genre and Hollywood* (London: Routledge, 2000), 39.

31. Edward Small, *Direct Theory: Experimental Film/Video as Major Genre* (Carbondale: Southern Illinois University Press, 1995), xiv.

32. Neale, 27.

33. Barry Keith Grant, "Introduction," in *Film Genre Reader*, ed. Barry Keith Grant (Austin: University of Texas Press, 1986), ix.

34. Andrew, 23.

Chapter 2

1. Bill Nichols, *Engaging Cinema: An Introduction to Film Studies* (New York: Norton, 2010), 190.

2. Scott MacDonald, *Avant-Garde Film: Motion Studies* (Cambridge: Cambridge University Press, 1993), 2–3.

3. Jeffrey Skoller, *Shadows, Specters, Shards: Making History in Avant-Garde Film* (Minneapolis: University of Minnesota Press, 2005), xxviii.

4. Duncan Reekie, *Subversion: The Definitive History of Avant-Garde Cinema* (London: Wallflower Press, 2007), 76.

5. A.L. Rees, *A History of Experimental Film and Video* (London: BFI Publishing, 1999), 2.

6. Reekie, 81.

7. Michael O'Pray, *Avant-Garde Film: Forms, Themes and Passions* (London: Wallflower Press, 2003), 9.

8. Jan-Christopher Horak, "The First American Film Avant-Garde, 1919–1945," in *Lovers of Cinema: The First American Film Avant-Garde, 1919–1945*, Ed. Jan-Christopher Horak (Madison: The University of Wisconsin Press, 1995), 15.

9. Ibid., 19.

10. Ibid., 29.

11. O'Pray, 8.

12. Reekie, 77.

13. O'Pray, 48.

14. P. Adams Sitney, *Visionary Film: The American Avant-Garde, 1943–2000* (Oxford: Oxford University Press, 2002), 15.

15. O'Pray, 49.

16. Rees, 58.

17. Reekie, 135.

18. Sitney, 18.

19. David Bordwell and Kristin Thompson, *Film History: An Introduction* (Boston: McGraw-Hill, 2010), 92.

20. Susan Hayward, *Cinema Studies: The Key Concepts* (London: Routledge, 2000), 172.

21. David Cook, *A History of Narrative Film* (New York: Norton, 2004), 94.

22. Ibid., 95.

23. Sitney, 11.

24. MacDonald, 3.

25. Rees, 43.

26. Ibid., 43.

27. Graeme Harper and Rob Stone, "Introduction: The Unsilvered Screen," in *The Unsilvered Screen: Surrealism on Film*, eds. Graeme Harper and Rob Stone (London: Wallflower Press, 2007), 2–3.

28. Skoller, xviii.

29. Reekie, 121.

30. O'Pray, 12.

31. Reekie, 58–59.

32. Robert Stam, *Film Theory: An Introduction* (Malden, MA: Blackwell Publishers, 2000), 38.

33. Ibid., 86.

Chapter 3

1. Bill Nichols, *Engaging Cinema: An Introduction to Film Studies* (New York: Norton, 2010), 81.

2. A.O. Scott, "The Reassuring Shock of

the Early Buñuel," *The New York Times* (January 25, 2004). No page numbers. http://www.nytimes.com/2004/01/25/movies/film-the-reassuring-shock-of-the-early-bunuel.html.

3. Rob Stone, *Spanish Cinema* (London: Pearson Longman, 2002), 52.

4. Ramona Fotiade, "From Ready-Made to Moving Image: The Visual Poetics of Surrealist Cinema," in *The Unsilvered Screen: Surrealism on Film*, eds. Graeme Harper and Rob Stone (London: Wallflower Press, 2007), 14.

5. Sophy Williams, "*L'Age d'Or*: Faux-Raccord," *Senses of Cinema* (January 23, 2008). No page numbers. http://www.sensesofcinema.com/contents/cteq/00/5/age.html.

6. Allen Weiss, "Between the Sign of the Scorpion and the Sign of the Cross: *L'Age d'Or*," in *Dada and Surrealist Film*, ed. Rudolf Kuenzli (New York: Willis Locker and Owens, 1987), 159.

7. Williams.

8. Weiss, 160.

9. Fotiade, 20.

10. Chris Jenks, *Transgression* (London: Routledge, 2003), 154–155.

11. Weiss, 161.

12. Stone, 24.

13. Williams.

14. Nichols, 81.

15. Jean Cocteau, *The Blood of a Poet* (DVD), Liner Notes. Criterion, 2000.

16. Julia Levin, "The Blood of a Poet," *Senses of Cinema*. No page numbers. http://www.sensesofcinema.com/2003/cteq/blood_of_a_poet/.

17. Bill Nichols, *Engaging Cinema: An Introduction to Film Studies* (New York: Norton, 2010), 80.

18. Cocteau.

19. Roy Armes, "The Blood of a Poet," *Film Reference*. No page numbers. http://www.filmreference.com/Films-Ro-Se/Le-Sang-D-Un-Poete.html.

20. André Fraigneau, *Cocteau on the Film: Conversations with Jean Cocteau Recorded by André Fraigneau* (New York: Dover Publications, 1972), viii-ix.

21. Rudolf Kuenzli, "Introduction," in *Dada and Surrealist Film*, ed. Rudolf E. Kuenzli (New York: Willis Locker and Owens, 1987), 10.

22. A.L. Rees, *A History of Experimental Film and Video* (London: BFI Publishing, 1999), 46.

23. Fraigneau, 60.

24. Rees, 47.

25. Richard Suchenski, "Hans Richter,"

Senses of Cinema. No page numbers. http://www.sensesofcinema.com/2009/great-directors/hans-richter/.

26. Ibid.

27. A.L. Rees, *A History of Experimental Film and Video* (London: BFI Publishing, 1999), 56.

28. Ibid., 55.

29. Suchenski.

30. Bret Wood, "Jean-Isidore Isou: *Venom and Eternity*." April 4, 2007. No page numbers. http://bretwood.blogspot.com/2007/04/venom-and-eternity.html.

31. A.L. Rees, *A History of Experimental Film and Video* (London: BFI Publishing, 1999), 63.

32. Laura Rascaroli, *The Personal Camera: Subjective Cinema and the Essay Film* (London: Wallflower Press, 2009), 22.

Chapter 4

1. P. Adams Sitney, *Visionary Film: The American Avant-Garde, 1943–2000* (Oxford: Oxford University Press, 2002), 14.

2. Ibid., 14.

3. Ibid., 18–19.

4. A.L. Rees, *A History of Experimental Film and Video* (London: BFI Publishing, 1999), 58.

5. Michael O'Pray, *Avant-Garde Film: Forms, Themes and Passions* (London: Wallflower Press, 2003), 49.

6. Rees, 59.

7. Jonas Mekas, "Notes on the New American Cinema," in *Experimental Cinema: The Film Reader*, eds. Wheeler Winston Dixon and Gwendolyn Audrey Foster (London: Routledge, 2002), 54.

8. Ibid., 62.

Chapter 5

1. Noel Carroll, "Mind, Medium and Metaphor in Harry Smith's *Heaven and Earth Magic*," *Film Quarterly* Vol. 31, No. 2 (Winter 1977–78), 37.

2. P. Adams Sitney, *Visionary Film: The American Avant-Garde, 1943–2000* (Oxford: Oxford University Press, 2002), 236.

3. Fred Camper, "Heaven and Earth Magic." *Chicago Reader*. No page numbers. http://www.chicagoreader.com/chicago/calendar/Content?oid=914484.

4. P. Adams Sitney, "Harry Smith Interview," in *Film Culture Reader*, ed. P. Adams

Sitney (New York: Cooper Square Press, 2000), 272.

5. Carroll, 42.

6. Ibid., 39.

7. Sitney, *Visionary Film*, 249.

8. Carroll, 37.

9. Ibid., 38.

10. Ibid.

11. Ibid., 43.

12. Sitney, *Visionary Film*, 238.

13. Michael O'Pray, *Avant-Garde Film: Forms, Themes and Passions* (London: Wallflower Press, 2003), 86.

14. A.L. Rees, *A History of Experimental Film and Video* (London: BFI Publishing, 1999), 69.

15. P. Adams Sitney, *Visionary Film: The American Avant-Garde, 1943–2000* (Oxford: Oxford University Press, 2002), 349.

16. Ibid., 351.

17. Thom Andersen, "The '60s Without Compromise: Watching Warhol's Films," *Rouge* (2006). No page numbers. http://www.rouge.com.au/8/warhol.html.

18. Ibid.

19. O'Pray, 86.

20. Sitney, 351.

21. O'Pray, 88–89.

22. P. Adams Sitney, "Structural Film," in *Film Culture Reader*, ed. P. Adams Sitney (New York: Cooper Square Press, 2000), 327.

23. Sitney, *Visionary Film*, 350.

24. Sitney, "Structural Film," 327.

25. Henry Geldzahler, "Some Notes on Sleep," in *Film Culture Reader*, ed. P. Adams Sitney (New York: Cooper Square Press, 2000), 300.

26. Ibid., 301.

27. Sitney, *Visionary Film*, 351.

28. Ibid., 351–352.

29. Scott MacDonald, *A Critical Cinema 2: Interviews with Independent Filmmakers* (Berkeley: University of California Press, 1992), 78.

30. David James, "Film Diary/Diary Film: Practice and Product in *Walden*," in *To Free the Cinema: Jonas Mekas and the New York Underground*, ed. David E. James (Princeton: Princeton University Press, 1992), 147.

31. Sitney, P. Adams, *Eyes Upside Down: Visionary Filmmakers and the Heritage of Emerson* (London: Oxford University Press, 2008), 85.

32. MacDonald, 98.

33. Ibid., 101.

34. Ibid., 78–79.

35. Sitney, 89.

36. James, 151.

37. Jerome Sans, "Just Like a Shadow: Jerome Sans Speaks to Jonas Mekas," *The Vilnius* 11 (2001). No page numbers. http://test.svs.lt/?Vilnius;Number%2816%29;Article%2824%29.

38. Ibid.

39. James, 154.

40. Sitney, 92.

41. James, 164–165.

42. Ibid., 157.

43. Mark Segal, "Hollis Frampton/*Zorns Lemma*," *Film Culture* 52 (1971): 88–95.

44. Scott MacDonald, *Avant-Garde Film: Motion Studies* (Cambridge: Cambridge University Press, 1993), 71.

45. P. Adams Sitney, *Visionary Film: The American Avant-Garde, 1943–2000* (Oxford: Oxford University Press, 2002), 27.

46. Ibid., 285.

47. Ibid., 306.

48. Ibid., 306.

49. Ibid., 348.

50. Peter Gidal, "Introduction," *Structural Film Anthology* (London: BFI Publishing, 1976). http://www.luxonline.org.uk/articles/theory_and_definition%281%29.html.

51. MacDonald, 69.

52. Sitney, 369.

53. Segal.

54. MacDonald, 70.

55. Segal.

Part III

1. Barbara Wilinsky, *Sure Seaters: The Emergence of Art House Cinema* (Minneapolis: University of Minnesota Press, 2001), 28.

2. Geoffrey Nowell-Smith, "Art Cinema," in *The Oxford History of World Cinema*, ed. Geoffrey Nowell-Smith (Oxford: Oxford University Press, 1996), 567.

3. Elizabeth Ezra, "Introduction: A Brief History of Cinema in Europe," in *European Cinema*, ed. Elizabeth Ezra (Oxford: Oxford University Press, 2004), 1.

4. Wilinsky, 18.

5. Rosalind Galt and Karl Schoonover, "Introduction: The Impurity of Art Cinema," in *Global Art Cinema*, eds. Rosalind Galt and Karl Schoonover (Oxford: Oxford University Press, 2010), 6.

6. Angela Ndalianis, "Art Cinema," in *The Cinema Book*, ed. Pam Cook (London: BFI Publishing, 2007), 83.

7. Galt and Schoonover, 6.

8. Matei Calinescu, *Five Faces of Modernity* (Durham: Duke University Press, 1987), 5.

9. Ibid.

10. See Greenberg, *The Collected Essays and Criticism* (1986); here, cited in Kovacs, *Screening Modernism* (2007)

11. Quoted in Andras Balint Kovacs, *Screening Modernism: European Art Cinema, 1950-1980* (Chicago: University of Chicago Press, 2007), 11.

12. Dudley Andrew, *Concepts in Film Theory* (London: Oxford University Press, 1984), 62.

13. Kovacs, 31.

14. Ben Singer, *Melodrama and Modernity: Early Sensational Cinema and Its Contexts* (New York: Columbia University Press, 2001), 20.

15. Calinescu, 95.

Chapter 6

1. David Schwartz, "Visions of New York: Films from the 1960s Underground," in *Underground U.S.A.: Filmmaking Beyond the Hollywood Canon*, eds. Xavier Mendik and Steven Jay Schneider (London: Wallflower Press, 2002), 203.

2. A.L. Rees, *A History of Experimental Film and Video* (London: BFI Publishing, 1999), 62–63.

3. Parker Tyler, *Underground Film: A Critical History* (New York: Da Capo Press, 1995), 35.

4. J. Hoberman and Jonathan Rosenbaum, *Midnight Movies* (New York: Harper and Row, 1983), 39.

5. Ibid., 40.

6. Lauren Rabinovitz, "Wearing the Critic's Hat: History, Critical Discourses, and the American Avant-Garde Cinema," in *To Free the Cinema: Jonas Mekas and the New York Underground*, ed. David E. James (Princeton: Princeton University Press, 1992), 277–278.

7. Duncan Reekie, *Subversion: The Definitive History of Avant-Garde Cinema* (London: Wallflower Press, 2007), 136.

8. Ibid., 139.

9. Jonas Mekas, "Notes on the New American Cinema," in *Experimental Cinema: The Film Reader*, eds. Wheeler Winston Dixon and Gwendolyn Audrey Foster (London: Routledge, 2002), 60.

10. Ibid., 66.

11. Wheeler Winston Dixon, *The Exploding Eye: A Re-Visionary History of 1960s American Experimental Cinema* (Albany: State University of New York Press, 1997), 2.

12. Walter Metz, "'What Went Wrong?': The American Avant-Garde Cinema of the 1960s," in *The Sixties: 1960–1969*, ed. Paul Monaco (Berkeley: University of California Press, 2001), 259.

13. Michael O'Pray, *Avant-Garde Film: Forms, Themes and Passions* (London: Wallflower Press, 2003), 96.

14. Rees, 64.

15. Dixon, *The Exploding Eye*, 5.

16. Tyler, 10.

17. Xavier Mendik and Steven Jay Schneider, "Explorations Underground: American Film (Ad)ventures Beneath the Hollywood Radar," in *Underground U.S.A.: Filmmaking Beyond the Hollywood Canon*, eds. Xavier Mendik and Steven Jay Schneider (London: Wallflower Press, 2002), 2.

18. O'Pray, 107.

19. Ernest Mathijs and Xavier Mendik, "What Is a Cult Film?" in *The Cult Film Reader*, eds. Ernest Mathijs and Xavier Mendik (London: Open University Press, 2008), 11.

20. Ibid., 1–9.

21. Ernest Mathijs and Xavier Mendik, "The Concept of Cult," in *The Cult Film Reader*, eds. Ernest Mathijs and Xavier Mendik (London: Open University Press, 2008), 15.

22. Ibid., 18.

23. Reekie, 206.

24. Ibid., 204.

25. Ibid., 204–206.

26. Ibid., 206.

Chapter 7

1. Jeffrey Skoller, *Shadows, Specters, Shards: Making History in Avant-Garde Film* (Minneapolis: University of Minnesota Press, 2005), xxiii.

2. Alexandre Astruc, "The Birth of a New Avant-Garde: La Camera-Stylo," in *Film and Literature: An Introduction and Reader*, ed. Timothy Corrigan (Upper Saddle River, NJ: Prentice-Hall, 1999), 159.

3. Robert Stam, *Film Theory: An Introduction* (Malden, MA: Blackwell Publishers, 2000), 83.

4. Timothy Corrigan, "The Essay Film as a Cinema of Ideas," in *Global Art Cinema*, eds. Rosalind Galt and Karl Schoonover (Oxford: Oxford University Press, 2010), 222.

5. Laura Rascaroli, *The Personal Camera: Subjective Cinema and the Essay Film* (London: Wallflower Press, 2009), 106.

6. Bill Nichols, *Engaging Cinema: An Introduction to Film Studies* (New York: Norton, 2010), 100.

7. Rascaroli, 106.

8. Timothy Corrigan, "Expression, the Essayistic, and Thinking in Images." No Page Numbers. http://www.facstaff.bucknell.edu/efaden/ms5/corrigan1.htm.

9. Rascaroli, 23.

10. Quoted in Timothy Corrigan, *New German Film: The Displaced Image* (Bloomington: Indiana University Press, 1994), 151.

11. Ibid., 156.

12. Susan Sontag. "Syberberg's Hitler," in *Under the Sign of Saturn* (New York: Farrar, Strauss, Giroux, 1980), 138–139.

13. Quoted in Timothy Corrigan, *Film and Literature: An Introduction and Reader* (Upper Saddle River, NJ: Prentice-Hall, 1999), 58.

14. Skoller, xxvi.

15. Rascaroli, 22–23.

16. Kaja Silverman and Harun Farocki, "I Speak, Therefore I'm Not —*Gay Knowledge/Le Gai Savoir* (1968)," in *Speaking About Godard* (New York: New York University Press, 1998), 113.

17. James Monaco, "*Le Gai Savoir:* Picture and Act —Godard's Plexus," *Jump Cut* 7 (1975), 15.

18. Silverman and Farocki, 127.

19. Rascaroli, 87.

20. Rosenstone, Robert A., *History on Film/Film on History* (London: Pearson Longman, 2006), 19.

21. David Sterritt, "*A Grin Without a Cat*— Web Exclusive," *Cineaste* vol. XXXIV, no.4 (2009). No Page Numbers. http://www.cineaste.com/articles/ema-grin-without–a-catem.

22. Rascaroli, 64.

23. Sterritt.

24. Jean Petrolle and Virginia Wright Wexman, "Introduction: Experimental Filmmaking and Women's Subjectivity," in *Women and Experimental Filmmaking*, eds. Jean Petrolle and Virginia Wright Wexman (Urbana: University of Illinois Press, 2005), 3.

25. Robin Blaetz, "Introduction: Women's Experimental Cinema: Critical Frameworks," in *Women's Experimental Cinema*, ed. Robin Blaetz (Durham: Duke University Press, 2007), 11.

26. Ibid., 12.

27. Petrolle and Wexman, 1.

28. Ibid., 5.

29. Nichols, 91.

30. Janet Cutler, "Su Friedrich: Breaking the Rules," in *Women's Experimental Cinema*, ed. Robin Blaetz (Durham: Duke University Press, 2007), 322.

31. Scott MacDonald, *A Critical Cinema 2: Interviews with Independent Filmmakers* (Berkeley: University of California Press, 1992), 284.

32. Cecelia Muhlstein, "Su Friedrich in Conversation with Cecelia Muhlstein," *New York Arts Magazine* (May-June 2008). No page Numbers. http://www.nyartsmagazine.com/index.php?option=com_content&task=view&id=177282&Itemid=747.

33. Cutler, 312.

34. MacDonald, 295.

35. Jean Petrolle and Virginia Wright Wexman, "Chantal Akerman," in *Women and Experimental Filmmaking*, eds. Jean Petrolle and Virginia Wright Wexman (Urbana: University of Illinois Press, 2005), 45.

36. Jonathan Rosenbaum, "Romance of the Ordinary [on Chantal Akerman]," *Chicago Reader* (January 26, 1990). No page Numbers. http://www.jonathanrosenbaum.com/?p=7472.

37. Ivone Margulies, *Nothing Happens: Chantal Akerman's Hyperrealist Everyday* (Durham: Duke University Press, 1996), 7.

38. Jerry White, "Chantal Akerman's Revisionist Aesthetic," in *Women and Experimental Filmmaking*, Eds. Jean Petrolle and Virginia Wright Wexman (Urbana: University of Illinois Press, 2005), 47.

39. Ibid., 67.

40. Margulies, 118.

41. White, 66.

42. Judith Mayne, "Women in the Avant-Garde: Germaine Dulac, Maya Deren, Agnes Varda, Chantal Akerman, and Trinh T. Minh-ha," in *Experimental Cinema: The Film Reader*, eds. Wheeler Winston Dixon and Gwendolyn Audrey Foster (London: Routledge, 2002), 89.

43. Jan-Christopher Horak, "The First American Film Avant-Garde, 1919–1945," in *Lovers of Cinema: The First American Film Avant-Garde, 1919–1945*, ed. Jan-Christopher Horak (Madison: The University of Wisconsin Press, 1995), 33.

44. Corrigan, "The Essay Film as a Cinema of Ideas," 219.

Chapter 8

1. Karla Oeler, "A Collective Interior Monologue: Sergei Paradjanov and Eisenstein's Joyce-Inspired Vision of Cinema," *The

Modern Language Review 101, no. 2 (April 2006): 479.

2. Andras Balint Kovacs, *Screening Modernism: European Art Cinema, 1950–1980* (Chicago: University of Chicago Press), 175.

3. Oeler, 480.

4. James Steffen, book review: "*Seven Visions,*" *Film Quarterly* 54, no. 1 (Autumn 2000): 60.

5. Ibid., 61.

6. Kovacs, 175.

7. Oeler, 485.

8. James Steffen, "Paradjanov's Playful Poetics: On the 'Director's Cut' of *The Color of Pomegranates,*" *Journal of Film and Video* 47, no. 4 (Winter 1995–1996): 21.

9. Oeler, 480.

10. Ibid., 481.

11. Ibid., 483.

12. Steffen, "Paradjanov's Playful Poetics," 24.

13. J. Hoberman and Jonathan Rosenbaum, *Midnight Movies* (New York: Harper and Row, 1983), 214.

14. Chris Rodley, ed., *Lynch on Lynch* (London: Faber and Faber, 2005), 64.

15. Steven Jay Schneider, "The Essential Evil in/of *Eraserhead* (or, Lynch to the Contrary)," in *The Cinema of David Lynch: American Dreams, Nightmare Visions*, eds. Erica Sheen and Annette Davison (London: Wallflower Press, 2004), 7.

16. Tim Hewitt, "Is There Life After *Dune*?" in *David Lynch: Interviews*, ed. Richard A. Barney (Jackson: University of Mississippi Press, 2009), 30.

17. Rodley, 55–56.

18. Stephen Saban and Sarah Longacre, "*Eraserhead*: Is There Life After Birth?" in *David Lynch: Interviews*, ed. Richard A. Barney (Jackson: University of Mississippi Press, 2009), 5.

19. Ibid., 5.

20. Hoberman and Rosenbaum, 214.

21. Rodley, 72.

22. Schneider, 8.

23. K. George Godwin, "*Eraserhead,*" *Film Quarterly* 39 (Autumn 1985), 37.

24. Todd McGowan, *The Impossible David Lynch* (New York: Columbia University Press, 2007), 27.

25. Rodley, 56.

26. McGowan, 47.

27. Hoberman and Rosenbaum, 251.

28. Erica Sheen and Annette Davison, "Introduction: American Dreams, Nightmare Visions," in *The Cinema of David Lynch: American Dreams, Nightmare Visions*, eds. Erica Sheen and Annette Davison (London: Wallflower Press, 2004), 3.

29. Rodley, 78.

30. Hoberman and Rosenbaum, 242.

31. Schneider, 8.

32. Godwin, 38–39.

33. Rodley, 54.

34. Joel Siegel, "Greenaway by the Numbers," in *Peter Greenaway: Interviews*, eds. Vernon Gras and Marguerite Gras (Jackson: University Press of Mississippi, 2000), 73.

35. Amy Lawrence, *The Films of Peter Greenaway* (Cambridge: Cambridge University Press, 1997), 3.

36. Bart Testa, "Tabula for a Catastrophe: Peter Greenaway's *The Falls* and Foucault's Heterotopia," in *Peter Greenaway's Postmodern/Poststructuralist Cinema*, eds. Paula Willoquet-Maricondi and Mary Alemany-Galway (Lanham, MD: Scarecrow, 2008), 91.

37. Lawrence, 23.

38. Robert Brown, "Greenaway's Contract," in *Peter Greenaway: Interviews*, eds. Vernon Gras and Marguerite Gras (Jackson: University Press of Mississippi, 2000), 10.

39. David Pascoe, *Peter Greenaway: Museums and Moving Images* (London: Reaktion Books, 1997), 58.

40. Lawrence, 3.

41. Testa, 14.

42. Lawrence, 24.

43. Michael Ciment, "Interview with Peter Greenway: *Zed and Two Noughts (Z.O.O.)*," in *Peter Greenaway: Interviews*, eds. Vernon Gras and Marguerite Gras (Jackson: University Press of Mississippi, 2000), 35.

44. Testa, 87.

45. Ibid., 97.

46. Lawrence, 27.

47. Ibid., 20.

48. Testa, 83.

49. Lawrence, 43.

50. Paula Willoquet-Maricondi, "From British Cinema to Mega Cinema," in *Peter Greenaway's Postmodern/Poststructuralist Cinema*, eds. Paula Willoquet-Maricondi and Mary Alemany-Galway (Lanham, MD: Scarecrow, 2008), 3.

51. Testa, 96–97.

52. Lawrence, 21.

53. Pascoe, 57–58.

54. Lawrence, 17–18.

55. Pascoe, 58.

56. Tom Mes, *Iron Man: The Cinema of Shinya Tsukamoto* (Surrey: FAB Press, 2005), 59.

57. Quoted in Mes, 59.
58. Mes, 63.
59. Ibid.
60. Ibid., 10.
61. Ibid., 12.
62. Scott MacDonald, *A Critical Cinema 3: Interviews with Independent Filmmakers* (Berkeley: University of California Press, 1998), 285.
63. Ibid., 292.
64. Ibid., 288.
65. Ibid., 289.
66. Ibid., 290.
67. Ramona Fotiade, "From Ready-Made to Moving Image: The Visual Poetics of Surrealist Cinema," in *The Unsilvered Screen: Surrealism on Film*, eds. Graeme Harper and Rob Stone (London: Wallflower Press, 2007), 18.
68. Richard Corliss, "A Happy Birthday for the Kids of Kane," *Time* (May 13, 1991). No page numbers. http://www.time.com/time/magazine/article/0,9171,972906,00.html.
69. Robert Enright, "Far From the Maddin Crowd," in *Guy Maddin: Interviews*, ed. D.K. Holm (Jackson: University Press of Mississippi, 2010), 3.
70. Ibid., 3.
71. David Chute, "Weird Art and Science: Guy Maddin's Primitive Genius," in *Guy Maddin: Interviews*, ed. D.K. Holm (Jackson: University Press of Mississippi, 2010), 29.
72. William Beard, *Into the Past: The Cinema of Guy Maddin* (Toronto: University of Toronto Press, 2010), 56.
73. Mark Peranson, "Guy Maddin," in *Exile Cinema: Filmmakers at Work Beyond Hollywood*, ed. Michael Atkinson (Albany: State University of New York Press, 2008), 140.
74. Will Straw, "Reinhabiting Lost Languages: Guy Maddin's *Careful*," in *Playing with Memories: Essays on Guy Maddin*, ed. David Church (Winnipeg: University of Manitoba Press, 2009), 60.
75. Mike White, "Tales of Guy Maddin," in *Guy Maddin: Interviews*, ed. D.K. Holm (Jackson: University Press of Mississippi, 2010), 45.
76. Caelum Vatnsdal, *Kino Delirium: The Films of Guy Maddin* (Winnipeg: Arbeiter Ring Publishing, 2000), 65.
77. Alan Jones, "Far from the Maddin Crowd: Guy Maddin Interviewed," in *Guy Maddin: Interviews*, ed. D.K. Holm (Jackson: University Press of Mississippi, 2010), 24.
78. Beard, 51.
79. Vatnsdal, 62.
80. David Church, "Bark Fish Apprecia-tion: An Introduction," in *Playing with Memories: Essays on Guy Maddin*, ed. David Church (Winnipeg: University of Manitoba Press, 2009), 8.
81. Dana Cooley, "Demented Enchantments: Guy Maddin's Dis-eased Heart," in *Playing with Memories: Essays on Guy Maddin*, ed. David Church (Winnipeg: University of Manitoba Press, 2009), 184.
82. Geoff Pevere, "Guy Maddin: True to Form," in *Playing with Memories: Essays on Guy Maddin*, ed. David Church (Winnipeg: University of Manitoba Press, 2009), 55.
83. Jones, 25.
84. Stephen Snyder, "Sexuality and Self in the Guy Maddin Vision," in *Playing with Memories: Essays on Guy Maddin*, ed. David Church (Winnipeg: University of Manitoba Press, 2009), 125.
85. Beard, 40.
86. Jones, 19.
87. Ibid., 26.
88. Beard, 66.
89. Nancy Kapitanoff, "Thickening the Plot: 'Bullets for Breakfast,' an Experimental Film, Cracks Open Typical Story Lines on the West and Women's Place in the World," *Los Angeles Times*, September 18, 1992. No page Numbers. http://articles.latimes.com/1992-09-18/news/va-508_1_experimental-film.
90. Ibid.
91. Ibid.
92. André Habib, "Ruin, Archive and the Time of Cinema: Peter Delpeut's 'Lyrical Nitrate,'" *SubStance* 35, no. 2 (2006): 122.
93. Ibid., 127–128.
94. Ibid., 123.
95. Bill Nichols, *Engaging Cinema: An Introduction to Film Studies* (New York: Norton, 2010), 88.
96. Habib, 129.
97. Jonathan Rosenbaum, "Clip Art" 6 August, 1993. No page numbers. http://www.jonathanrosenbaum.com/?p=7073.
98. Ibid.
99. Habib, 128–129.
100. Ibid., 129.
101. Ibid., 136.
102. Ibid., 128.
103. Rosenbaum, "Clip Art."
104. Ibid.
105. Habib, 133.
106. Ibid, 136.
107. André Habib, "Thinking in Ruins: Around the Films of Bill Morrison," *Offscreen*, November 30, 2004. No page Num-

bers. http://www.horschamp.qc.ca/new_off screen/cinematic_ruins.html.

108. Ibid.

109. Tony Peake, *Derek Jarman: A Biography* (Woodstock: The Overlook Press, 1999), 398.

110. Ibid., 399.

111. Tim Ellis, *Derek Jarman's Angelic Conversations* (Minneapolis: University of Minnesota Press, 2009), 233.

112. Ibid., xiii.

113. Peter Wollen, *"Blue,"* *New Left Review* 6 (November/December 2000), 121.

114. Peake, 476.

115. Ellis, 245.

116. Peake, 511.

117. Ellis, 245.

118. Ibid., 241.

119. Ibid., 240.

120. Ibid., 247.

121. Jim Clark, "Jim's Reviews—*Blue.*" Jim's Reviews, June 24, 2008. No page Numbers. http://jclarkmedia.com/jarman/jarman 11.html.

122. Peter Hames, "The Core of Reality: Puppets in the Feature Films of Jan Svankmajer," in *Dark Alchemy: The Cinema of Jan Svankmajer*, ed. Peter Hames (London: Wallflower Press, 2008), 95.

123. Frantisek Dryje, "The Force of Imagination," in *Dark Alchemy: The Cinema of Jan Svankmajer*, ed. Peter Hames (London: Wallflower Press, 2008), 187.

124. Hames, "The Core of Reality," 102.

125. Peter Hames, "Interview with Jan Svankmajer," in *Dark Alchemy: The Cinema of Jan Svankmajer*, ed. Peter Hames (London: Wallflower Press, 2008), 129.

126. Hames, "Interview with Jan Svankmajer," 137.

127. Hames, "The Core of Reality," 95.

128. Dryje, 189.

129. Ibid., 190.

130. Hames, "The Core of Reality," 95.

131. Quoted in Hames, "Interview with Jan Svankmajer," 129.

132. Chris Jenks, *Transgression* (London: Routledge, 2003), 5.

133. Ibid., 186.

134. Hames, "The Core of Reality," 99.

135. Michael O'Pray, "The Animated Film," in *World Cinema: Critical Approaches*, eds. John Hill and Pamela Church Gibson (Oxford University Press, 2000), 52.

136. Hames, "Interview with Jan Svankmajer," 112.

137. Dryje, 188.

138. Wendy Jackson, "The Surrealist Conspirator: An Interview with Jan Svankmajer," *Animation World Magazine* online, June 1997, no page numbers. http://www.awn.com/mag/issue2.3/issue2.3pages/2.3jacksonsvankmajer.html.

139. Hames, "The Core of Reality," 101.

140. Dryje, 187.

141. Peter Hames, *The Czechoslovak New Wave* (London: Wallflower Press, 2005), 256.

142. Hames, "The Core of Reality," 102.

143. Dryje, 190.

144. Paul Wells, *Animation: Genre and Authorship* (London: Wallflower Press, 2002), 50.

145. Julie Sanders, *Adaptation and Appropriation* (London: Routledge, 2006), 82–83.

146. Michael Atkinson, "On DVD: Lech Majewski, 'Brand Upon the Brain!'" *IFC*, August 19, 2008. No page Numbers. http://www.ifc.com/news/2008/08/the-garden-of-earthly-delights.php.

147. Philip Kennicott, "Four Films, One Singular Talent: Majewski Is the Surreal McCoy." *The Washington Post*, August 10, 2007. No Page Numbers. http://www.washingtonpost.com/wpdyn/content/article/2007/08/09/AR2007080902233.html.

148. Magdalena Lebecka, "Glass Lips," *KINO Polish Cinema* 2008, 73–74. http://kino.org.pl/index.php?option=com_content&task=view&id=160&Itemid=134.

149. Dagmara Drzazga, "Lech Majewski: The World According to Bruegel." No page Numbers. http://www.themillandthecross.com/files/bruegel2.pdf.

150. Lebecka.

151. Joe Leydon, *"Glass Lips." Variety*, November 8, 2007. No page Numbers. http://www.variety.com/review/VE1117935367?refcatid=31.

152. Jeannette Catsoulis, *"Glass Lips*: Telling a Tale of Torment, Wordlessly." *New York Times*, November 7, 2007. No page Numbers. http://query.nytimes.com/gst/fullpage.html?res=9402EFDC1138F934A35752C1A9619C8B63.

153. Quoted in Drzazga.

Conclusion

1. Paul Arthur, *A Line of Sight: American Avant-Garde Film Since 1965* (Minneapolis: University of Minnesota Press, 2005), xii.

Bibliography

Altman, Rick. *Film/Genre*. London: British Film Institute, 1999.

Andersen, Thom. "The '60s Without Compromise: Watching Warhol's Films." *Rouge* (2006). No page numbers. http://www.rouge.com.au/8/warhol.html. Accessed 12 January 2011.

Anderson, Steve. "Seeing Is Believing: Unseen Cinema Unearths a New History of the Early American Avant-Garde." *Independent Film and Video Monthly* 24, no. 6 (July, 2001): 33–35.

Andrew, Dudley. *Concepts in Film Theory*. London: Oxford University Press, 1984.

Armes, Roy. "The Blood of a Poet." *Film Reference*. No page numbers. http://www.filmreference.com/Films-Ro-Se/Le-Sang-D-Un-Poete.html. Accessed 20 December 2010.

Arthur, Paul. *A Line of Sight: American Avant-Garde Film Since 1965*. Minneapolis: University of Minnesota Press, 2005.

Astruc, Alexandre. "The Birth of a New Avant-Garde: La Camèra-Stylo from *The New Wave*." In *Film and Literature: An Introduction and Reader*, edited by Timothy Corrigan, 158–162, Upper Saddle River: Prentice-Hall, 1999.

Atkinson, Michael. "On DVD: Lech Majewski, 'Brand Upon the Brain!'" *IFC* (August 19, 2008). No page Numbers. http://www.ifc.com/news/2008/08/the-garden-of-earthly-delights.php. Accessed 24 January 2011.

Beard, William. *Into the Past: The Cinema of Guy Maddin*. Toronto: University of Toronto Press, 2010.

Blaetz, Robin. "Avant-garde Cinema of the Seventies." *Lost Illusions: American Cinema in the Shadows of Watergate and Vietnam, 1970–1979*, edited by David Cook, 453–478. Berkeley: University of California Press, 2002.

_____. "Introduction: Women's Experimental Cinema: Critical Frameworks." In *Women's Experimental Cinema*, edited by Robin Blaetz, 1–19. Durham: Duke University Press, 2007.

Bordwell, David. *On the History of Film Style*. Cambridge: Harvard University Press, 1997.

_____, and Kristin Thompson. *Film Art: An Introduction*. New York: McGraw Hill, 2010.

Brakhage, Stan. *Film at Wit's End: Eight Avant-Garde Filmmakers*. Kingston, NY: Documentext, 1989.

Brown, Robert. "Greenaway's Contract." In *Peter Greenaway: Interviews*, edited by Vernon Gras and Marguerite Gras, 6–12. Jackson: University Press of Mississippi, 2000.

Burger, Peter. *Theory of the Avant-Garde*. Minneapolis: University of Minnesota Press, 1984.

Calinescu, Matei. *Five Faces of Modernity: Modernism, Avant-Garde, Decadence, Kitsch, Postmodernism*. Durham: Duke University Press, 1987.

Camper, Fred. "The End of Avant-Garde Film." *Millennium Film Journal* 16/17/18 (Fall/Winter 1986–87): 99–124.

_____. "Heaven and Earth Magic." *Chicago Reader*. No page numbers. http://www.chicagoreader.com/chicago/calendar/

Content?oid=914484. Accessed 11 November 2010.

Cardullo, Bert. *Cinematic Illusions: Realism, Subjectivity, and the Avant-Garde.* Cambridge: Cambridge Scholars Press, 2008.

Carroll, Noel. "Mind, Medium and Metaphor in Harry Smith's *Heaven and Earth Magic.*" *Film Quarterly* 31, no. 2 (Winter 1977–78): 37–44.

Catsoulis, Jeannette. "*Glass Lips*: Telling a Tale of Torment, Wordlessly." *New York Times*, November 7, 2007. No page Numbers. http://query.nytimes.com/gst/fullpage.html?res=9402EFDC1138F9 34A35752C1A9619C8B63. Accessed 2 February 2011.

Christie, Ian. "The Avant-Garde and European Cinema before 1930." In *The Oxford Guide to Film Studies*, edited by John Hill and Pamela Church Gibson, 449–454. Oxford: Oxford University Press, 1998.

_____. "Histories of the Future: Mapping the Avant-Garde." *Film History* 20, no. 1 (2008): 6–13.

Church, David. "Bark Fish Appreciation: An Introduction." In *Playing with Memories: Essays on Guy Maddin*, edited by David Church, 1–25. Winnipeg: University of Manitoba Press, 2009.

Chute, David. "Weird Art and Science: Guy Maddin's Primitive Genius." In *Guy Maddin: Interviews*, edited by D.K. Holm, 28–30. Jackson: University Press of Mississippi, 2010.

Ciment, Michael. "Interview with Peter Greenway: *Zed and Two Noughts (Z.O.O.)*." In *Peter Greenaway: Interviews*, edited by Vernon Gras and Marguerite Gras, 28–41. Jackson: University Press of Mississippi, 2000.

Clark, Jim. "Jim's Reviews—*Blue*." *Jim's Reviews*, June 24, 2008. No page Numbers. http://jclarkmedia.com/jarman/jarman11.html. Accessed 21 February 2011.

Cocteau, Jean. *The Blood of a Poet.* DVD Liner Notes. Criterion, 2000.

Cook, David. *A History of Narrative Film, Fourth Edition.* New York: Norton, 2004.

Cooley, Dana. "Demented Enchantments: Guy Maddin's Dis-eased Heart." In *Playing with Memories: Essays on Guy Maddin*, edited by David Church, 171–189. Winnipeg: University of Manitoba Press, 2009.

Corliss, Richard. "A Happy Birthday for the Kids of Kane." *Time* (May 13, 1991). No page Numbers. http://www.time.com/time/magazine/article/0,9171,972 906,00.html. Accessed 3 March 2011.

Corrigan, Timothy. "The Essay Film as a Cinema of Ideas." In *Global Art Cinema: New Theories and Histories*, edited by Rosalind Galt and Karl Schoonover, 218–237. Oxford: Oxford University Press, 2010.

_____. "Expression, the Essayistic, and Thinking in Images." No Page Numbers. http://www.facstaff.bucknell.edu/efaden/ms5/corrigan1.htm. Accessed 3 March 2011.

_____. *Film and Literature: An Introduction and Reader.* Upper Saddle River: Prentice-Hall, 1999.

_____. *New German Film: The Displaced Image.* Bloomington: Indiana University Press, 1994.

_____, and Patricia White. *The Film Experience: An Introduction, Second Edition.* Boston: Bedford/St. Martin's, 2009.

Curtis, David. *Experimental Cinema: A Fifty Year Evolution.* London: Studio Vista, 1971.

Cutler, Janet. "Su Friedrich: Breaking the Rules." In *Women's Experimental Cinema*, edited by Robin Blaetz, 312–338. Durham: Duke University Press, 2007.

Derrida, Jacques. "The Law of Genre." In *Acts of Literature*, edited by Derek Attridge, 221–252. London: Routledge, 1992.

Dittmar, Linda. "The Voice of the Other: Women in Third World and Experimental Film." In *Double Vision: Perspectives on Gender and the Visual Arts*, edited by Natalie Harris Bluestone, 125–137. Madison: Fairleigh Dickinson Press, 1995.

Dixon, Wheeler Winston. *The Exploding Eye: A Re-Visionary History of 1960s American Experimental Cinema.* Albany: State University of New York Press, 1997.

_____. "Performativity in the 1960s American Experimental Cinema: The Body as

Site of Ritual and Display." *Film Criticism* 23.1 (1998 Fall): 48–60.

Dixon, Wheeler Winston, and Gwendolyn Audrey Foster, eds. *Experimental Cinema: The Film Reader*. London: Routledge, 2002.

Dryje, Frantisek. "The Force of Imagination." In *Dark Alchemy: The Cinema of Jan Svankmajer*, edited by Peter Hames, 143–203. London: Wallflower Press, 2008.

Drzazga, Dagmara. "Lech Majewski: The World According to Brueghel." No page Numbers. http://www.themillandthecross.com/files/bruegel2.pdf. Accessed 12 February 2011.

Enright, Robert. "Far from the Maddin Crowd." In *Guy Maddin: Interviews*, edited by D.K. Holm, 3–18. Jackson: University Press of Mississippi, 2010.

Ellis, Tim. *Derek Jarman's Angelic Conversations*. Minneapolis: University of Minnesota Press, 2009.

Ezra, Elizabeth, ed. *European Cinema*, Oxford: Oxford University Press, 2004.

Fotiade, Ramona. "From Ready-Made to Moving Image: The Visual Poetics of Surrealist Cinema." In *The Unsilvered Screen: Surrealism on Film*, edited by Graeme Harper and Rob Stone, 9–22. London: Wallflower Press, 2007.

Fraigneau, André. *Cocteau on the Film: Conversations with Jean Cocteau Recorded by André Fraigneau*. New York: Dover Publications, 1972.

Fuller, Greg S. "'Unquiet Years': Experimental Cinema in the 1980s." In *Transforming the Screen, 1950–1959*, edited by Peter Lev, 279–302. New York: Charles Scribner's Sons, 2003.

Fullerton, John. "Introduction: Experiment in Film Before World War II." *Film History* 20.1 (2008): 3–5.

Galt, Rosalind, and Karl Schoonover. *Global Art Cinema: New Theories and Histories*. Oxford: Oxford University Press, 2010.

Geldzahler, Henry. "Some Notes on *Sleep*." In *Film Culture Reader*, edited by P. Adams Sitney, 300–301. New York: Cooper Square Press, 2000.

Gidal, Peter. "Introduction." *Structural Film Anthology*. London: BFI Publishing,

1976. http://www.luxonline.org.uk/articles/theory_and_definition%281%29.html. Accessed 12 February 2011.

———. *Materialist Film*. London: Routledge, 1989.

Godwin, K. George. "*Eraserhead*." *Film Quarterly* 39 (Autumn 1985): 37–43.

Graf, Alexander, and Dietrich Scheunemann. *Avant-Garde Film*. New York: Rodopi, 2007.

Grant, Barry Keith, ed. *Film Genre Reader*. Austin: University of Texas Press, 1986.

Greenberg, Clement. "Where Is the Avant-Garde?" In *Collected Essays and Criticism*, 259–264. Chicago: University of Chicago Press, 1993.

Gunning, Tom. "The Cinema of Attraction: Early Film, Its Spectator, and the Avant-Garde." In *Film and Theory: An Anthology*, edited by Robert Stam and Toby Miller, 229–235. Malden: Blackwell Publishers, 2000.

Habib, André. "Ruin, Archive and the Time of Cinema: Peter Delpeut's 'Lyrical Nitrate.'" *SubStance* 35, no. 2 (2006): 120–139.

———. "Thinking in Ruins: Around the Films of Bill Morrison." *Offscreen*, November 30, 2004. No page Numbers. http://www.horschamp.qc.ca/new_offscreen/cinematic_ruins.html. Accessed 25 February 2011.

Hames, Peter. "The Core of Reality: Puppets in the Feature Films of Jan Svankmajer." In *Dark Alchemy: The Cinema of Jan Svankmajer*, edited by Peter Hames, 83–103. London: Wallflower Press, 2008.

———. *The Czechoslovak New Wave*. London: Wallflower Press, 2005.

———. "Interview with Jan Svankmajer." In *Dark Alchemy: The Cinema of Jan Svankmajer*, edited by Peter Hames, 104–139. London: Wallflower Press, 2008.

Hatfield, Jackie. "Expanded Cinema and Its Relationship to the Avant-Garde: Some Reasons for a Review of the Avant-Garde Debates Around Narrativity." *Millennium Film Journal* 39/40 (Winter 2003): 50–65.

———. *Experimental Film and Video: An Anthology*. Bloomington: Indiana University Press, 2006.

Harper, Graeme, and Rob Stone, eds. *The Unsilvered Screen: Surrealism on Film.* London: Wallflower Press, 2007.

Hawkins, Joan. *Cutting Edge: Art-Horror and the Horrific Avant-Garde.* Minneapolis: University of Minnesota Press, 2000.

Hayward, Susan. *Cinema Studies: The Key Concepts.* London: Routledge, 2000.

Hewitt, Tim. "Is There Life After *Dune?*" In *David Lynch: Interviews,* edited by Richard A. Barney, 29–33. Jackson: University of Mississippi Press, 2009.

Hoberman, J. "After the Avant-Garde Film." In *Art After Modernism: Rethinking Representation,* edited by Brian Wallis. New York: New Museum of Contemporary Art, 1984.

_____. "Three Myths of Avant-Garde Film." *Film Comment* 17 (May/June 1981): 34–35.

_____, and Jonathan Rosenbaum. *Midnight Movies.* New York: Harper and Row, 1983.

Horak, Jan-Christopher. "The First American Film Avant-Garde, 1919–1945." In *Lovers of Cinema: The First American Film Avant-Garde, 1919–1945,* edited by Jan-Christopher Horak, 14–66. Madison: The University of Wisconsin Press, 1995.

Jackson, Wendy. "The Surrealist Conspirator: An Interview with Jan Svankmajer," *Animation World Magazine* 2.3 (June 1997). No page numbers. http://www.awn.com/mag/issue2.3/issue2.3 pages/2.3jacksonsvankmajer.html. Accessed 10 October 2010.

Jacobs, Lewis. *The Rise of the American Film: A Critical History.* New York: Teachers College Press, 1968.

James, David. *Allegories of Cinema: American Film in the Sixties.* Princeton: Princeton University Press, 1989.

_____. *The Most Typical Avant-Garde: History and Geography of Minor Cinemas in Los Angeles.* Berkeley: University of California Press, 2005.

_____, ed. *To Free the Cinema: Jonas Mekas and the New York Underground.* Princeton: Princeton University Press, 1992.

Jenks, Chris. *Transgression.* London: Routledge, 2003.

Jones, Alan. "Far from the Maddin Crowd: Guy Maddin Interviewed." In *Guy Maddin: Interviews,* edited by D.K. Holm, 19–27. Jackson: University Press of Mississippi, 2010.

Kapitanoff, Nancy. "Thickening the Plot: 'Bullets for Breakfast,' an Experimental Film, Cracks Open Typical Story Lines on the West and Women's Place in the World." *Los Angeles Times* (September 18, 1992). No page Numbers. http://articles.latimes.com/1992-09-18/news/va-508_1_experimental-film. Accessed 25 February 2011.

Kennicott, Philip. "Four Films, One Singular Talent: Majewski Is the Surreal McCoy." *The Washington Post* (August 10, 2007). No Page Numbers. http://www.washingtonpost.com/wpdyn/content/article/2007/08/09/AR20070809 02233.html. Accessed 25 February 2011.

Kleinhaus, Chuck. "Reading and Thinking About the Avant-Garde." *Jump Cut* 6 (1975): 21–25.

Kovacs, Andràs Balint. *Screening Modernism: European Art Cinema, 1950–1980.* Chicago: Chicago University Press, 2007.

Kuenzli, Rudolf. *Dada and Surrealist Film.* New York: Willis Locker and Owens, 1987.

Lawrence, Amy. *The Films of Peter Greenaway.* Cambridge: Cambridge University Press, 1997.

Lebecka, Magdalena. "Glass Lips." *KINO Polish Cinema,* 2008: 73–74. http://kino.org.pl/index.php?option=com_content&task=view&id=160&Itemid=134. Accessed 20 February 2011.

Le Grice, Malcolm. *Abstract Film and Beyond.* Cambridge: MIT Press, 1977.

_____. *Experimental Cinema in the Digital Age.* London: BFI Publishers, 2001.

Levin, Julia. "The Blood of a Poet." *Senses of Cinema.* No page numbers. http://www.sensesofcinema.com/2003/cteq/blood_of_a_poet/. Accessed 10 October 2010.

Levy, Emanuel. *Cinema of Outsiders: The Rise of American Independent Film.* New York: New York University Press, 1999.

Lewis, Jon, ed. *The End of Cinema as We*

Know It: American Film in the Nineties. New York: New York University Press, 2001.

Leydon, Joe. *"Glass Lips."* Variety, November 8, 2007. No page Numbers. http://www.variety.com/review/VE1117935367?refcatid=31. Accessed 3 February 2011.

MacDonald, Scott. *Adventures of Perception: Cinema as Exploration–Essays/Interviews.* Berkeley: University of California Press, 2009.

_____. "Avant-Doc: Eight Intersections." *Film Quarterly* 64.2 (December 2010): 50–57.

_____. "Avant-Garde Film: Cinema as Discourse." *Journal of Film and Video* 40.2 (Spring 1988): 33–42.

_____. *Avant-Garde Film: Motion Studies.* Cambridge: Cambridge University Press, 1993.

_____. "Cinema 16: Documents Toward a History of the Film Society." *Wide Angle* 19.1 (January 1997), 28–30.

_____. *A Critical Cinema 2: Interviews with Independent Filmmakers.* Berkeley: University of California Press, 1992.

_____. *A Critical Cinema 3: Interviews with Independent Filmmakers.* Berkeley: University of California Press, 1998.

_____. "Poetry and Avant-Garde Film: Three Recent Contributors." *Poetics Today* 28.1 (Spring 2007): 1–41.

Macrae, David. "Painterly Concepts and Filmic Objects: The Interaction of Expression and Re-Production in Early Avant-Garde Film." In *European Avant-Garde: New Perspectives*, edited by Dietrich Scheunemann, 137–154. Amsterdam: Rodopi, 2000.

Margulies, Ivone. *Nothing Happens: Chantal Akerman's Hyperrealist Everyday.* Durham: Duke University Press, 1996.

Mathijs, Ernest, and Xavier Mendik. "The Concept of Cult." In *The Cult Film Reader*, edited by Ernest Mathijs and Xavier Mendik. London: Open University Press, 2008.

_____. "What Is a Cult Film?" In *The Cult Film Reader*, edited by Ernest Mathijs and Xavier Mendik. London: Open University Press, 2008.

Mayne, Judith. "Women in the Avant-Garde: Germaine Dulac, Maya Deren, Agnes Varda, Chantal Akerman, and Trinh T. Minh-ha." In *Experimental Cinema: The Film Reader*, edited by Wheeler Winston Dixon and Gwendolyn Audrey Foster, 81–112. London: Routledge, 2002.

McCabe, Susan. *Cinematic Modernism: Modernist Poetry and Film.* Cambridge: Cambridge University Press, 2005.

McGowan, Todd. *The Impossible David Lynch.* New York: Columbia University Press, 2007.

Mekas, Jonas. "Notes on the New American Cinema." In *Experimental Cinema: The Film Reader*, edited by Wheeler Winston Dixon and Gwendolyn Audrey Foster, 53–70. London: Routledge, 2002.

Mellencamp, Patricia. *Indiscretions: Avant-Garde Film, Video, and Feminism.* Bloomington: Indiana University Press.

Mendik, Xavier, and Steven Jay Schneider. "Explorations Underground: American Film (Ad)ventures Beneath the Hollywood Radar." In *Underground U.S.A.: Filmmaking Beyond the Hollywood Canon*, edited by Xavier Mendik and Steven Jay Schneider, 1–12. London: Wallflower Press, 2002.

Mes, Tom. *Iron Man: The Cinema of Shinya Tsukamoto.* Surrey: FAB Press, 2005.

Metz, Walter. "'What Went Wrong?': The American Avant-Garde Cinema of the 1960s." In *The Sixties: 1960–1969*, edited by Paul Monaco, 231–260. Berkeley: University of California Press, 2001.

Miller, Tyrus. "Avant-Garde and Theory: A Misunderstood Relation." *Poetics Today* 20.4 (Winter 1999): 549–479.

Moine, Raphaelle, and Pierre Taminioux. "From Surrealist Cinema to Surrealism in Cinema: Does a Surrealist Genre Exist in Film?" *Yale French Studies* 109 (2006): 98–114.

Monaco, James. *"Le Gai Savoir:* Picture and Act — Godard's Plexus." *Jump Cut* 7 (1975), 15–17.

Muhlstein, Cecelia. "Su Friedrich in Conversation with Cecelia Muhlstein." *New York Arts Magazine* (May-June 2008). No page Numbers. http://www.nyarts-magazine.com/index.php?option=com_

content&task=view&id=177282&Itemid=747. Accessed 12 February 2011.

Ndalianis, Angela. "Art Cinema." In *The Cinema Book*, edited by Pam Cook, 83–87. London: BFI Publishing, 2007.

Neale, Steve. "Art Cinema as Institution." *Screen* 22.1 (Spring 1981), 11–39.

_____. *Genre and Hollywood*. London: Routledge, 2000.

Nichols, Bill. "Documentary Film and the Modernist Avant-Garde." *Critical Inquiry* 27.4 (Summer 2001): 580–610.

_____. *Engaging Cinema: An Introduction to Film Studies*. New York: Norton, 2010.

Nowell-Smith, Geoffrey. "Art Cinema." In *The Oxford History of World Cinema*, edited by Geoffrey Nowell-Smith, 567–575. Oxford: Oxford University Press, 1996.

_____. *Making Waves: New Cinemas of the 1960s*. New York: Continuum Press, 2001.

Oeler, Karla. "A Collective Interior Monologue: Sergei Paradjanov and Eisenstein's Joyce-Inspired Vision of Cinema." *The Modern Language Review* 101, no. 2 (April 2006): 472–487.

O'Pray, Michael. "The Animated Film." In *World Cinema: Critical Approaches*, edited by John Hill and Pamela Church Gibson, 50–55. Oxford University Press, 2000.

_____. *Avant-Garde Film: Forms, Themes and Passions*. London: Wallflower Press, 2003.

_____. "'New Romanticism' and British Avant-Garde Film in the Early 80s." In *The British Cinema Book*, edited by Robert Murphy, 256–262. London: BFI Publishers, 2001.

Orr, John. *Cinema and Modernity*. Cambridge: Polity Press, 1993.

_____, and Olga Taxidou, eds. *Post-War Cinema and Modernity*. New York: New York University Press, 2001.

Pascoe, David. *Peter Greenaway: Museums and Moving Images*. London: Reaktion Books, 1997.

Peake, Tony. *Derek Jarman: A Biography*. Woodstock: The Overlook Press, 1999.

Peranson, Mark. "Guy Maddin." In *Exile Cinema: Filmmakers at Work Beyond Hollywood*, edited by Michael Atkinson, 137–144. Albany: State University of New York Press, 2008.

Peterson, James. *Dreams of Chaos, Visions of Order: Understanding the American Avant-Garde Cinema*. Detroit: Wayne State University Press, 1994.

_____. "Is a Cognitive Approach to the Avant-Garde Cinema Perverse?" In *Post-Theory: Reconstructing Film Studies*, edited by David Bordwell and Noel Carroll, 108–129. Madison: University of Wisconsin Press, 1996.

Petrolle, Jean, and Virginia Wright Wexman. "Chantal Akerman." In *Women and Experimental Filmmaking*, edited by Jean Petrolle and Virginia Wright Wexman, 45–46. Urbana: University of Illinois Press, 2005.

_____. "Introduction: Experimental Filmmaking and Women's Subjectivity." In *Women and Experimental Filmmaking*, edited by Jean Petrolle and Virginia Wright Wexman, 1–17. Urbana: University of Illinois Press, 2005.

Pevere, Geoff. "Guy Maddin: True to Form." In *Playing with Memories: Essays on Guy Maddin*, edited by David Church, 48–57. Winnipeg: University of Manitoba Press, 2009.

Pidduck, Julianne. "New Queer Cinema and Experimental Video." In *New Queer Cinema: A Critical Reader*, edited by Michele Aaron, 80–100. New Brunswick: Rutgers University Press, 2004.

Pierson, Michele. "Avant-Garde Re-Enactment: World Mirror Cinema, *Decasia*, and *The Heart of the World*." *Cinema Journal* 49.1 (Fall 2009): 1–19.

Polan, Dana. "Discourses of Rationality and the Rationality of Discourse in Avant-Garde Political Film Culture." *Wide Angle* 6.2 (1984): 12–17.

Rabinovitz, Lauren. "Experimental and Avant-Garde Cinema in the 1940s." In *Boom and Bust: The American Cinema in the 1940s*, edited by Thomas Schatz, 445–460. New York: Scribner's, 1997.

_____. *Points of Resistance: Women, Power and Politics in the New York Avant-Garde Cinema, 1943–1971*. Urbana: University of Illinois Press, 2003.

_____. "Wearing the Critic's Hat: History,

Critical Discourses, and the American Avant-Garde Cinema." In *To Free the Cinema: Jonas Mekas and the New York Underground*, edited by David E. James, 268–283. Princeton: Princeton University Press, 1992.

Rascaroli, Laura. *The Personal Camera: Subjective Cinema and the Essay Film*. London: Wallflower Press, 2009.

Ray, Robert. *How a Film Theory Got Lost and Other Mysteries in Cultural Studies*. Bloomington: Indiana University Press, 2001.

Reekie, Duncan. *Subversion: The Definitive History of Underground Cinema*. London: Wallflower Press, 2007.

Rees, A.L. *A History of Experimental Film and Video*. London: Palgrave MacMillan, 1999.

Rodley, Chris, ed. *Lynch on Lynch*. London: Faber and Faber, 2005.

Rodowick, David. "Politics, Theory and the Avant-Garde." In *The Undercut Reader: Critical Writings on Artist's Film and Video*, edited by Nina Danino and Michael Maziere, 34–37. London: Wallflower, 2003.

Rosen, Philip. *Change Mummified: Cinema, Historicity, Theory*. Minneapolis: University of Minnesota Press, 2001.

Rosenbaum, Jonathan. "Clip Art." 6 August 1993. No page numbers. Http://www.jonathanrosenbaum.com/?p=7073. Accessed 16 January 2011.

———. "Romance of the Ordinary [on Chantal Akerman]," *Chicago Reader* (January 26, 1990). No page Numbers. Http://www.jonathanrosenbaum.com/?p=7472. Accessed 25 January 2011.

Rosenstone, Robert. *History on Film/Film on History*. Harlow: Pearson Longman, 2006.

Russell, Catherine. *Experimental Ethnography: The Work of Film in the Age of Video*. Durham: Duke University Press, 1999.

Saban, Stephen, and Sarah Longacre, "*Eraserhead*: Is there Life after Birth?" In *David Lynch: Interviews*, edited by Richard A. Barney, 3–8. Jackson: University of Mississippi Press, 2009.

Sanders, Julie. *Adaptation and Appropriation*. London: Routledge, 2006.

Sans, Jerome. "Just Like a Shadow: Jerome Sans Speaks to Jonas Mekas," *The Vilnius* 11 (2001). No page numbers. Http://test.svs.lt/?Vilnius;Number%2816%29;Article%2824%29; Accessed 2 October 2010.

Sargeant, Jack. *Naked Lens: An Illustrated History of Beat Cinema*. London: Creation Books, 2001.

Schneider, Steven Jay. "The Essential Evil in/of *Eraserhead* (or, Lynch to the Contrary)." In *The Cinema of David Lynch: American Dreams, Nightmare Visions*, edited by Erica Sheen and Annette Davison, 5–18. London: Wallflower Press, 2004).

Schwartz, David. "Visions of New York: Films from the 1960s Underground." In *Underground U.S.A.: Filmmaking Beyond the Hollywood Canon*, edited by Xavier Mendik and Steven Jay Schneider, 201–203. London: Wallflower Press, 2002.

Scott, A.O. "The Reassuring Shock of the Early Buñuel." *The New York Times* (January 25, 2004). No page numbers. Http://www.nytimes.com/2004/01/25/movies/film-the-reassuring-shock-of-the-early-bunuel.html. Accessed 2 October 2010.

Segal, Mark. "Hollis Frampton/*Zorns Lemma*." *Film Culture* 52 (1971): 88–95.

Sheen, Erica, and Annette Davison. "Introduction: American Dreams, Nightmare Visions." In *The Cinema of David Lynch: American Dreams, Nightmare Visions*, edited by Erica Sheen and Annette Davison, 1–4. London: Wallflower Press, 2004.

Siegel, Joel. "Greenaway by the Numbers." In *Peter Greenaway: Interviews*, edited by Vernon Gras and Marguerite Gras, 66–90. Jackson: University Press of Mississippi, 2000.

Silverman, Kaja, and Harun Farocki. "I Speak, Therefore I'm Not — *Gay Knowledge/Le Gai Savoir* (1968)." In *Speaking About Godard*, 112–140. New York: New York University Press, 1998.

Singer, Ben. *Melodrama and Modernity: Early Sensational Cinema and Its Contexts*. New York: Columbia University Press, 2001.

Sitney, P. Adams. *Eyes Upside Down: Vi-*

sionary Filmmakers and the Heritage of Emerson.* London: Oxford University Press, 2008.

_____. "Harry Smith Interview." In *Film Culture Reader,* edited by P. Adams Sitney, 260–276. New York: Cooper Square Press, 2000.

_____. "Structural Film." In *Film Culture Reader,* edited by P. Adams Sitney, 326–348. New York: Cooper Square Press, 2000.

_____. *Visionary Film: The American Avant-Garde, 1943–2000.* Oxford: Oxford University Press, 2002.

Sklar, Robert. *A World History of Film.* New York: Harry N. Abrams, 2002.

Skoller, Jeffrey. *Shadows, Specters, Shards: Making History in Avant-Garde Film.* Minneapolis: University of Minnesota Press, 2005.

Small, Edward. *Direct Theory: Experimental Film/Video as Major Genre.* Carbondale: Southern Illinois University Press, 1995.

Smelik, Anneke. *And the Mirror Cracked: Feminist Cinema and Film Theory.* Hampshire: Palgrave, 1998.

Smith, Murray. "Modernism and the Avant-Gardes." In *The Oxford Guide to Film Studies,* edited by John Hill and Pamela Church Gibson, 395–412. London: Oxford University Press, 1998.

Snyder, Stephen. "Sexuality and Self in the Guy Maddin Vision." In *Playing with Memories: Essays on Guy Maddin,* edited by David Church, 119–132. Winnipeg: University of Manitoba Press, 2009.

Sontag, Susan. "Syberberg's Hitler." In *Under the Sign of Saturn,* 138–158. New York: Farrar, Strauss, Giroux, 1980.

Stam, Robert. *Film Theory: An Introduction.* Malden: Blackwell Publishers, 2000.

Steffen, James. "Book Review: Seven Visions." *Film Quarterly* 54, no. 1 (Autumn 2000): 60–61.

_____. "Paradjanov's Playful Poetics: On the 'Director's Cut' of *The Color of Pomegranates.*" *Journal of Film and Video* 47, no. 4 (Winter 1995–1996): 17–32.

Sterritt, David. "*A Grin Without a Cat*— Web Exclusive," *Cineaste* XXXIV, no.4 (2009). No page Numbers. Http://www. cineaste.com/articles/ema-grin-without–a-catem. Accessed 4 December 2010.

_____. *Guiltless Pleasures: A David Sterritt Reader.* Jackson: University of Mississippi Press, 2005.

_____. *Mad to Be Saved: The Beats, the 50s, and Film.* Carbondale: Southern Illinois University Press, 1998.

Steven, Peter, ed. *Jump Cut: Hollywood, Politics, and Counter Cinema.* New York: Praeger, 1985.

Stone, Rob. *Spanish Cinema.* London: Pearson Longman, 2002.

Straw, Will. "Reinhabiting Lost Languages: Guy Maddin's *Careful.*" In *Playing with Memories: Essays on Guy Maddin,* edited by David Church, 58–69. Winnipeg: University of Manitoba Press, 2009.

Suarez, Juan Antonio. *Bike Boys, Drag Queens, and Superstars: Avant-Garde, Mass Culture, and Gay Identities in the 1960s Underground Cinema.* Bloomington: Indiana University Press, 1996.

Suchenski, Richard. "Hans Richter." *Senses of Cinema.* No page numbers. Http://www.sensesofcinema.com/2009/greatdirectors/hans-richter/. Accessed 23 October 2010.

Testa, Bart. "Tabula for a Catastrophe: Peter Greenaway's *The Falls* and Foucault's Heterotopia." In *Peter Greenaway's Postmodern/Poststructuralist Cinema,* edited by Paula Willoquet-Maricondi and Mary Alemany-Galway, 79–114. Lanham, MD: Scarecrow Press, 2008.

Tyler, Parker. *Underground Film: A Critical History.* New York: Da Capo Press, 1995.

Vatnsdal, Caelum. *Kino Delirium: The Films of Guy Maddin.* Winnipeg: Arbeiter Ring Publishing, 2000.

Wees, William. *Light Moving in Time: Studies in the Visual Aesthetics of Avant-Garde Film.* Berkeley: University of California Press, 1992.

Wells, Paul. *Animation: Genre and Authorship.* London: Wallflower Press, 2002.

Weiss, Allen. "Between the Sign of the Scorpion and the Sign of the Cross: *L'Age d'or.*" In *Dada and Surrealist Film,* edited by Rudolf Kuenzli, 159–175. New York: Willis Locker and Owens, 1987.

White, Jerry. "Chantal Akerman's Revisionist Aesthetic." In *Women and Experimental Filmmaking*, edited by Jean Petrolle and Virginia Wright Wexman, 47–68. Urbana: University of Illinois Press, 2005.

White, Mark. "Tales of Guy Maddin." In *Guy Maddin: Interviews*, edited by D.K. Holm, 45–52. Jackson: University Press of Mississippi, 2010.

Wilinsky, Barbara. *Sure Seaters: The Emergence of Art House Cinema.* Minneapolis: University of Minnesota Press, 2001.

Williams, Sophy. "*L'Age d'or*: Faux-Raccord" *Senses of Cinema* (January 23, 2008). No page numbers. Http://www.sensesofcinema.com/contents/cteq/00/5/age.html. Accessed 13 October 2010.

Willis, Holly. *New Digital Cinema: Reinventing the Moving Image.* London: Wallflower Press, 2005.

Willoquet-Maricondi, Paula. "From British Cinema to Mega Cinema." In *Peter Greenaway's Postmodern/Poststructuralist Cinema*, edited by Paula Willoquet-Maricondi and Mary Alemany-Galway, 3–36. Lanham, MD: Scarecrow, 2008.

Wollen, Peter. *Paris Hollywood: Writings on Film.* New York: Verso, 2002.

_____. "Popular Culture and Avant-Garde." *Wide Angle* 7 (1–2) (1985): 102–104.

_____. "The Two Avant-Gardes." *Studio International* 190, no. 978 (November/December 1975), 171–175.

Wood, Bret. "Jean-Isidore Isou: *Venom and Eternity.*" April 4, 2007. No page numbers. Http://bretwood.blogspot.com/2007/04/venom-and-eternity.html. Accessed 14 October 2010.

Youngblood, Gene. *Expanded Cinema.* New York: Dutton, 1970.

Zyrd, Michael. "The Academy and the Avant-Garde: A Relationship of Dependence and Resistance." *Cinema Journal* 45.2 (Winter 2006), 26–28.

Index

219